Changing Information Technologies: Research Challenges in the Economics of Information

Nouvelles Technologies de l'Information: Les Défis pour la Recherche en Economie de l'Information

Also available in this series:

Information Technology and the Research Process
edited by Mary Feeney and Karen Merry

Information UK 2000
edited by John Martyn, Peter Vickers and Mary Feeney

Scholarly Communication and Serials Prices
edited by Karen Brookfield

Scholarship and Technology in the Humanities
edited by May Katzen

Multimedia Information
edited by Mary Feeney and Shirley Day

Decision Support Systems and Performance Assessment in Academic Libraries
Roy Adams, Ian Bloor, Mel Collier,
Marcus Meldrum and Suzanne Ward

Teaching Information Skills: A Review of the Research and its Impact on Education
edited by Rick Rogers

Innovation in Information: Twenty Years of the British Library Research and Development Department
Jack Meadows

National Information Policies and Strategies: an Overview and Bibliographic Survey
Michael Hill

Changing Information Technologies: Research Challenges in the Economics of Information

**The Third International Information Research Conference,
Centre de Télécommunications, Poigny la Forêt,
Rambouillet, France,
11-13 July 1993**

**Edited by Mary Feeney
and Maureen Grieves**

British Library Research

BOWKER
SAUR

London • Melbourne • Munich • New Jersey

British Library Cataloguing in Publication Data

A catalogue record for this book is available from the British Library.

Library of Congress Cataloging-in-Publication Data

A catalog record for this book is available from the Library of Congress.

Published by Bowker Saur Limited.
Maypole House, Maypole Road,
East Grinstead, West Sussex RH19 1HH, UK.
Tel: +44(0)342 330100 Fax: +44(0)342 330191
E-mail: lis@bowker-saur.co.uk
Bowker-Saur is a division of REED REFERENCE PUBLISHING

ISBN 1-85739-069-5

Cover design by John Cole
Desktop published by Mary Feeney, The Data Workshop, Bury St Edmunds
Printed on acid-free paper
Printed and bound in Great Britain by Antony Rowe Ltd, Chippenham.

Nouvelles Technologies de l'Information: Les Défis pour la Recherche en Economie de l'Information

Troisième Conférence Internationale sur la Recherche en Information,
Centre des Télécommunications, Poigny la Forêt,
Rambouillet, France,
11-13 juillet 1993

**Edité par Mary Feeney
et Maureen Grieves**

British Library Research

BOWKER
SAUR

London • Melbourne • Munich • New Jersey

Préface

La Troisième Conférence Internationale sur la Recherche en Information, *Nouvelles Technologies de l'Information: Les Défis pour la Recherche en Economie de l'Information*, s'est tenue en juillet 1993 au Centre des Télécommunications de Poigny la Forêt à Rambouillet, France. La Conférence a été organisée par le Centre National de la Recherche Scientifique, Meudon, France, Le Conservatoire National des Arts et des Métiers, Paris, France, le Département R&D de la British Library, Londres, Grande-Bretagne, et l'Ecole des sciences des bibliothèques et de l'information de l'Université de Pittsburgh, Pittsburgh, Etats-Unis.

Nous tenons à remercier tout particulièrement les membres français de Comité d'organisation pour tout le travail difficile d'organisation qu'ils ont effectué ainsi que Madame Liliane Neck pour son efficace gestion. Nous remercions également le Ministère de la Recherche et de la Technologie (Département de l'Information Spécialisée) pour l'appui financier apporté. Nous remercions aussi Freda Klipstein qui a traduit les résumés et Judy Batchelor qui a rédigé l'index.

Les communications présentées en anglais sont publiées in extenso, accompagnées d'un résumé en français. Les communications présentées en français sont sont publiées in extenso, accompagnées d'un résumé en anglais. Index anglais et index français correspondent respectivement aux textes anglais et aux textes français.

Brian Perry et Maureen Grieves
The British Library
Research and Development Department
1994

Preface

The Third International Information Research Conference, *Changing Information Technologies: Research Challenges in the Economics of Information*, was held at the Centre des Télécommunications, Poigny la Forêt, Rambouillet, France in July 1993. The Conference was organized by the Centre National de la Recherche Scientifique, Meudon, France; The Conservatoire National des Arts et des Métiers, Paris, France; The British Library Research and Development Department, London, UK; and the University of Pittsburgh, School of Library and Information Science, Pittsburgh, USA.

We would particularly like to thank the French members of the organizing committee for all their hard work in arranging the conference and Madame Liliane Neck for handling the administration so efficiently. We are most grateful to the Département de l'Information Spécialisée in the Ministry of Research and Technology for their very generous support. Thanks are also due to Freda Klipstein for the translations and to Judy Batchelor who compiled the indexes.

English language papers are printed in full in English and followed by a summary in French. French language papers are printed in full in French and followed by a summary in English. The English and French indexes cover the English and French text respectively.

Brian Perry and Maureen Grieves
The British Library
Research and Development Department
1994

Contents

Introduction

Yves F. Le Coadic
CNAM, Paris, France

On behalf of the organizing committee, I am very pleased to welcome you to this third International Information Research Conference on the Economics of Information. The two preceeding conferences took place in the UK, in Cranfield in 1989 on Information Technology and the Research Process, and in Cambridge in 1991 on Multimedia Information; both were co-organized by the British Library Research and Development Department and the School of Library and Information Science of the University of Pittsburgh. The proceedings of both conferences have been published by Bowker-Saur.

The idea of the founders, Toni Carbo Bearman and Brian Perry, was to continue the famous Cranfield Conferences—milestones in the history of information science—small-scale, in informal settings, and a relaxed environment. I hope you will appreciate this conference's formula during these three days.

This year, we decided to work on an important dimension in the information sector, the economic dimension—more precisely, the economics of information technology. This dimension has been neglected by both economists and information scientists. However, as we said in our call for papers, information professionals, economists, librarians, sociologists, managers, computer scientists and many others are confronted by a new reality: the changing nature of information economics and policies emerging from dramatic technological advances. Palmtop computers, personalized information services, converging telecommunications systems and other technological advances provide new alternatives for creating, organizing, managing, disseminating and using information.

These advances drive changes in economics. So new ways are needed:

- to measure the economic value of information
- to study the role of information in competitiveness and innovation

- to evaluate its impact on libraries and other organizations in both the public and private sectors.

But these advances are also changing research practice, the process of the scholarly communication of research results, sharing of information within and across organizations and borders, and delivery of information in all forms of media.

So, academics and practitioners are becoming increasingly interested in the economics of information technology. In part, this interest stems from the increased role that information technology now plays in the strategic thinking of most large organizations and from the significant costs expended by these organizations on information technology.

Naturally enough, researchers are turning to economics as a reference discipline in their attempt to answer questions concerning both the value added by information technology and the true cost of providing information technology resources. This increased interest in the economics of information technology is manifested in the application of a number of aspects of economic theory in recent information systems research, leading to results that have appeared in a wide variety of publication outlets. Some of these areas of economic theory are, for example:

- information economics
- production economics (industrial)
- economic models of organization performance
- industrial organization
- institutional economics
- macroeconomics studies of information technology impact.

Some research questions and practical applications related to these areas are to be discussed during the conference. I hope with great success.

Introduction

Au nom du comité d'organisation de la troisième Conférence Internationale sur la Recherche en Information, j'ai le plaisir de vous souhaiter la bienvenue, à Poigny la Forêt dans cet établissement de France-Telecom. Les deux précédentes conférences se sont tenues en Grande-Bretagne, à Cranfield en 1989 sur la Technologie de l'Information et les Processus de Recherche, et à Cambridge en 1991 sur l'Information Multimédia. Elles étaient organisées conjointement par le R&D Department de la British Library et la School of Library and Information Science de l'University of Pittsburgh. Les actes de ces deux conférences ont été publiés par Bowker-Saur.

L'idée des fondateurs de ces conférences, Toni Carbo Bearman et Brian Perry, était de donner une suite aux fameuses Conférences de Cranfield—qui ont été des jalons importants de l'histoire de la science de l'information—sous la forme de petites réunions où régneraient l'informel et l'agréable. J'espère que vous aurez l'occasion, pendant ces trois jours, d'apprécier cette formule.

Cette année, nous avons décidé d'aborder une dimension importante du secteur de l'information, la dimension économique, plus précisément l'économie de la technologie de l'information. Cet aspect est peu étudié par les économistes et les chercheurs en science de l'information. Cependant, comme nous l'évoquions dans notre appel à communications, les professionnels de l'information, les économistes, les bibliothécaires, les sociologues, les gestionnaires, les informaticiens sont confrontés à une nouvelle réalité: la nature évolutive de l'économie de l'information et des politiques de l'information résultant des étonnantes avancées technologiques. Stations de travail, services personnalisés d'information, systèmes intégrés de télécommunications, etc....fournissent de nouvelles alternatives à la création, l'organisation, la gestion, la dissémination et l'usage de l'information.

Ces avancées ont d'importantes conséquences économiques:

- moyens de mesure de la valeur économique de l'information
- rôle de l'information dans la compétitivité et l'innovation
- impact sur les bibliothèques et les centres de documentation, dans les secteurs publics et privés...

Mais elles ont aussi comme résultats de changer les pratiques de recherche, les processus de communication scientifique et technique, le partage de l'information à l'intérieur et à l'extérieur des organisations et sa distribution dans de multiples médias.

On comprend donc l'intérêt nouveau qu'accordent universitaires et professionnels à l'économie de la technologie de l'information. Pour une bonne part, cet intérêt provient du rôle important que joue maintenant la technologie de l'information dans la stratégie des organisations et des coûts grandissants des investissements occasionnés par cette technologie.

Et tout naturellement, les chercheurs se tournent vers la science économique pour trouver des réponses aux questions qui concernent la valeur ajoutée apportée par la technologie de l'information et les coûts réels engendrés par les investissements qui sont consentis. Cet intérêt accru pour l'économie de la technologie de l'information se traduit par des tentatives d'applications des théories économiques aux systèmes d'information, conduisant à des résultats maintenant largement publiés. Sont ainsi appliqués les théories et modèles suivants:

- économie de l'information
- économie de la production (économie industrielle)
- modèles économiques de performance
- organisation industrielle
- économie des institutions publiques et privées
- modèles macro-économiques de l'impact de la technologie de l'information.

Un certain nombre de questions vives et d'applications pratiques liées à ces sujets feront l'objet de présentations et de discussions pendant la Conférence; avec beaucoup de succès, je l'espère.

GENERAL OVERVIEW

Perspective Générale

The Economics of Information: General Overview

L'Economie de l'Information: Perspective Générale

Michael W. Hill
Director (Retired), Science Reference Information Service,
The British Library, UK

Introduction

As the opening paper to a Conference entitled *Changing Information Technologies: Research Challenges in the Economics of Information,* the aim of this paper is primarily to delineate the field within which those which follow are set. However, since I am not an economist, some of the areas of that field will be less distinct than others.

In March 1992, Walter Wriston, the former Chairman of the American Citibank gave a Nationhood Lecture on the topic of 'The Twilight of Sovereignty' (Wriston, 1992). It was an impressive dissertation and I would like to quote several excerpts from it that are relevant to our theme. He said:

> In the last few decades the information revolution is changing the very source of wealth, and even more dramatically than did the Industrial Revolution. The new source of wealth is not material, it is information, knowledge applied to work to create value. The pursuit of wealth is now largely the pursuit of information, and the application of information to the means of production...... The world desperately needs a model of the economics of information that will schematize its forms and functions...... [there's a research challenge to us at this Conference]. The information economy changes the very definition of an asset, transforms the nature of wealth, cuts

> a new path to prosperity. The information economy changes everything from how we make a living to how and by whom the world is run..... The information revolution not only makes the microeconomy more difficult to regulate, it makes the macroeconomy—the world of GNP, aggregate demand and seasonally adjusted statistics—harder to measure and therefore harder to control..... How does a national government measure capital formation when much new capital is intellectual? How does it measure the productivity of knowledge workers whose product cannot be counted on our fingers? If it cannot do that how can it track productivity growth? How does it track or control the money supply when the financial markets create new financial instruments faster than the regulators can keep track of them? And if it cannot do any of these things with the relative precision of simpler times, what becomes of the great mission of modern governments: controlling and manipulating the national economy?..... The convergence of computers and telecommunications has created a new international monetary system..... The global market makes and publishes judgements about each currency in the world every minute and every hour of the day. The forces are so powerful that government intervention can only result in expensive failure over time.

That was said a few months before currency movements forced sterling out of the European ERM (Exchange Rate Mechanism) and caused devaluation despite heavy government intervention. Thus an eminent American banker nicely sets the scene for this Conference.

It will be apparent that in the above there are several different aspects of information and its interaction with the economy. For this audience I need not define information, but it may be helpful to remember that it is a word which is used to embrace a number of very different forms and types of information, and that each has very different properties. In what follows will be included not only data but also knowledge, which has been neatly defined by the late Michael Oakeshott as 'information partnered by judgement'.

It is my intention first to discuss the nature of information as an economic entity and then its role in commercial activities and its impact on them. This should lead logically on to its impact on government and socio-economic management. After that, sections will deal with the information market, the information industry, the generation of information and the consequences of developments in IT. Finally, I will address some social and other economically relevant questions which need our attention.

The nature of information

Almost the first question with which any study of our topic is faced is how well does information fit into the definitions of an economic good? A standard textbook (Burningham, et al, 1991) states that 'Economics is the study of the arrangements that societies make for the use and development of their scarce resources'! Taken as a whole, information is not a scarce resource. Indeed, a large part of the efforts of the information profession is devoted to establishing ways of reducing information overload to a manageable level.

So what is scarce that gives it value? The answer is obviously the specific information that one needs for a particular purpose at the time and in the form one wants it. A partial analogy is books. There is an excess of these, far more than any person can want. Most are of no interest at all; some have sufficient interest to be worth borrowing; some sufficient to be worth buying to keep for everyday purposes; and a few, such as early first editions, of such rarity to be worth specialist collectors' paying huge sums for them. The analogy should not, however, be pushed any further.

Information, we are told, is a commodity. However, I suspect I would find some difficulty trading in information on the Commodities Market. To repeat my earlier point, it is not a sufficiently homogeneous entity that it can be traded in bulk like wheat or oil. It can be, and has to be, managed in modest quantities in compartmentalized information systems and, when required for use, an information package has to be produced by assembling and tailoring the material.

In national terms, the GDP may include a measure of the sales of information services but it does not directly include any measure of new information produced, nor of the information content of a country. But then, GDP does not include measures of unmined coal or oil reserves, nor of investment, nor of increase in those quite unmeasurables health, leisure (real not enforced) and welfare. How should we measure national investment in information reserves? Is it sufficient to take expenditure on research as the measure of investment in the creation of new information? Information can form part of a company's capital. When studies were being undertaken of the Hecksher-Ohlin theory of inter-country trade it was found that often the equations for opportunity costs could be made to work only if capital were taken as including not only tangibles, such as machinery, but also intangibles, such as knowledge.

Patents are well established as part of a company's capital assets but other forms of information are not. Charles Oppenheim wondered, when we were talking once, whether information could be treated in the same way as Goodwill. I have talked since with several accountants but they cannot see a way of doing so. Yet, what about that unpatented type of information which is so valuable, namely Know-how? Some companies do know how to value it. Most patented processes are useless without it. It is a cornerstone of technology transfer. When the engineering companies from industrialized countries are selling manufacturing plant to other countries they are, as they admit, selling Know-how as a very substantial part of the package.

What about that very different type of company information, so different it may be impossible to treat in the same way as patents and know-how? I refer, of course, to management information or, as it—or part of it—is sometimes called, intelligence? Some of it is formed by simply maintaining records of the activities of the organization, the value of which depends only on when they are needed again and for what. Part will be information brought in by and from the staff. Some will have been purchased, for example from market research institutions, and at least bears the value of the purchase price. It has cost labour or money to acquire but are accounts ever kept in such a way that the cost of acquiring information can be isolated?

We are all familiar with the cry that information should be free. As Professor Bearman pointed out at the FID (International Federation for Documentation) discussion in Helsinki on National Information Policies, it is not that it is free, it is only a question of who pays for it. This is quite true, but, confusing economic studies even more, it is also a question of *how* it is paid for. Information is commonly an object of barter, both barter for more information and barter for influence—not forgetting singing for one's free lunch. Is the level of barter such that the information economy has to be treated as a 'dual economy' like the market sector of developing countries?

Of course, we expect government information and the public library service to be available without charge, i.e. that it should be paid for out of taxes, national or local. We as a community should share the cost, irrespective of who benefits most, though under most tax systems those who are richer pay more than the poorer. I shall return to this aspect when discussing the information industry, because such provision, whether socially beneficial or not, distorts the unimpeded competition which the classic economists, Adam Smith and Ricardo, regarded as an essential component of being able to establish proper prices for goods.

An example of an apparently free information service, (actually it is subsidized from the television licence or paid for by advertising), is the News Bulletin on UK Radio. Anyone who has a radio can listen to the news without paying any fee. To watch television one must pay a licence fee, but not to listen to radio. Yet there is more news, certainly of no worse quality and often better and of a less repetitious nature than on television. It may be that this phenomenon has been studied and successfully explained. If so, I should like to know what the reasons are, as I suspect factors such as the producer's perception of the audience may override considerations of cost-effectiveness and consumer need.

With that minor digression, though perhaps it was useful in illustrating further the need to approach differently the economics of each different category of information, let me conclude this section on the properties of information by raising the question of perishability and value change. In the scientific and technical field, studies have been made of the decay with time in interest in journal articles, but I am not aware whether this has been done for STI (Scientific and Technical Information) as such. Some information, such as technical data, remains valid permanently—or anyway for a very long time. Some does not. This is particularly true of theory which masquerades as data (one is nowadays only too familiar with scientific data, so-called, on the nutritional or harmful nature of foods). But without this, correct information may be correct at a certain time only (for example, a takeover can totally change information about a commercial market). However, this situation is not without parallel in other commodities or pieces of capital equipment. Fashion goods are an obvious example. But even in other fields a product can suddenly be superseded by something entirely new, a piece of manufacturing plant can breakdown irreparably. In each case something of value has suddenly gone, just as information and its value suddenly goes.

It will be apparent that when we try to examine the economic properties of information, let alone the impact of information on economic activities, we shall find ourselves dealing with a multidimensional matrix which it is a major challenge to present clearly.

The impact of information

Let us briefly remind ourselves of some of the many ways information of one sort or another affects industry, commerce and other activities of economic importance generally. It is, for example, an obvious truism that information is the life-blood of industry and commerce. Trying to manufacture something without any information would be like trying to play bridge with blank cards. Information tells one what to make, how, when, how many and so on, and new information tells one how to make better or cheaper ones, what to charge, etc., etc. At all levels in both industry and commerce, employees of all ranks are continually seeking information. Much of it is to enable routine tasks to continue but more and more is for decision making, especially decisions aimed at improving profitability or reducing costs.

At this point it is impossible to consider information without at the same time including the effects of modern information and communication technologies as well. As the information economy has developed, the provision and handling of information by industrial and commercial organizations have become more and more intensive. Very large numbers of white collar workers have been employed in what has been termed 'paper-pushing'. The cost, an overhead, has become enormous. At first calculators and typewriters were seen as a way of getting more sophisticated output. Then as a better output per worker. Photocopy machines allowed even more paper to be produced and stored. Then, just as in the factories machines that had at first helped the workers replaced them as the market limits were reached, so computerized systems were devised which reduced dramatically the number of clerks (as most executives and junior managers used to be called) needed.

IT, rather than information, has dramatically changed the employment market both in the office and in the factory as machines have become computer-driven. Telecommunications have compounded the changes. We are all now familiar with remote, direct ordering systems whether for a flight ticket, to find the car one wants, or, with much greater economic impact on the components market, just-in-time ordering systems . Some labour is still needed, though the growth of self-entry of data by customers will minimize even this, at least for data entry points. But now much data entry and software design can be done where labour is cheapest. Reading *La Dépêche* recently, I saw concern expressed not merely that manufacturers were being moved to Taiwan, Vietnam, the Philippines, etc., but also that service industries were moving their centres to these countries leaving, in effect, only a terminal in the West.

Even without such dramatic moves, firms have been able to take a new attitude to staff location and move many activities out of city centres, even if home working is rather slow catching on, with a consequent reduction in their costs and a dramatic effect on the economies of the very large cities and their transport systems. Urban planning not only uses IT but also has to take into account the effect of the information society on town life.

The impact of IT on national and international economies has been studied over a long period with sets of excellent reports produced by the Information Policy, Computer and Communications Committee of OECD (Organisation for Economic Co-operation and Development), and I would refer any of you not already familiar with them to those reports.

It hardly needs me to point out that, against the very considerable economic gains from the greater information efficiency that IT brings, there must be set large economic and social losses. However, the lesson of history, drawn from the development of agriculture and of industry, is that the losses are short term and that eventually there is economic gain for most members of society.

On the other hand, it may be that Malthus was correct and the first natural resource that will be exhausted is gainful employment. Many developing countries would claim, justifiably, that there never has been enough to go round. Should we reverse Parkinson's Law and require that the population of the world shrink to match the work-hours available? Or shall we, in the industrialized countries, as we spend our enforced leisure tending our gardens, growing not only flowers but fruit and vegetables, find we are reversing the agricultural revolution?

Turning from such thoughts to the way the resilience of the human being contrives to turn any ready resource to profit, let us ponder for a moment on those sectors of activity in which the need for or availability of information has been exploited. Publishing nowadays is big business. In the UK over 60,000 non-fiction titles were published in 1992. The value of the non-fiction market two years earlier, 1990, was estimated as £1,500,000,000 (*The L.I.S.T.*, 1992). Then there is the magazine market. There is a huge number of magazines published on almost any conceivable subject, as a visit to any newsagent reveals. It seems that literate man has a desire to add to his knowledge of any subject that interests him.

This has been further exploited by the holiday industry, in which there has been a sharp increase in study tours, and even by universities which contrive to maintain occupancy during vacations by running holiday courses to supplement the declining number of conferences.

Radio, television and the media generally find a use for information in their product, though they are careful not to overdo it. Incidentally, the news media provide an interesting example of the ephemeral value of information. A story that will sell a newspaper today is merely a space-filler tomorrow and omitted the day after even though the event described may still be occurring.

That information can be merely entertainment is further exemplified by quiz games on the media and even for purchase, such as the very successful *Trivial Pursuits*.

In any review of industries that have developed out of our need for information, advertising and public relations must hold an important place. They have grown in scale and impact enormously during this century, so much so that some regulation to prevent sharp practice has had to be introduced. The effect has certainly been to increase sales of products marketed on a national scale and sometimes to decrease sales of local products but sometimes to increase sales of those too (the 'coat-tails' effect). The economic effects are too complex to consider now, but should not be overlooked in any national information audit.

Then there are activities which are very information-sensitive. The Stock Exchange is an excellent example, many millions of pounds in value suddenly being gained or lost as a piece of information about a company, an intended take-over perhaps, suddenly becomes known. As indicated in the introductory section, the effect of IT has been to make the whole financial sector liable to sudden change and to make it very difficult for government to control. At the personal level, the information held and supplied by credit rating agencies can be very damaging to one's personal economy while Switch and Smart Cards make it impracticable to exploit the delay, as one used, between cheques being given and being cleared.

Government and society

Another impact of the greater use of greater amounts of information and the need to be able to use the new information technologies is that the economy has to support a higher level of secondary and tertiary education. As the Finnish Prime Minister Harri Holkeri said at an FID Congress, 'The only unlimited natural resource we have is that between our ears' (sadly, it was not included in the printed text of his speech). As labouring and paper-pushing jobs have decreased in number in western countries, it has become necessary to develop inherent intellectual abilities as far as is practicable. Not only have the numbers staying longer at school and those going on to university risen, but so too have the numbers of adults going to evening classes and of those taking post-experience training. This is a heavy but necessary cost on the national budget and one that will pose special difficulties for developing countries. The UK government is trying to contain the cost by increasing teacher/student ratios to keep the number of teachers from rising.

Governments are longing to find something they can control and manipulate so that it will change the economy in the intended way. Wage policies have failed. Attempts to reduce unemployment by creating jobs have, in the end, resulted in the same level of unemployment plus added inflation. In the UK, the policy seems to be centred on keeping inflation low—but not zero—and hoping that the private sector and competition will between them give rise to real economic growth. Interest has focused more on Supply Side economics than on Demand Management policies with particular encouragement being given to develop a willingness among both management and labour to adopt the most efficient technologies, which in most cases means the latest IT, available. Labour mobility has been a problem addressed more through retraining schemes to ensure a supply of skills in any part of the country rather than tackling the more difficult question of moving people around the country. Enabling industry to locate itself anywhere that there is a pool of unemployed people has been an important if not well publicized part of official strategy that IT developments have facilitated.

At one time concern was, understandably, expressed in the US that the export of technical information could be harmful to the proper development of the national economy. So far, however, it seems that governments have not explored in any depth the scope for manipulating information supply as an economic lever, though some small steps have been taken. Of course, government has greatly increased the amount of information it demands from the citizens and from organizations of all types. This has to be the raw material for whatever economic strategy it adopts. And, realizing its potential value to the country, it releases much of it back as exploitable information. It also, however, as a result of the ever increasing numbers of laws, rules, regulations, codes of conduct, etc., which citizens and firms must observe, has to accept the cost of doing their best to keep people informed of changes, though keeping the population abreast of it all is an impossible task.

The UK Government has seen that a requirement to provide information can influence behaviour. This worked well in the Companies Acts which have required a great deal more openness about each company's affairs. Indeed, there are those who argue that government intervention in company affairs, e.g. by the Monopolies Commission, would be less often justified were there an even greater amount of information available in the market through company disclosure. Given this, they say, the market would operate more efficiently. However, as recent scandals have revealed, it is still possible to keep crucial information hidden. Legislation on Trade Descriptions has been required to ensure a reasonable level of honesty about items for sale.

The Citizen's Charters and several similar requirements to publish data on efficiency are also examples of using a demand that information be published to improve the performance of organizations which cost the tax-payer money and are shielded from the normal spur of competition.

The information profession has long argued the need for governments to adopt coherent information policies. Would it be worth considering research to find out if and how information could be managed to nudge the economy in a desired direction?

The information market and the information industry

As said earlier, the development of the information market has always been dogged by the belief, still heard in some quarters, that information should be free, meaning that the recipient should not have to pay directly for it. Even when the categories of social and welfare information, which it is entirely reasonable to provide at the State's expense, are excluded, the belief still exists. In practice, even when the value of information is recognized and there is willingness to pay the cost of information services, it has not been possible to establish a market wherein prices are based on competitive market forces. One aspect is that much commercial information is obtained by barter and by intelligence methods (both have a cost, of course, but it is not explicit). Another is that the huge cost of maintaining a store of published information is greatly reduced by a free library service, though modern charges for photocopies which contain a contribution to the cost of the source are reducing the distortion. Nevertheless, the market for information and modern information services has developed, helped by several factors.

To take just one part of the sector, the OECD estimated the 1990 worldwide online market of the US, Western Europe and Japan to amount to US$ 10.3 billion with an anticipated annual growth rate of between 9 and 16 per cent. To get that into proportion, it may be helpful to note that the turnover of one UK pharmaceutical company, Boots the Chemists, amounted to US$ 6 billion in 1992. Of course, the information industry includes much more than just online activities. However, the traditional publishing industry in the EC, excluding fiction and education products, earns only about 10 billion ECU (Report EUR 14925 EN).

In times of recession companies are particularly keen to bring down overhead costs. Some have seen in the ability to engage the services of outside professionals who can utilize a range of library and other information sources an opportunity to keep down internal library services to what is essential, often integrating them with in-house information management. Probably more important has been the rapid development and normalization of telecommunications networks, reduced costs, databanks containing primary information and the rapid expansion of in-house working with computer systems and terminals.

As the OECD has pointed out, it has been led by the financial services market with that for economic and business information following close behind. Although much of the early work involved STI, that field is now much less important. Even now, the return on capital investment by the database industry is poor and long term horizons are needed but the telecommunications industry seems to be profiting. On the technical side, CD-ROMs (Compact Disc Read Only Memory) are gaining ground and there is some in-house mounting of databases where the frequency of online searching is so high that costs are significant. Applications of multimedia also seem to be growing but some technologies either fail or are slow to catch on. CDI (Compact Disc Interactive) appears to be one such.

One consequence of the growth of disc systems is that the highly concentrated online industry, a mere five or so players, has had to accept competition from a much more diffuse industry, for almost anyone can get their database put on a disk and market it as they do a book. The recent CEC Report quoted above emphasizes that the traditional publishing industry should be moving more deeply than it has into the electronic sector.

As mentioned in an earlier context, the scope for remote accessing of information has proved attractive. There are no distance or frontier barriers. Satellites and fibre optics have made distance irrelevant. Broadband networking within and between countries will homogenize information resources and communication still further. The more serious matters are the natural language and search language barriers, for there is a great reluctance among many people to become multilingual in either capacity.

One major consequence economically is the saving of time which, as Benjamin Franklin wrote in 1748, is money.

Governments have involved themselves in the information market. On the one hand they make much of the information they amass readily available to the industry and even buy it back from the industry. Apparently, three governments actually subsidize the production of databases and the provision of host services but in other countries there are research grants and other indirect subsidies so that, as commented earlier, exposure to the discipline of natural competition is not experienced.

With the new communication technologies and the ability to access readily information held anywhere in the world, it would seem as though the domestic market should be no more important than a foreign one. This is not so, however, save in the financial information sector. In the STI field the not-invented-here syndrome is still operative. It is not just in the UK. When in the US not many years ago, I was intrigued to discover in several locations a total lack of interest in foreign patents as a source of information. The language barrier has already been mentioned. Even if one can read a foreign language fluently one still has a slight anxiety whether one has understood correctly. Thus it remains important to have a good base of customers within one's own country as well as trying to sell abroad.

Next let us consider briefly the creation of new information. The publishing, database, library, etc., services are concerned with storing, transmitting, selecting and repackaging existing information. But government, industry and commerce need new or updated information. In addition to receiving and handling masses of returns from both citizens and institutions of all sorts, government and the private sector commission research. Information polls on political trends are well known but in practice there is a sizeable industry involved in producing reports, i.e. information, on all manner of topics. Well known to us are market research reports but there are many other sectors and quite a large workforce, including consultancy firms, often branches of accountants, engaged in producing them. Modern society has such a need for information to improve the quality of its decisions—since the consequences of bad decisions can be very dramatic and costly—that there is a large and growing information generating workforce.

Having mentioned the consequences of not having information when wanted, let me now touch on one other problem, namely the quality of information. Good information can become bad by being superseded. Printed directories are the standard example of a product which is often already partly out of date by the time it is sold. There is no redress if loss results from relying on it.

In general, as the demand for goods increases, so the supply of poor quality goods increases even more rapidly (cheap toys are a good example) until at a certain point quality demand begins to rise, often accompanied by legislation. As we all know, there is plenty of poor quality information around and some of it even gets accepted as reliable data. Reports in the popular media are a notorious source of incomplete and hence unreliable information. Yet many accept them even though casting doubt at the same time. The economic consequences of partially correct information can be considerable, as the salmonella in eggs scare illustrated. Sales of eggs fell sharply. Some poultry farmers went out of business. On the other hand, as can easily be illustrated in the case of car servicing, deteriorating services may be reflected in accounts as additional expenditure and hence an increase in GNP! Any studies of the economics of information must include the consequences of failure to maintain proper quality control of our information resource. Finally, traditional research in laboratories also continues to produce new information which, in the right hands, can be converted into innovation. As Schumpeter said, 'As a result of innovations a flow of income arises that cannot be traced either to the contribution of labour or to that of resource owners'. Heilbronner (1991), discussing the great economic theories of the past, says, 'Their failure was due to their failure to anticipate the advent, or the consequences, of technological change'. So, although my concern has in general been with information and only secondarily with IT, it is appropriate that this Conference should start with 'Changing Information Technologies' and ensure that any new theories which come from research take its impact fully into account.

Résumé

L'Economie de l'Information: Perspective Générale

La révolution dans les nouvelles technologies de l'information a transformé la distribution de la richesse dans l'économie. Il y a un besoin de développer un modèle de l'information pour décrire les activités concernées et les effets sur la productivité industrielle. La convergence des technologies des ordinateurs et des télécommunications est de la plus grande importance.

Des questions se posent concernant la nature de l'information: Est-il possible de la considérer en 'produit commercial', bien qu'il ne s'agit pas d'une entité physique? L'information de gestion, ou 'l'intelligence', s'achète souvent chez des fournisseurs externes. Si l'information n'est pas gratuite, qui doit payer, et quels sont les modes de paiement? Le 'produit d'information' est-il un produit périssable? Certaines catégories de l'information deviennent surannées et ne sont plus utiles. D'autres informations retiennent leur valeur.

Les effets de l'information sur la prise de décision au sein de l'organisation contemporaine sont étudiés, en considérant les implications pour l'économie nationale et internationale. La transformation du main d'oeuvre à la suite de l'introduction de l'automatisation et des nouvelles technologies de télécommunication est évaluée. La plus grande efficacité de l'information a produit des gains économiques, bien qu'elle a introduit en même temps des problèmes économiques et sociaux. Certains secteurs en particulier ont réussi à exploiter les possibilités offertes par le besoin de l'information et par l'accès à cette information. Le secteur d'édition, le secteur de vacances, les média, la publicité et le secteur financier ont profité du développement de l'industrie de l'information.

Il est également important d'évaluer les effets sur la société de la révolution de l'information. Un niveau plus élevé d'enseignement secondaire et tertiaire est exigé. La mobilité du main d'oeuvre a influencé la localisation de l'industrie. D'un côté, les gouvernements veulent souligner les risques de l'exportation des informations techniques. De l'autre côté, la provision de l'information peut être considérée comme une valeur économique. Les politiques nationales de l'information doivent prendre en compte le besoin du développement d'une stratégie capable d'incorporer toutes les exigences de la situation.

Le développement du marché de l'information a facilité l'application des mécanismes de prix et de valeur aux 'produits de l'information'. Dans les entreprises, les coûts de provision de l'information ont été réduits à force d'intégrer les contractants externes au personnel interne de l'organisation. C'est le secteur financier qui a pris l'initiative en ce qui concerne les développements dans les technologies de l'information, telles que le CD-ROM, le multimédia, les systèmes d'exploitation sur disque, les satellites, les fibres optiques, qui ont éliminé les barriéres de la communication.

Il reste encore le problème de la qualité de l'information. A l'origine, la qualité de l'information décroît avec la croissance de la demande. Plus tard, il y a une amélioration de la qualité de l'information qui correspond au niveau élevé des exigences de l'utilisateur. L'abandon d'un niveau élevé dans la provision de l'information a des conséquences économiques extrèmement défavorables, et l'importance des prévisions basées sur les tendances économiques est soulignée.

References

Burningham, D. et al (1991). **Economics** (3rd edn.). Sevenoaks, UK: Hodder & Stoughton.

Heilbronner, R.L. (1991). **The worldly philosophers. The lives, times and ideas of the great economic thinkers** (6th edn.). London: Penguin Books.

The L.I.S.T. (1992). Library & Information Statistics Tables for the United Kingdom. Compiled and published for the British Library Research and Development Department by the Library & Information Statistics Unit (LISU), Loughborough University.

Wriston, W. (1992). The twilight of sovereignty. **RSA Journal**, CXL (5432), 568-577.

ECONOMIC IMPLICATIONS OF INFORMATION TECHNOLOGY

La Portée Economique de la Nouvelle Technologie de l'Information

The Information Industry in the Republic of Ireland: a Critical Examination of a Possible Model for Information Sector Development

Le Secteur de l'Information dans la République d'Irlande: Analyse Critique d'un Modèle de Développement Eventuel

William J. Martin
Belfast University, UK

Introduction

Successive Irish governments have pursued a vigorous policy aimed at the attraction of foreign direct investment to the country. A significant proportion of this investment is in the information industry. This paper will consider the Irish information industry, assessing its strengths and weaknesses and its potential value as a model for information sector development in other less favoured regions of the European Community and elsewhere. Faced with a potentially limitless landscape, the paper bases its treatment of the industry upon certain divisions and subdivisions of the International Standard Classification of all Economic Activities (United Nations, 1990):

3210	Integrated circuits/components
3000	Computer hardware, peripherals and related products
7210/7290	Computer software/computer services
3220	Telecommunications equipment

This ignores such key areas as telecommunications services and the entire spectrum of electronic information services. However, it has the virtue of manageability and is defensible in terms of its actual contribution to the Irish economy.

The Irish economy

In any assessment of Irish economic performance, the demography is critical. The Republic of Ireland has a population of around 3.5 million, 45 per cent of which is under the age of 25 years, the largest proportion for any country in the European Community. During the period from 1981 to 1986, the population grew by 2.8 per cent and although the pace of growth has slowed down, with a birth rate of 14.6 per 1000, Ireland is one of the very few countries in the European Community whose population is growing (Central Statistics Office, 1990). This has proved to be something of a mixed blessing.

The Irish economy still suffers from the effects of certain structural characteristics, including the small size of the domestic market and the distance from large centres of population. The country must also face up to more recent challenges, such as the increasing globalization of competition and completion of the internal European market. Despite such difficulties, the economy continues to benefit from policies geared to the attraction of inward investment in key sectors such as electronics, engineering, pharmaceuticals and health care, as well as recent renewed emphasis on the need for simultaneous development of indigenous industry (National Economic and Social Council, 1990). The most serious economic problem facing the country, however, is that of unemployment, where Ireland, with 294,618 persons or 16.8 per cent of the workforce currently out of work, has one of the worst records in the European Community.

Transfer payments

Ireland's merchandise trade balance improved sharply between 1986 and 1988, while from 1988 to 1991, exports of goods exceeded imports by £2 billion a year. Much of the credit for this performance lay in the extraordinary export growth exhibited by branches of multinational companies located in Ireland. The problem is that along with this growth of export profits went a vast export of cash from the country in the form of profits, dividends, royalties and interest payments. Previous estimates put this outflow of funds for 1986-1990 at £9.016 million. Recent revision indicates that by 1991, it had reached the figure of £2,377 million (Tansey, 1993).

The root cause of such transfer payments lies in the tax regime that obtains in Ireland. With corporation tax at a mere 10 per cent, compared to perhaps 30 per cent in the United States, multinational companies find it profitable to concentrate their profits in Ireland then repatriate what is left. Furthermore, with overseas tax authorities hardening their attitudes towards transfer pricing, the multinationals find it makes sense to bill their Irish subsidiaries for a wide range of corporate services such as advertising, public relations, marketing and research and development. As a result, the outflow of cash from Ireland on the import of these services rose from £212 million in 1986 to £800 million in 1991 (Tansey, 1993). These figures are germane both because of the role played by multinational companies in the Irish information industry, and because of the importance of the tax regime in Irish industrial development policy.

Industrial policy in Ireland

Industrial policy in Ireland over the last twenty years can be characterized by two constantly recurring themes, inward investment and grants for industrial development. The Industrial Development Authority (IDA) has been in the vanguard of such activity, aiding first overseas industry seeking to locate in Ireland and later, indigenous companies seeking to start up or expand.

The IDA's record has been criticized in government and other circles for its alleged high technology bias and for its weakness in relying on foreign direct investment, often to the detriment of indigenous industry (*Culliton Report*, 1992). The facts are that during the period 1987-1991, the total grant expenditure funded by the IDA, at 1991 prices, was of the order of £699,773,000. The net change in employment levels, once indigenous and foreign companies, jobs gains and job losses have been balanced, came to 27,600 per year over the period at an overall average cost of £13,403 per job (*Culliton Report*, 1992). According to figures produced by the European Community, this level of aid to industry is equivalent to 35 per cent of Gross Fixed Capital Formation in manufacturing, or a rate of subsidy that is twice the EC norm (*Employment through Enterprise*, 1993). The obvious question is whether or not such a high level of expenditure is justified in terms of return to the Exchequer.

The Industrial Development Authority is confident that it is fulfilling its major responsibility, which is to bring employment to Ireland. The facts here are quite plain. There are currently 1,050 overseas firms located in Ireland, including five of the top fifteen US insurance giants and six of the world's top ten software companies. Outside the areas served by the Shannon Development Authority and Udaras na Gaeltachta (which deals with Irish-speaking districts) a total of some 194,000 manufacturing jobs have been created by the IDA. These workers take home and spend wages and the companies employing them purchase goods and services, both of which, it is estimated, result in about one extra job for each manufacturing job. Hence as a result of manufacturing activity, including an estimated 30,000 jobs in non-IDA areas, there are about 230,000 jobs in Ireland (*Multinationals in Ireland*, 1993).

Nor are these manufacturing jobs by any means all provided by overseas companies. Indeed, of the 194,000 jobs reported above, the majority—some 106,165—are located within indigenous companies. Moreover, for the 1,000 plus overseas companies there are a further 6,000 indigenous companies supplying them with goods and services. A recent drive by An Bord Trachtala (The Export Board) to promote sales from Irish manufacturers to the major industrial buyers located in the country is expected to net some £30 million in additional business (*Multinationals in Ireland*, 1993).

However, IDA executives are keen to stress that the dichotomy between overseas and indigenous companies is not all that helpful. Ireland needs both types of investment and both offer different things. In any case, with globalization changing the character of multinational firms, the distinction between foreign and indigenous companies will be increasingly blurred. The policy focus should, therefore, be on those companies that are integrated into the Irish economy and undertaking core decision making functions within the country, rather than based on a simple definition of ownership.[1]

Criticism of inward investment policy

Much is made in the media and elsewhere of the so-called 'take the

---

1. Interview with IDA executive, IDA Headquarters, Dublin, May 14 1993.

money and run' syndrome whereby, it is alleged, overseas companies come to Ireland, take the grants available, then depart at the earliest opportunity. Although there may have been instances of such behaviour, the IDA remains confident that there is no real case to answer. Grant availability is based on the output of a sophisticated financial model, posited on quantifiable returns to the national exchequer within two years and taking account of specific items such as utility payments, transport and other service charges, consumer spending, taxes and so on. If the model does not indicate the likelihood of such a return then the grant is not given. In any case, the multiplier effect of their contribution to the local economy far exceeds the amounts paid in grants. Moreover in addition to such spinoff, there is frequently a major dividend in the form of managerial expertise. There has been a clear trend for Irish people formerly employed by multinational companies, to take their expertise and set up in business on their own account. This has been particularly noticeable in the software industry and represents a very substantial benefit from the inward investment programme.[2]

There is a serious problem, however, in the demographic patterns within the country. While the IDA is creating of the order of 10,000 new jobs a year, some 25,000 new job seekers enter the labour market annually. Moreover, in a worldwide recession the traditional option of emigration is severely limited and many migrants have, in fact, returned to Ireland. This renders the task of industrial development at once more critical and more daunting.

Overview of the information industry in Ireland

Manufacture of computers

Within the past twenty years, Ireland has been transformed from a predominantly agricultural country into a vibrant industrial economy. Much of the thrust behind economic growth has come from within the information industry. However, along with the dynamism associated with these sectors goes a considerable degree of market volatility, a fact brought home to Ireland with brutal clarity in February 1993, with the

2. Interview with IDA executive, IDA Headquarters, Dublin, May 14 1993.

announcement that Digital Equipment Corporation (DEC) was ceasing the production of minicomputers at its Galway plant and moving to South Queenferry, near Edinburgh. The immediate impact of closure was the loss of 800 of the 1,150 jobs in the factory, but the wider implications for the city of Galway were near catastrophic, as a kind of reverse multiplier situation immediately came into operation.

Although Digital was the nineteenth overseas hardware manufacture to shut down manufacturing in the Republic, it was much more than just another casualty of recession. In many ways it was the flagship of the Irish information industry, its very presence a selling point for the attraction of other overseas companies to the country. Wang, Prime and Amdahl all followed to manufacture mainframe and minicomputers during the 1970s. Not only was this a major source of employment in itself, but it also created the first opportunities for smaller, local companies in the electronics sub-assembly business. Since the 1970s, direct employment in the Irish electronics sector grew to 18,200. Today, the sector's annual wage bill is £284 million and it generates corporation tax of at least £34 million annually (*Digital*, 1993).

By any criteria, the loss of Digital to the Irish economy was a serious blow. As recently as 1990 its annual operating profits in Ireland were said to be of the order of US$ 206 million. What is certain, moreover, is that in any one year, Digital paid back in taxes and wages alone more than four times the total of the £13.2 million it received in IDA grants during its 22 years in Ireland (*Digital*, 1993).

Furthermore, while Digital was the most spectacular casualty of recession in the information industry, its problems are no different from those of other multinational corporations attracted to Ireland by a combination of generous grants and low corporation tax. The IDA directly grant-aided the 14 largest foreign hardware firms to the extent of £89.5 million since 1980. Six of these firms have since ceased manufacturing in Ireland, while at most five have reached their job targets. The two largest recipients of grants, Wang (with £16.6 million) and DEC (with £15.5 million) have reduced their workforces by four-fifths since 1989 (*Digital*, 1993)

Although such statistics are discouraging, the situation is a complex one. In the information industry rapid change is the norm rather than the exception, and products are expected to be outmoded within several years of their introduction. In the circumstances, no single plant was ever expected to stay in production as long as did the Digital plant in Galway. In fact, only the Dataproducts factory in Dublin, now owned by Hitachi, has survived into a third decade (O'Keefe, 1992). Also, despite having to close down its manufacturing operation in Galway, Digital has retained its European software supply business there, where it currently employs 350 staff. There are hopes for expansion both in employment and in the key areas of research and development.

Moreover, despite the short-term impact of the Digital retrenchment, the consensus within the Irish electronics industry is that it is probably strong enough to survive the virtual loss of any single operator, even one of such magnitude as Digital. Hence, despite recession, the electronics sector has continued to grow and despite individual closures employment has remained reasonably stable. In the information industry, the key determinant of survival has probably been technological change rather than the business cycle. In the short term, this has resulted in less rosy prospects for that array of mainframe and minicomputer manufacturers attracted to Ireland at considerable cost to the exchequer. The phenomenon of 'downsizing', where compact and increasingly cheaper personal computers can pack the power to compete with all but the biggest mainframes, has been one aspect of this technological revolution. Another has been the development of open systems, which means that computer users are no longer tied to their original suppliers and can mix equipment from different manufacturers quite freely.

In response to this situation, the IDA has refocused its strategy in several key respects. First, it has encouraged overseas companies such as Apple, Dell and Wang to begin the manufacture of personal computers in Ireland. Although this to some extent tackled the problems arising from the growing trend toward 'downsizing', there remains the further problem of increasingly cut-throat competition in the market for personal computers. This, along with trends in costs which, in effect, results in a considerable comparative advantage for lower cost Far East countries, has already seen Wang pull out of a loss-making situation in Ireland, and Apple has contemplated moving work to the Far East in an effort to maintain profitability. Second, the IDA has stepped up its efforts to develop specialist and high-growth niches in areas such as advanced microchip production. The largest project in this category is the £200 million Intel factory now under construction at Leixlip in County Kildare. This is a highly sophisticated operation involving a technology that is regarded as crucial to the future of the company and of the industry.

Other niche markets such as those for computer networking and telecommunications equipment will be considered below. However, a third major element of the changing IDA strategy focuses upon the software sector of the information industry. Employment in the software sector has grown by 40 per cent during the last five years. Software will be the driving force behind the future development of the Irish information industry. For ease of exposition, the sector will be treated here as two separate but overlapping areas, computer software and computer services.

Computer software

The software industry is currently worth £1.74 billion a year in Ireland, which amounts to about 10 per cent of total export earnings. In the early 1980s, the decision by IBM to locate a software development centre in Ireland was the first major success of an IDA marketing programme to attract mobile investment from the international software industry. This decision was akin to the one taken by Digital in the hardware field and it did much to help establish Ireland as a credible centre for software development.

Jobs in the software industry tend in the main to be highly-skilled, and something like 60 per cent of the industry's workforce in Ireland has a third level education. The pace of expansion has been impressive in recent years. In 1987, the industry employed 2,750 people in Ireland, a figure which had grown to 7,000 by 1991. Today, approximately 8,000 people are employed, divided almost equally between overseas and indigenous firms. This figure is expected to reach at least 14,000 by 1996. Ireland is the European centre for independent software localization and production and approximately 40 per cent of all European personal computer software is produced in the country.

Two thirds of indigenous companies are engaged in developing end user application products ranging from straightforward accounting systems to specialized niche market products. The rest obtain most of their revenue from the supply of services and specialist software systems such as software tools, communications software and software for dedicated hardware devices. The overseas sector has established Ireland as a world centre for software localization and manufacturing, and has developed a complete infrastructure for these functions. In addition, companies who originally established localization centres are now starting to attach software development units. Some key facts about the indigenous and overseas sectors of the Irish software industry are as follows (National Software Directorate, 1992):

The indigenous sector

- 65 per cent of indigenous companies have under 10 employees
- 71 per cent of indigenous companies are concentrated around the capital city, Dublin
- 10 per cent of indigenous companies are located in the South West, around Cork
- almost 33 per cent of indigenous companies are between six and ten years old
- the average age of indigenous companies is 5.25 years
- the indigenous sector is strongly export oriented; of the £153.2 million generated by indigenous companies in 1990, £61.3 million was generated abroad
- 45 companies accounted for 80 per cent of employment growth 1983-91

The overseas sector

- 76 per cent of overseas companies are concentrated around the capital city, Dublin
- Almost 10 per cent of overseas companies are located in the South West, around Cork
- Overseas companies export 95 per cent of their output
- Output of overseas companies is currently estimated at £1.58 million

Overall assessment of the software industry in Ireland
(National Software Directorate, 1992)

The industry's success in job creation and in the export market would support the many claims for its positive development. As a destination for inward investment, Ireland has proved popular on account of a number of factors, including:

- availability of an English-speaking workforce
- the 10 per cent corporation tax rate
- access to the European marketplace
- Irish technical skills in communications, database and C++ programming

- infrastructure of software manufacturing support services: translation, disc duplication printing, etc.

There are opportunities for both local and overseas companies in the key multimedia and telecommunications software sectors. Multimedia is a combination of hardware and software techniques which allow photographic and computer-generated images, recorded and synthesized sound sequences, text and so on, to be used interactively on a single screen. Multimedia applications offer enhanced accessibility and user-friendliness and Ireland's existing expertise in Computer Based Learning and software localization makes it a serious player.

It is estimated that between 70 per cent and 80 per cent of the cost of network development is now attributable to software costs. Telecommunications is one of the fastest growing areas of software development and already employs significant numbers of people in Ireland. Furthermore, the rapid growth of telecommunications technologies and services will create additional management and control problems, which will fuel the demand for more sophisticated software.

The support infrastructure in terms of both telecommunications and the higher education sector are already in place, while the efforts of bodies such as the IDA, An Bord Trachtala and the National Software Directorate, as well as a wide range of European Community (EC) funded programmes, can be used to exploit such opportunities to the full.

Before this can happen properly, however, the areas of quality and marketing need to be addressed as a matter of urgency. These are usually achieved by having good professional staff, being aware of one's customers, working with a well-defined methodology and using the best available development and test tools. The emphasis in general must be on total quality management, with certification being an important factor. ISO 9000 can be a useful framework for guiding quality improvement, while an important milestone has been the establishment of a Quality Forum for the Irish software industry.

However, marketing remains a major weakness for Irish companies, given the small size of their home market and the relative difficulty of accessing other markets. Irish companies need to strengthen the longer term aspects of their marketing activities, probably through the forging of strategic alliances in order to enable Irish companies to compete more easily in world markets.

Computer services

A recent categorization of the software and computer services sector divided it into five broad areas of activity: consulting services, processing services, professional services, software packages and systems integration. In Europe alone this involves a small number of large companies and perhaps as many as 16,000 small firms competing for a share of the ECU 85 billion sales expected by 1995 (Cane, 1992). The software services market remains one of the bright spots in an information industry hit by recession and market saturation. Hence, the large computer manufacturers are expanding their services activities to compensate for declining hardware sales. In March 1993, IBM UK announced the creation of a separate computer services company with 1,500 staff to undertake facilities management and consultancy work. Indeed, IBM is one of the biggest providers of international services in Ireland, with a portfolio which includes electronic forms processing, data warehousing, software delivery and consultancy (*IBM in Ireland*, 1992). Indigenous firms are extremely active in the 'Professional services' segment of this market, notably in software provision and training, while overseas companies based in Ireland are prominent in the other four areas.

Components, peripherals and related products

There are over 40 overseas component manufacturers in Ireland and at least 20 more producing peripherals and related products. The names read like a 'Who's Who' of the respective industries. They include in the component sector, Analog Devices, Fujitsu Microelectronics, General Semiconductor, Intel, NEC and Unitrode; and in the peripherals and related products sector, Keytronic, SysGen Industries, Leeds & Northrup, Verbatim and Wescan. There is also a strong local element to both sectors involving mainly small firms, some of which are producing for export while others are supplying multinational companies in Ireland.

Two major trends in world electronics are clearly detectable in Ireland. The first is towards Contract Electronics Manufacturing (CEM), where specialist sub-contract manufacturers deliver quality products to major players. The second involves 'outsourcing', or the buying in of a wide range of services and other peripheral corporate functions, including manufacturing, in order to ensure concentration on the core competencies of the organization—for example, market research, product definition, product planning, marketing and sales. Contracting out of manufacturing and assembly is well-established in Japan, where it is said to account for over one-third of total manufacturing costs (Taylor, 1993). Companies such as Melchert Electronics in Listowel, County Kerry, are establishing themselves as outsourcing companies for major players such as IBM, AT&T and Northern Telecom, while SCI of Huntsville, Alabama, has set up a major CEM operation employing 300 people making electronic assemblies at Fermoy, County Cork (Taylor, 1993). Another leading example in Ireland is that of IBM, which in 1989 decided to use Ireland as a source of supply for its European manufacturing plants, particularly for the large facility at Greenock in Scotland (*IBM in Ireland*, 1992). Trends towards downsizing, cost competitiveness and reduced product cycles all point in the direction of increased opportunity for Irish companies in contract manufacturing and particularly in outsourcing. The IDA is aiming to support the creation of at least another 3,000 new jobs in component sourcing by the end of 1994 (*Multinationals in Ireland*, 1993).

Telecommunications equipment

There are nearly 100 companies, both indigenous and overseas, engaged in the manufacture, service and distribution of telecommunications equipment in Ireland (Kompass, 1990). The overseas companies include such familiar names as AT&T, Alcatel, Ericcson, Motorola, Northern Telecom, Philips and Tellabs. The local operations would be much less familiar outside Ireland but, together, indigenous and overseas companies are covering a wide and growing range of telecommunications products, including: transmission and switching equipment, handsets, mobile and fax hardware, networking equipment and communications software.

The telecommunications infrastructure

Although the Irish Republic has an advanced digital telecommunications network, its monopoly telecommunications carrier is saddled with crippling debts and a lack of competitiveness (Murphy, 1993). With telecommunications increasingly featuring at the heart of international business, this is a serious disadvantage in the competition for markets and jobs. Indeed, the IDA is seeking to encourage job creation in telecommunications-based services companies, in telemarketing and related areas, and is aiming for an extra 2,000 jobs by 1997 (Murphy, 1993).

Assessment of the Irish information industry

1992 was not a good year for the Irish information industry. Hundreds of jobs were lost at the plants of foreign multinationals such as Amdahl, Pulse, Digital and Wang, and even worse was to follow at Digital's Galway plant in 1993. Nevertheless, by 1992, there were 300 electronics companies in Ireland, employing 28,000 people and exporting goods to the value of £4 billion (Long, 1992). Moreover, the software sector is thriving, with over 300 companies, and growing at an annual rate in excess of 20 per cent. The level of start ups and the steady increase in size of indigenous software companies are particularly encouraging. There are problems, of course, including those of profitability, a low level of investment and the management of change (National Software Directorate, 1992). However, given the strength of international competition and the emergence of information industries in traditionally low cost regions of the world, no part of the Irish information industry can afford to sit back on its laurels.

Threats to Ireland's position as a destination for inward investment

The threat of competition from low wage areas in the Caribbean and the Far East, particularly following enhancements to their telecommunications infrastructures, could certainly tempt potential investors away from Ireland, and could even lead to an outflow of existing jobs to cheaper locales. Fortunately for countries like Ireland, there is more to this issue than a simple matter of costs. On the basis of labour costs alone, Far Eastern manufacturers would have an advantage over Europe and North America, but the gap is narrowing and the use of automated equipment means that the cost of labour is often relatively insignificant. It is important to look at total costs in these matters, which would include shipping costs, delays in transport and loss of design flexibility. Having worked out such details ICL, for instance, stopped buying its systems from Acer in Taiwan and resorted to its own plant at Ashton-Under-Lyne (Taylor, 1993).

Can the Irish experience be replicated?

Ireland's success in the software industry has encouraged other countries to adopt a more aggressive marketing stance. For example, Holland now offers substantial grant incentives, including free buildings, and tax structures which can be competitive with Ireland; France has a very strong software industry and has been actively promoting places such as Sophia in the South with substantial financial incentives (National Software Directorate, 1992). For other countries to repeat the Irish performance it will be necessary to match it in terms of educational infrastructure, labour market conditions and, not least, demographic patterns.

Is Ireland a useful model for information industry development?

The 1,000 plus overseas companies currently contributing to Irish prosperity are a plausible argument for the kinds of inward investment policies pursued by successive Irish governments. Even in Ireland, however, there remain serious reservations as to the cost and value implications of a technology-oriented inward investment policy. There are similar reservations about the social implications of the continuing gulf between the sectoral and skill backgrounds of many unemployed people on the one hand, and plans to target advanced manufacturing operations on the other. In response to such concerns, the IDA is to be reorganized into separate divisions for the attraction of inward investment and the development of indigenous industry. There is also the problem of vulnerability to the actions of foreign corporations and governments, an issue that is highlighted by the United States Congresses' recent deliberations on the tax regime for US multinationals operating abroad. However, the information industry is only one strand in industrial development policy, albeit an important one. Sectors such as financial services, agribusiness, health and tourism will continue to be targeted. There is obviously no simple answer to industrial development but Ireland, through the development of its information industry as one of a growing portfolio of policy measures, is doing its best.

Résumé

Le Secteur de l'Information dans la République d'Irlande: Analyse Critique d'un Modèle de Développement Eventuel

Une évaluation du secteur de l'information dans la république d'Irlande est présentée, en considérant les effets de l'investissement direct étranger, de l'économie, et de la politique industrielle nationale, ainsi que les facteurs démographiques. Serait-il possible d'adapter l'expérience irlandaise à la situation des autres pays de la Communauté Européenne?

Le secteur de l'information en Irlande est évalué dans le contexte de la politique industrielle nationale. Il faut considérer deux éléments principaux: l'investissement direct et les allocations destinées au développement industriel. Le niveau de l'aide en Irlande est le double du taux normal des pays de la Communauté Européenne. Il faut souligner ici le rôle important de l'Industrial Development Authority (organisme pour le développement industriel ou IDA). Un niveau de dépenses ainsi élevé serait-il justifié?

La politique de l'investissement direct étranger a été critiquée en vue de son biais technologique et en vue de l'industrie nationale ainsi compromise. En dépit de l'amélioration de la balance commerciale et de la croissance des exportations à la fin des années 1980 et au début des années 1990—un tel développement étant lié à l'existence des entreprises multinationales en Irlande, ce sont ces entreprises mêmes qu'il faut condamner pour avoir provoqué le problème des paiements de transfert industriels et commerciaux envers les pays d'origine.

L'importance de la fabrication des ordinateurs est considérée. Des entreprises étrangères telles que Digital Equipment Corporation, Wang, Prime sont attirées à l'Irlande en 1970-1 en particulier par les allocations et par l'impôt réduit sur les sociétés. La récession économique a obligé plusieurs de ces entreprises à réduire le main d'oeuvre, et même souvent d'arrêter la fabrication. Néanmoins, il faut remarquer la croissance continue de l'industrie électronique, dont la survie dépend plutôt sur l'adaptation aux changements technologiques, ainsi que sur l'évolution des procédés de fabrication qui détermine, par example, la suppression des mini-ordinateurs et les unités centrales de traitement en faveur des ordinateurs personnels. L'IDA a développé une stratégie pour encourager l'investissement direct étranger en Irlande, à force de créer des spécialismes tels que la fabrication des microplaquettes avancées, la communication par réseaux informatiques, les télécommunications et le logiciel.

Au début des années 1980, la localisation du centre de développement logiciel IBM dans la république d'Irlande a encouragé l'investissement par les entreprises étrangères dans le secteur logiciel. L'Irlande représente aujourd'hui le centre du développement, de la localisation et de la fabrication indépendante du logiciel en Europe. Les entreprises domestiques sont pour la plupart orientées vers les exportations, les applications d'utilisateur final, les services d'informatique, les systèmes de logiciel spécialisés, tandis que les entreprises étrangères spécialisent dans la localisation et dans la fabrication du logiciel, et dernièrement, dans l'établissement des centres de développement du logiciel. Le secteur logiciel a encouragé la croissance d'un main d'oeuvre bien formé et bien qualifié.

L'introduction du multimédia, ainsi que l'expertise irlandaise dans l'enseignement assisté par ordinateur, a offert de nombreuses possibilités d'exploitation aux entreprises nationales et étrangères. La croissance des technologies de télécommunications a provoqué une demande de logiciel. En même temps, le succès de celui-ci a été facilité par la création d'une infrastructure de soutien dans les télécommunications et dans l'enseignement supérieur, et par l'assistance des organismes tels que l'Industrial Development Authority, le National Software Directorate, ainsi que les programmes financés par la CE. Cependant, il existe toujours des désavantages sérieux en ce qui concerne la qualité des produits et le marketing.

Le secteur des services ordinateur comporte cinq sections indépendantes: la consultation, le traitement de données, les services professionnels, les progiciels, et l'intégration des systèmes, dont le secteur logiciel a connu le plus grand succès. Les entreprises étrangères et nationales ont participé à la fabrication des périphériques. Deux tendances principales ont été notées: la fabrication des produits électroniques sous contrat, et les services contractés à l'extérieur. Dans le domaine des télécommunications, près de 100 entreprises irlandaises et étrangères sont en train de fabriquer une gamme entière de produits de télécommunications, y compris les installations de transmission et de commutation, le matériel pour postes de téléphone mobile et pour téléfax, les installations de communication par réseaux informatiques, et le logiciel de communication. L'infrastructure de télécommunications s'appuie sur un réseau de télécommunications numérique avancé; pourtant, elle souffre l'inconvénient de l'endettement et d'une compétitivité affaiblie.

Malgré la récession, l'industrie électronique en Irlande connait à présent une époque de croissance, surtout dans le secteur logiciel. Pourtant, il faut reconnaître les problèmes de profitabilité, de sous-investissement, de l'adaptation aux changements technologiques, et de la compétitivité des zones industrielles des îles Caraïbes et de l'Extrême-Orient, qui offrent un main d'oeuvre bon marché ainsi qu'une infrastructure de télécommunications améliorée.

L'expérience irlandaise dans le secteur de l'information a été étudiée en vue de l'adaptation éventuelle dans d'autres pays, surtout en ce qui concerne l'investissement direct étranger. L'exemple de l'Irlande a été suivi par la France et par la Hollande, qui ont fait des efforts pour développer une infrastructure tout en offrant des incitations financières. Les avantages irlandaises de l'enseignement, du main d'oeuvre et du marché, ainsi que les facteurs démographiques, doivent également être pris en considération.

References

Cane, A. (1992). Software and computer services: Battleground where giants contend. **Financial Times**, March 17. Financial Times Survey, Section III, IT in Europe, i-viii.

Central Statistics Office (1990). **Ireland, a statistical abstract**. Dublin: Stationery Office.

Culliton Report (1992). A time of change: industrial policy for the 1990s. Report of the Industrial Policy Review Group. Dublin: Stationery Office.

Digital (1993). **Sunday Tribune**, Dublin, Feb 28.

Employment through enterprise (1993). The response of the Government to the Moriarty Task Force on the implications of the Culliton Report. Dublin: Stationery Office.

IBM in Ireland (1992). **Sunday Tribune**, Dublin, June 7, C15.

Kompass (1990). **Irish engineering, electronics and construction directory, 1990.** (3rd edn.) Dublin: Kompass Ireland.

Long, A. (1992). Electronics remain healthy. **Financial Times**. Survey: Ireland. November 6, 33-35.

Multinationals in Ireland (1993). **Sunday Tribune**, Dublin, May 16, C11.

Murphy, C. (1993). Telecom's monopoly: extension to be sought. **Sunday Tribune**, Dublin, May16, C7.

National Economic and Social Council (1990). **Strategy for the Nineties: economic stability and structural change**. Dublin: Stationery Office.

National Software Directorate (1992). The software industry in Ireland: a strategic review. Dublin: IDA.

O'Keefe, B. (1992). Ireland: Europe's software capital. **Irish Times**, Dublin, March 13.

Tansey, P. (1993). Pop goes the surplus: inaccuracy in data wipes out £3,013 million. **Sunday Tribune**, Dublin, March 7, C4.

Taylor, P. (1993). Partnership in age of technical complexity. **Financial Times**, Survey. March 16, 35.

United Nations (1990). **International Standard Industrial Classification of All Economic Activities**. 3rd. Revision. New York: United Nations.

Nouvelles Technologies de l'Information et Structures Matricielles

Information Technology and Matrix Structures

Alain Bompard
Université de Lyon, France

C'est à la NASA, à la fin des années cinquante, que fut expérimentée, semble-t-il, pour la première fois l'organisation matricielle. Le projet de faire marcher l'homme sur la lune a entraîné un énorme chantier pour lequel ont travaillé un très grand nombre d'entreprises. La NASA, responsable des contrats passés avec les différentes firmes, demanda à chacune d'elle de nommer un directeur de projet, interlocuteur privilégié de la NASA. Ce directeur de projet matriciel détenait l'autorité conjointe, de manière durable, pour coordonner les ressources (humaines, matérielles et financières) dépendant hiérarchiquement de divers directeurs fonctionnels.

Les structures matricielles mises en place se différencient alors des '*task-forces*' dans lesquels des moyens sont rassemblés momentanément au service du projet, ou des structures par projets dans lesquelles les ressources sont regroupées pour une longue période sur un projet, mais sous la seule autorité hiérarchique du chef de projet.

Cependant les partisans de la structure matricielle (Wolff, 1982), les adeptes de la structure par projets (cf. AFITEP, 1992) et certains théoriciens des organisations (Mintzberg, 1990) admettent l'existence d'autres formes intermédiaires, telle les structures fonctionnelles croisées ('*cross-functional structure*') décrites par J.R. Galbraith (1971).

L'arrivée de nouvelles technologies de l'information et de la communication semble avoir stimulé le développement de telles '*structures hybrides*' (Kalika, 1988), recommandées par les cabinets de conseil anglo-saxons.

Les organisations matricielles ont eu de nombreux détracteurs (Peters et Waterman, 1982) car leur gestion complexe nécessitait des investissements informatiques coûteux seulement à la portée de puissantes firmes.

Depuis les Trente Glorieuses, le coût de l'accès aux technologies de l'information et de la communication ('hardware et software') a notablement diminué, et de nombreuses entreprises ont adopté la forme matricielle. Les organisations matricielles en place continuent à se doter de nouvelles technologies de l'information tel le groupe ESC (appelé ici Formagestion) où nous avons enquêté.

Nous retiendrons, comme hypothèse, que les technologies d'information au sein de la matrice organisationnelle permettent une augmentation de la fréquence de communication latérale dans l'organisation (Galbraith, 1971; Davis et al, 1977; Joyce, 1986) et une augmentation de la quantité de traitement de l'information (Davis et al, 1977; Kolodny, 1979).

Ce papier se propose d'apporter, à l'aide d'une approche originale s'appuyant sur la théorie de l'agence et le paradigme transactionnel, des éléments de réponse à la question suivante: en quoi les nouvelles technologies ont-elles modifié l'organisation matricielle ?

En particulier, les systèmes d'information mis en oeuvre dans la matrice engendreront-ils un nouveau modèle organisationnel?

Dans ce qui suit, nous présenterons d'abord l'évolution de l'organisation matricielle du Groupe Formagestion face aux nouvelles technologies de l'information. Ensuite, nous examinerons à la lumière de la théorie de l'agence et du paradigme transactionnel les diverses mutations des systèmes formels et informels de la matrice organisationnelle.

L'évolution de la structure matricielle face aux nouvelles technologies de l'information

Rappel concernant les structures matricielles

Nous définirons sommairement la structure d'organisation matricielle (cf. Bompard, 1991) comme type de structure dans laquelle un individu travaille sous la coupe d'une autorité hiérarchique multiple (cf. Davis et al, 1977). Le schéma organisationnel possède au moins deux axes qui partagent le pouvoir entre des responsables fonctionnels, des chefs de produits ou de projets, ... , des responsables de zones (cf. Figure 1). La combinaison au plan vertical des fonctions et au plan horizontal des produits (par exemple) fait apparaître une dualité d'autorité; les mécanismes de coordination seront essentiellement latéraux. La forme matricielle se distingue donc des formes fonctionnelles et divisionnelles (cf.

***Figure 1:** La forme matricielle*

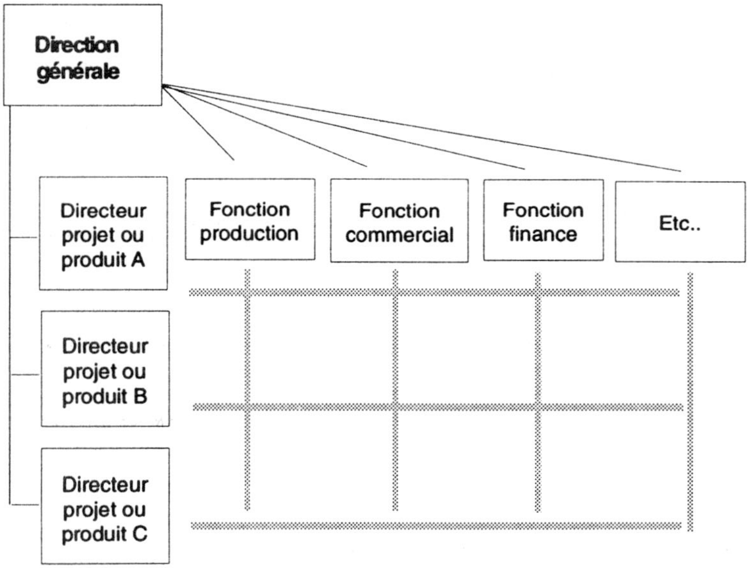

Figures 2 et 3) pour lesquelles la coordination entre les différentes spécialités transite par le canal hiérarchique. La structure matricielle est une structure multidimensionnelle particulière, c'est une organisation généralement organique possédant une culture propre.[1]

Un exemple de structure matricielle: les variables contextuelles

Le Groupe Formagestion[2] est un établissement privé d'enseignement supérieur qui a acquis sa réputation grâce à un diplôme en trois ans

1. Il n'est pas toujours évident pour un chef hiérarchique de partager son autorité avec un nouveau venu.
2. Nos enquêtes se sont déroulées sur quatre années dont une année entière passée sur le 'terrain'.

***Figure 2**: La forme fonctionnelle*

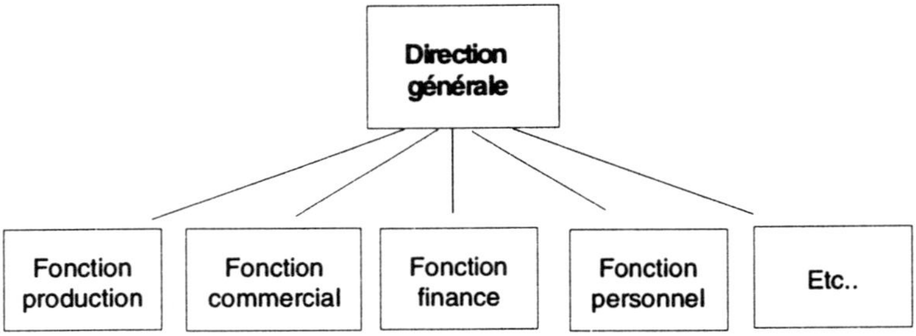

***Figure 3**: La forme divisionnelle*

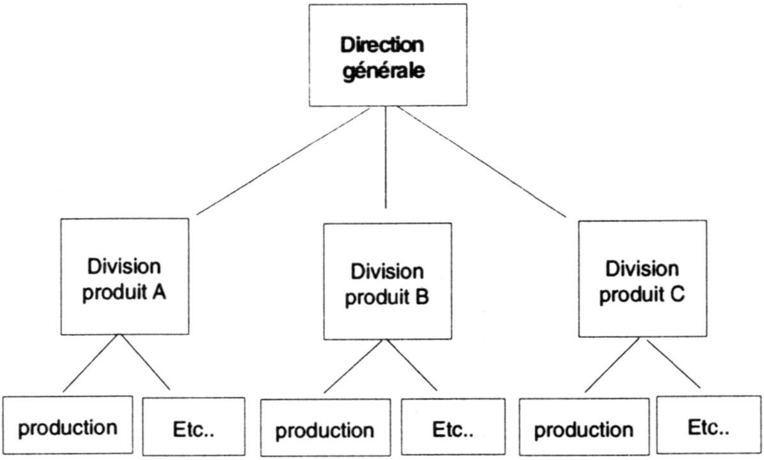

décerné par des enseignants, formateurs, chercheurs ou conseils reconnus comme compétents. Cette organisation développa d'autres diplômes pour des étudiants, des salariés, puis des formations courtes plus lucratives. Après avoir tissé de nombreux liens avec les entreprises de sa région, elle mit en place une activité de recherche et de conseil. Avec un corps enseignant d'une centaine de permanents, cet établissement est considéré comme une entreprise de formation importante en France; elle intervient maintenant à l'étranger. Son personnel enseignant, en majorité employé à temps partiel, travaille fréquemment pour son compte en tant que conseiller d'entreprises ou formateur ou encore pour d'autres établissements publics ou privés. La direction des ressources humaines considère trois filières professionnelles pour les enseignants: les enseignants-chercheurs, les enseignants-experts et les enseignants-managers. Elle dit pratiquer une direction participative par objectifs (DPPO). Le Groupe Formagestion a adopté une structure matricielle qui combine verticalement les départements enseignement-recherche et horizontalement les directions des différents diplômes ou formations (cf. Figure 4).

Si l'origine du Groupe Formagestion peut remonter à 1872, il ne prend sa dénomination de Formagestion qu'en 1946. En 1960, il se lançait dans l'activité de '*formation continue*'. Sa structure organisationnelle de type entrepreneurial se transformait en structure par projets. L'année 1972 est une date clef dans le développement de l'organisation. La direction crée un troisième cycle de management général, le '*CEMA*' (centre du management), et déménage du centre ville vers un village voisin. Le nouveau bâtiment et le terrain attenant permettent d'envisager une nouvelle dynamique dans l'expansion du Groupe. Dès lors son organisation est matricielle et la matrice s'enrichit de nouveaux axes avec la création du centre de recherche et de développement (1977), la mise en place de deux programmes doctoraux de gestion en collaboration avec deux Universités en 1977 et 1982, la création de mastères (en 1987, 1988, 1989, 1990 et 1992), la mise en oeuvre d'un centre des créateurs et des entrepreneurs (1989, depuis 1984 au sein de la direction du développement du Groupe), le développement de l'activité de formation dans des locaux de la région parisienne (1988).

La direction investit de plus en plus dans les technologies de l'information et de la communication nécessaires aux étudiants que le Groupe forme. Les nouvelles technologies s'intègrent à une politique d'enseignement d''*élite*'. La stratégie du Groupe à compter parmi les '*grandes business schools européennes*' passe par les nouvelles technologies, porteuses d'une image d'excellence.

***Figure 4**: L'organigramme du Group Formagestion*

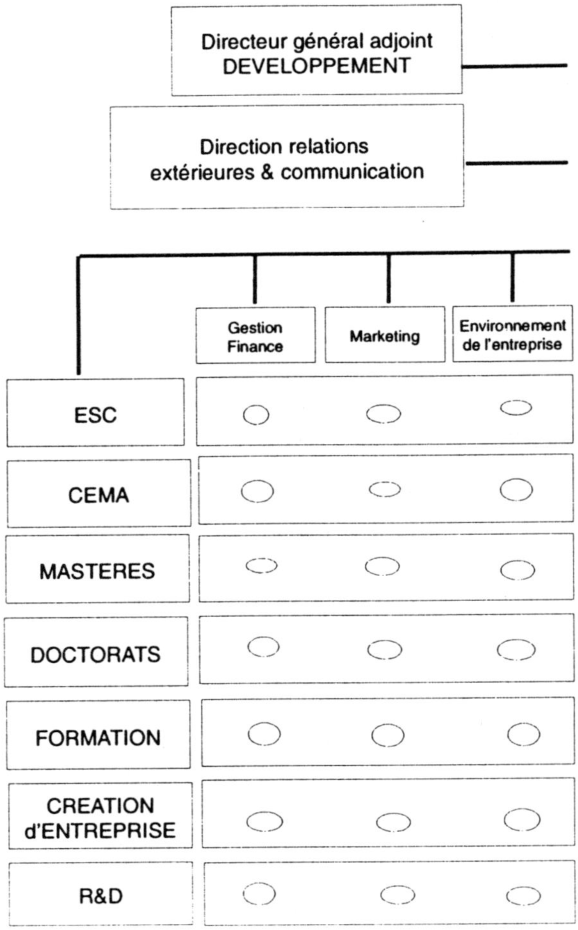

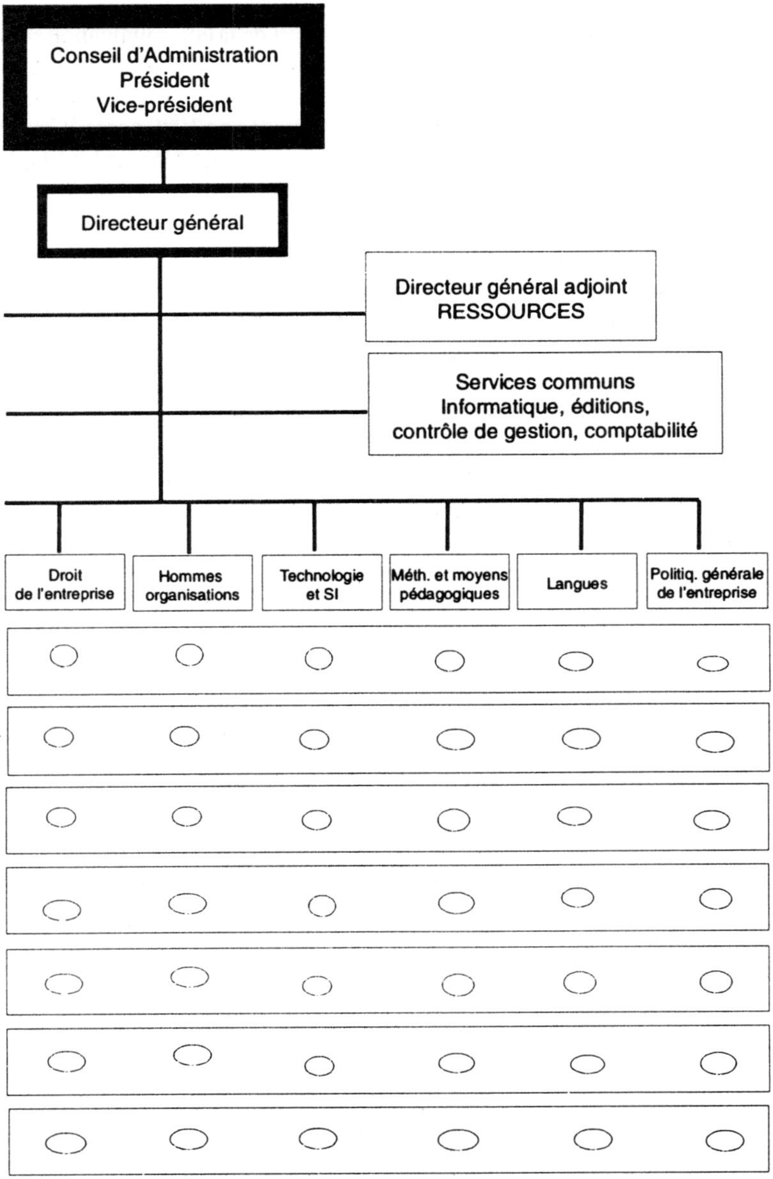
Conseil d'Administration
Président
Vice-président
Directeur général
Directeur général adjoint
RESSOURCES
Services communs
Informatique, éditions,
contrôle de gestion, comptabilité
Droit de l'entreprise
Hommes organisations
Technologie et SI
Méth. et moyens pédagogiques
Langues
Politiq. générale de l'entreprise

Les investissements en technologies de l'information et leurs conséquences sur le système d'information

Les nouvelles technologies de l'information et de la communication sont diverses et nombreuses. Elles peuvent s'apparenter à un produit ou à un service, être un moyen de recevoir de l'information ou d'en produire.

Dans une étude (citeé par Olivier, 1984) menée en 1980 par le '*Center for Information Policy Research*' de l'Université de Harvard intitulée '*Mapping the Information Business*', J.F. McLaughlin et A.E. Birinyi distinguent quatre grands segments de l'industrie de l'information:

- les canaux de distribution de l'information (*common carriers*)
- l'activité de services (*services*)
- l'édition (*publishing*)
- le matériel (*hardware*).

Dans la Figure 5, nous récapitulons ce que le Groupe a emprunté à l'industrie de l'information.

Dans un premier segment—*les canaux de distribution de l'information*—le Groupe a investi dans les réseaux de câbles, de téléphones, de télex ou de télécopies, de minitels, de transmissions par satellite pour ses télévisions. Dans un deuxième segment, le Groupe a fait appel aux *services* suivants: consultants informatiques (à noter que le Groupe possède aussi ses propres programmeurs et consultants), sociétés de services informatiques (démonstrations de logiciels) et de télécommunication, bases de données, les services de presse, photocomposition et autres services professionnels. Le troisième segment, *l'édition*, a permis au Groupe l'utilisation de la P.A.O. (Publication Assistée par Ordinateur), d'images scannérisées, la publication d'une lettre hebdomadaire, d'annuaires, l'accès à de nombreux ouvrages, magazines, revues, programmes audiovisuels. Le quatrième segment regroupe la totalité des *matériels* informatiques et télématiques, de l'ordinateur au rétroprojecteur en passant par les photocopieurs, les magnétophones, les dictaphones, les laboratoires de langues, les télévisions, camescopes, caméras, les machines de traitement de textes et les divers autres terminaux.

Ces investissements qui avaient pour but premier de satisfaire le client (étudiants, cadres, techniciens ...), de rivaliser avec les meilleures grandes écoles ont eu un impact sur l'organisation même de l'entreprise et son personnel.

Comme nous l'observons dans la Figure 6, avant 1972, Formagestion

Figure 5: *Segmentation des technologies de l'information rencontrées au Groupe Formagestion*

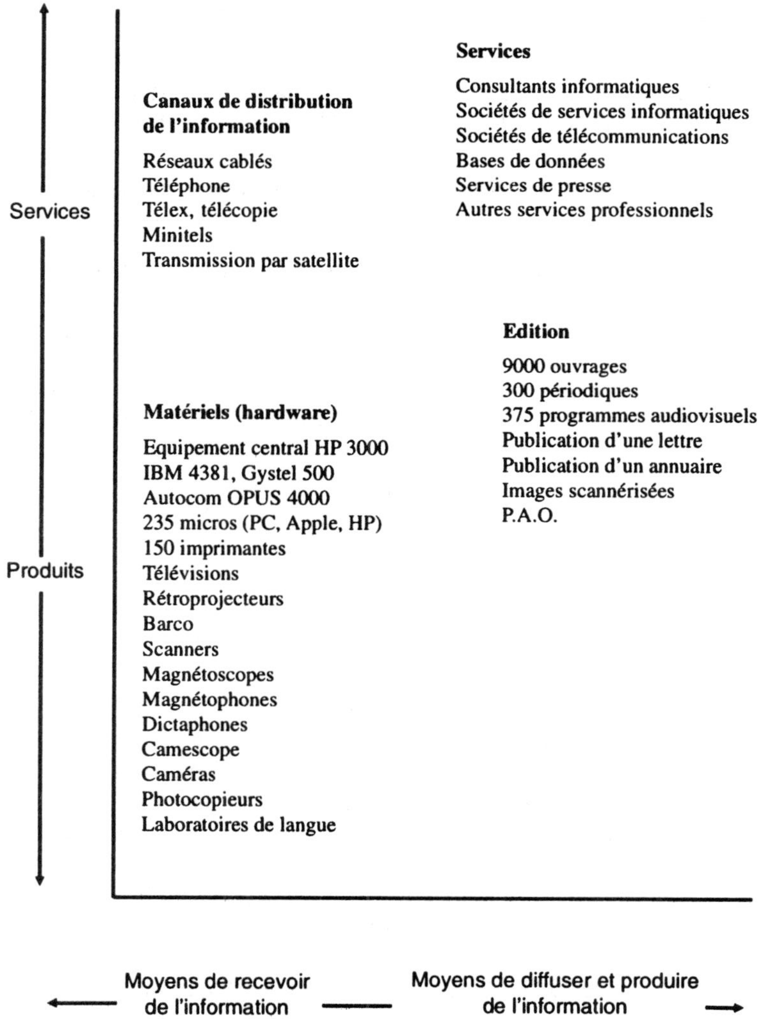

Figure 6

Avant 1972	De 1972 à 1985	De 1985 à 1992	A partir de 1992
Structure fonctionnelle	Structure matricielle	Structure matricielle	Structure matricielle
SI descendant	SI centralisé	SI décentralisé	SI communicant

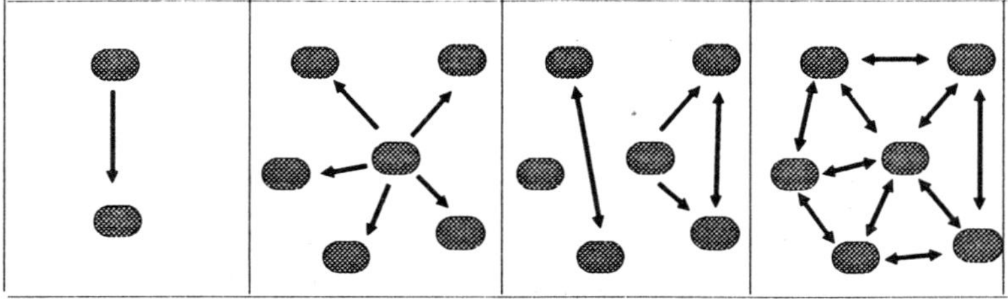

est une organisation de type fonctionnel, son système d'information est hiérarchique et l'information descendante. Les technologies de l'information sont peu évoluées. L'organisation témoigne d'une certaine flexibilité car à la structure hiérarchique s'ajoute la mise en place de structures additionnelles de liaison pour la réalisation de projets. De 1972 à 1985, le Groupe développe sa structure matricielle, son système d'information est centralisé et innerve sélectivement les différentes unités. Toutefois il faut noter qu'il existe d'importants échanges latéraux (inter-départements) d'information, très fréquents, plutôt informels (cafétéria...). De 1985 à 1992, la volonté est de décentraliser l'information et les décisions. Il s'agit d'ouvrir le personnel aux nouvelles technologies. Le Groupe prête même, sans intérêt, aux enseignants qui désirent acquérir un matériel informatique propre. Chaque unité investit de manière peu concertée dans les nouvelles technologies de l'information. Certaines unités adoptent des PC (compatibles IBM), d'autres des Macintosh, certaines se connectent en '*apple talk*'. La direction tente de rationaliser ce phénomène par l'achat d'un mini-ordinateur (HP 3000) pour le système administratif (services communs), puis l'achat d'un IBM 4381 pour le système pédagogique, d'un autocommutateur (JISTEL 500) pour le système de communication (qui relie les deux autres systèmes administratif et pédagogique). A partir de 1992, une grande tendance s'affiche: avoir un système communicant. Chaque unité a développé des bases de données, et doit pouvoir converser avec les autres, échanger des informations. Le Groupe décide d'investir deux millions de francs dans un autocommutateur performant (un OPUS 4000 d'ALCATEL) qui relie au plus faible coût chaque personne du Groupe (par téléphone, répondeur, messagerie...), effectue une facturation détaillée du service donné, s'ouvre vers l'extérieur.

S'il est intéressant de connaître les outils qui permettent de maîtriser les flux formels d'information, il nous paraît maintenant important d'analyser les mutations des systèmes d'information de la structure matricielle face à la théorie positive de l'agence et à la théorie des transactions. Le choix de ces deux théories semble permettre une approche originale (et non développée) dans l'explication de la structuration matricielle des organisations par leurs systèmes d'information.

Une analyse des mutations des systèmes d'information de la structure matricielle: de la théorie positive de l'agence à la théorie des transactions.

Rappel de la théorie de l'agence et de la théorie des transactions (cf. Martinet et al, 1987)

A son origine la relation d'agence (cf. Smith, 1776) s'attache aux problèmes de la séparation entre agents-propriétaires et agents de direction, et ses conséquences sur l'efficacité de la firme (Berle et Means, 1956).

Pour S.A. Ross (1973), une relation d'agence est constituée 'entre deux (ou plusieurs) parties lorsqu'une de ces deux parties désignée comme l'agent, agit soit de la part, soit comme représentant de l'autre, désignée comme le principal, dans un domaine décisionnel particulier'. M.C. Jensen et W.H. Meckling (1976) précisent que la relation d'agence est 'comme un contrat dans lequel une (ou plusieurs personnes) a recours aux services d'une autre personne pour accomplir en son nom une tâche quelconque, ce qui implique une délégation de nature décisionnelle à l'agent'. Ces relations entraînent des coûts, ces coûts d'agence sont constatés 'dans toute situation impliquant une coopération par deux ou plusieurs personnes même s'il n'y a pas de relation principal-agent bien définie'. Les tenants de la théorie de l'agence posent la double hypothèse que les individus agissent dans le but d'accroître leur fonction d'utilité et anticipent rationnellement les conséquences de ces relations d'agence sur la valeur future de leur patrimoine. Dès 1983, M.C. Jensen (1983) différencie deux courants au sein de la théorie de l'agence. Pour résumer,[3] la théorie normative s'attache essentiellement à définir des contrats optimaux par l'étude du fonctionnement au sein des organisations, la hiérarchie, le contrôle, et les incitations internes développées par la firme (cf. Stiglitz, 1975; Nalebuff et Stiglitz, 1983). La théorie positive, quant à elle, s'appuie sur les travaux de la théorie de l'agence pour expliquer le comportement réel des organisations (Jensen et Meckling, 1978). La branche positive, comme la branche normative, ne s'intéresse qu'à la structure formelle. La théorie des transactions offre alors un prolongement pertinent à la théorie de l'agence en considérant les phénomènes formels et informels dans l'organisation (Charreaux, 1990). L'unité d'analyse est la dyade ou acte d'échange entre deux agents économiques (Guilloux, 1992). O.E. Williamson (1985) parle d'un continuum de la structure de la relation dyadique. Une recherche entre deux entités peut être entreprise selon une analyse d'interactions entre les individus, des groupes, des organisations, entre des unités fonctionnelles et des départements produits, entre des étudiants et des enseignants. Ces théories peuvent nous mener vers une meilleure compréhension de la structure complexe de Formagestion et de l'implantation de ses nouvelles technologies de l'information.

L'apport de la théorie positive de l'agence à la compréhension de la structure matricielle

Dans les relations formelles inter-organisationnelles

L'existence de la structure est communément expliquée par les théories

---

3. Il ne s'agit ici que de tracer de grandes lignes pour expliquer où se situe notre réflexion, au risque d'être caricatural.

de la contingence comme la nécessité d'avoir une structure qui puisse réagir efficacement à un environnement complexe et incertain (cf. Davis et al, 1977). Cependant la création d'une unité produit avec un responsable donnant une nouvelle dimension à la matrice pourrait être remplacée par la mise en place d'un groupe (task-force) rattaché au responsable d'une autre unité produit, ou à un chef de programme. Lorsque le Groupe Formagestion décide de créer en 1977 le 'centre de Recherche et de Développement', il veut crédibiliser ses efforts dans la recherche. Ce centre est en fait une agence qui doit se faire valoir notamment auprès de la communauté scientifique en sciences de gestion, des entreprises qui embauchent les diplômés du Groupe et financent certaines recherches, les pouvoirs publics qui octroient des subventions, des autres unités de formations qui tireront des enseignements des travaux effectués. Lorsque le Ministère de la Recherche lance un appel d'offre concernant une étude importante, un enseignant-chercheur a peu de chance de remporter ce contrat. Le responsable de cette étude au ministère engage des fonds publics importants, il veut s'assurer du sérieux de son interlocuteur, l'étude doit se dérouler et s'achever selon les délais stipulés dans le contrat. Certes l'individu isolé peut se réclamer d'une institution connue à l'international. Toutefois il souffrira d'un manque de légitimité. Un centre qui a l'habitude de s'engager sur des contrats bénéficie d'une image, d'un crédit de confiance. Son responsable est à la tête d'un certain nombre de personnes, il utilise de la technologie de pointe, il fréquente les plus hauts responsables de son Groupe (cf. Zaleznik et Kets de Vries, 1975).[4]

Nous pouvons observer un tel phénomène au sein des multinationales qui préfèrent créer des agences ou des filiales à l'étranger, plutôt que de garder un responsable de zone export au siège social. Le responsable de l'agence peut ainsi traiter directement et en personne avec les plus hautes autorités de l'état d'accueil et les partenaires de la compagnie. Ce responsable est connu, et n'a plus l'impersonnalité de l'individu responsable avec qui les clients traitaient par téléphone. La thèse '*processus d'information*' de W.G. Egelhoff (1988), selon laquelle le responsable de zone géographique en place au siège social mondial de la compagnie pourrait, face aux diverses sollicitations de ses clients, agir

4. Pour le 'centre R&D', le montant des contrats de recherche passe de 1,32 à 9 millions de francs de 1979 à 1989. Nous qualifierons cette 'matricialisation' de proactive.

plus rapidement auprès de ses pairs pour résoudre un problème, ne nous semble plus très pertinente. En effet, les systèmes d'information reliant les agences des grandes multinationales occidentales (télécopies, vidéo-conférences, reportings et tableaux de bord, messageries électroniques) permettent une grande efficacité dans les communications entre les agences. La tendance est au décloisonnement de ces organisations (Wissler, 1992).

Dans les relations formelles intra-organisationnelles

Le Groupe Formagestion a un statut juridique particulier. Il ne dépend pas directement de la Chambre de Commerce et d'Industrie (CCI) mais d'un conseil d'administration où cette dernière est majoritaire. La Chambre Régionale de Commerce et d'Industrie est aussi représentée. Les statuts précisent que cette association est présidée par un industriel indépendant de la CCI. Le conseil d'administration mandate un directeur général qui dirige l'institution comme une entreprise, ce dirigeant étant responsable devant le conseil d'administration de la politique, de la mise en oeuvre des décisions, du budget et des résultats. Les salariés du Groupe ne comptent pas parmi le personnel consulaire. Les frontières de l'organisation sont complexes puisque les diplômes en formation initiale sont suivis par des étudiants, payés par les parents (essentiellement) et sanctionnés par le marché de l'emploi. Le Groupe a réussi à intégrer ses étudiants/clients en étudiants/coopérants (regroupés en associations, comités), ils animent une grande partie de la vie du Groupe et font sa publicité.

L'évolution du 'centre du management' (CEMA) relève d'une matrice que nous pourrions qualifier de 'réactive'; l'organisation a ajusté et adapté son fonctionnement interne par une stratégie de type défensif. Le CEMA aurait pu être géré par l'ESC, or les étudiants et les enseignants du Groupe ne veulent pas faire du CEMA un sous-diplôme d'un an de l'ESC. De même, jusqu'en 1976, ce diplôme s'appelle 'Centre d'Etudes des Techniques du Marketing' (CETM) car son but est d'ouvrir l'esprit des ingénieurs et scientifiques au marketing. Quand une option 'gestion-finance' est mise en place, le nom CETM n'a plus lieu d'être. L'unité du CETM se transforme en CEMA. En 1985, le CEMA se dote d'une option 'affaires internationales' et entame des relations durables avec une 'business school' britannique. En 1990, le CEMA devient un MBA. Durant toute l'évolution du CEMA, nous observons donc des relations d'agence entre l'unité CEMA, les diverses unités enseignement, les étudiants, le partenaire britannique, les 'financiers' du diplôme (entreprises, parents, étudiants).[5]

Ce phénomène de création d'unités matricielles entraîne une érosion de la ligne hiérarchique verticale au profit de pôles d'autorités qui sont les interlocuteurs directs du client (coopérant). Cela nous rappelle les observations de E.R. Corey et S.H. Star, à la division Lockheed-Georgia du groupe Lockheed. Sous la pression de son plus gros client (le Pentagone), la firme adoptait graduellement une dimension projet sous sa structure fonctionnelle. Le Pentagone voulait des interlocuteurs responsables-dirigeants et 'dignes de foi'.

Cette relation d'agence a des coûts, M.C. Jensen et W.H. Meckling en distinguent trois. Premièrement il existe des coûts de surveillance supportés par le principal (le Ministère de la Recherche, par exemple) pour restreindre le comportement opportuniste de l'agent. Deuxièmement, il peut être dans l'intérêt de l'agent (le centre R & D) d'assumer certains coûts (par exemple de structure, coûts d'information, de communication, de représentation), des 'coûts d'obligation', pour mettre en confiance le principal. Troisièmement, le coût d'opportunité que M.C. Jensen et W.H. Meckling nomment 'perte résiduelle', qui correspond à une perte d'utilité que pourrait connaître le principal du fait de la relation d'agence.

Formagestion doit donc être attentive aux différentes transactions qu'elle génère et qui l'entoure.

La structure matricielle à la lumière du paradigme transactionnel

Caractéristique et contexte des transactions au Groupe Formagestion
La structure matricielle est un lieu où se réalisent d'abondantes transactions à l'extérieur comme à l'intérieur (unités fonctionnelles, produits, services ...). Le paradigme transactionnel s'attache à étudier et à comprendre comment et pourquoi la coordination inter et intra-organisationnelle s'effectue dans un certain contexte.

Selon O.E. Williamson, les caractéristiques de la transaction et le contexte de cette transaction permettent à l'agent de choisir un mode de gestion approprié (intégration ou recours à une organisation spécialisée).

Comment se caractérisent les transactions du Groupe?

---

5. Lors de ces coopérations, chaque agence peut être tantôt proactive, réactive ou passive.

- La fréquence de la survenance des transactions sont différentes. Certaines se répètent régulièrement (élèves/enseignants), d'autres sont occasionnelles (élèves/directeur général du Groupe).
- Le recours à une transaction repose sur des supports spécifiques, O.E. Williamson en définit quatre.
  - » *L'implantation géographique* n'est plus unique comme à ses débuts. Le Groupe se compose de trois bâtiments séparés les uns des autres sur un même site, et d'une implantation en banlieue parisienne pour son centre de formation.[6]
  - » *Les attributs physiques originaux du produit* (par exemple un cours) demandent un appareillage spécifique pour leur réalisation[7] comme les nouvelles technologies de l'information.[8]
  - » *Les compétences du personnel* représentent des 'capitaux humains' spécifiques au Groupe. Les étudiants et les enseignants opèrent une relation d'échanges bilatéraux.
  - » *L'affectation de l'actif à un usage précis* (comme par des investissements en téléphonie, informatique—hardware et software—, l'audiovisuel) se fait dans l'intérêt d'usages particuliers.

Quel est le contexte des transactions du Groupe Formagestion ?

Selon O.E. Williamson, le contexte peut être étudié par deux séries de facteurs.

- Les facteurs d'environnement sont liés aux caractéristiques du marché. Le Groupe ne redoute pas trop la concurrence des autres établissements d'enseignement supérieur car il bénéficie d'une bonne image. Toutefois le développement de la collecte de la taxe d'apprentissage par ces établissements

---

6. La distance physique entre les différentes unités représente un coût en argent (appels téléphoniques ou billets de train pour rencontrer l'intervenant parisien), en temps (les relations avec son voisin de bureau sont normalement mieux entretenues que celles avec le collègue d'un autre bâtiment).
7. Les travaux dirigés en informatique sont liés à la disponibilité.
8. Cf. première partie.

peut entraîner une diminution des recettes. Plusieurs établissements et entreprises de formation constituent des concurrents sérieux.

De même les transactions sont modifiées par un environnement qui se complexifie par l'ouverture du Grand Marché Européen, l'internationalisation croissante, la diminution des débouchés sur le marché de l'emploi pour les étudiants sortant de Formagestion. Tout ceci augmente l'incertitude liée à l'évolution du marché.

- Les facteurs de comportements sont aussi sous l'influence de la complexité et de l'incertitude. Face à la complexité des événements, les agents agissent selon une rationalité limitée et sont parfois tentés par 'des liens de coopération mâtinés d'opportunisme individualistes' (Bienaymé, 1986).

L'individu au coeur du réseau communicant

O.E. Williamson emprunte partiellement à H. Simon le concept de rationalité limitée, l'agent économique reste un '*homo-economicus*' mais limité par ses aptitudes rationnelles et par l'information qu'il possède.

L'individu éprouve de la gêne à stocker et à traiter l'information avec fiabilité, ce qui explique pourquoi les organisations, comme Formagestion, se dotent de puissants matériels de traitement de l'information. Le Groupe tente ainsi de parer à toutes les éventualités quand il instaure un nouveau programme de formation. L'avantage du Groupe est de minimiser l'incertitude par la mise en place d'un réseau structuré de communication et son système hiérarchisé de décision. Le Groupe a réuni dans différents comités les hommes clefs possédant l'information stratégique. Ainsi il a été créé: un comité exécutif formé de l'équipe de direction générale et des principaux directeurs de centres, plus un représentant des responsables de département qui se rencontrent tous les quinze jours pour mettre en oeuvre des décisions opératoires et échanger des informations; un comité de direction composé du comité exécutif et du comité de départements qui se regroupe chaque mois pour préparer les décisions stratégiques; un comité de départements constitué de l'équipe de direction générale et les responsables de départements plus un représentant des directions de centres qui débattent sur la politique des départements et du corps professoral. Ici le Groupe tente de limiter l'incertitude grâce à l'ordre et la hiérarchie, en une procédure de rencontres qui étaient auparavant informelles. Ce calendrier de réunions élargit la connaissance des individus et autorise une meilleure rationalité dans la prise de décision. Selon O.E. Williamson, la notion de rationalité élargie peut s'expliquer par le fait que l'individu ne souhaite pas toujours maximiser ses gains monétaires et qu'il entend donner une attention particulière à l'*'atmosphère'*[9] au travail. Ainsi la structure matricielle reflète l'état d'esprit de certains dirigeants: ceux pour qui l'indépendance et la concurrence sont une double priorité privilégient le marché comme mode d'organisation (responsables produits), alors que d'autres, attirés par des plaisirs plus partagés font prévaloir des fonctions 'internalisées' (responsables fonctionnels).

Néanmoins certains individus peuvent être enclins à développer un comportement opportuniste. Leur objectif est (parfois par une conduite imprégnée de mauvaise foi) d'obtenir des gains individuels supérieurs à ce que l'échange normal aurait pu leur apporter. Cet opportunisme peut se manifester par une déformation de l'information ou le non respect d'une promesse ou d'un accord. Dans le cas du Groupe Formagestion, il est arrivé qu'une personne investie sur des contrats importants parte exercer ses compétences pour son propre compte ou celui d'une entreprise lui proposant un salaire élevé.[10] Pour éviter d'être lésé par un comportement opportuniste, la firme doit anticiper le remplacement éventuel d'un agent[11] et assurer une meilleure répartition de l'information. Si la firme doit rester vigilante face à l'opportunisme, ce comportement semble demeurer toutefois marginal.

En fait les individus ont dans la structure matricielle un '*comportement* sélectif' (cf. Breton et Wintrobe, 1982) qui se manifeste par une offre de services informels. Dans la structure matricielle, le subordonné se trouve placé sous l'autorité de deux ou plusieurs responsables hiérarchiques. Dans les rapports avec ses supérieurs hiérarchiques, le subordonné peut présenter à la fois un comportement coopératif (positif) et un comportement non coopératif (négatif). Ainsi le subordonné peut témoigner à un chef plutôt qu'à un autre de sa bonne volonté (ou de sa mauvaise volonté), prendre plus ou moins d'initiatives pour réaliser un travail défini par la structure formelle. Le subordonné détermine en

9. Selon O.E. Williamson, l''atmosphère' dépend des engagements quasi-moraux pris par les membres de l'équipe.
10. Le Groupe Formagestion n'a pas appliqué pour son personnel de politique de haut salaire.
11. Ce qui n'est pas toujours possible quand le marché offre peu d'opérateurs.

quelque sorte un degré d'efficacité à adopter dans le cadre de sa fonction formelle. Il décide alors du volume de services informels à fournir, de son efficacité (positif) ou de son inefficacité (négatif) ou de sa conformité à la norme (respect du cadre formel).

Évidemment les supérieurs hiérarchiques attendent généralement des services efficaces de la part de leurs subordonnés. Cependant il peut arriver qu'un supérieur hiérarchique encourage le laxisme de ses subordonnés pour freiner un autre responsable ou faire avorter une initiative qui lui est défavorable. Ainsi l'enjeu pour l'organisation matricielle est-il de s'assurer de la meilleure transmission possible de l'information à travers la structure hiérarchique multiple, de la qualité, de la quantité de l'information à fournir aux différents partenaires, et du suivi des décisions à appliquer (Harris et al, 1975).

La nature de l'offre de services informels, sa plus ou moins grande efficacité, dépendra du degré de confiance entre l'équipe de direction générale et les responsables des axes matriciels, entre les responsables fonctionnels, les responsables produits et les responsables de services, entre les différents responsables et leurs subordonnés.

A. Breton et R. Wintrobe définissent la confiance accordée par un individu à un autre comme

- la probabilité subjective d'honorer un engagement,
- un actif 'collectif" qui augmente chaque fois que les engagements sont honorés.

Au Groupe Formagestion, la confiance entre enseignants et enseignants-managers s'entretient par le biais d'échanges d'articles et d'ouvrages sur des thèmes de recherches communs, ainsi il se crée de véritables réseaux d'échanges.

L'accroissement des échanges entraîne une augmentation de la taille du réseau. La fréquence et la qualité des échanges dépendent alors d'un bon système d'information et de communication. Chaque échange augmente la productivité (cf. Breton et Wintrobe, 1986) du travail dans le Groupe.

Nous pouvons alors comprendre l'intérêt du Groupe dans un système EDI (Échanges de Données Informatisées) visant à réaliser une harmonieuse union de l'informatique et des communications, et assurant une bonne qualité de l'information, une gestion en temps réel et une disponibilité permanente.

Conclusion

Par l'étude du Groupe Formagestion, nous avons voulu connaître l'influence des nouvelles technologies de l'information et de la communication sur cette organisation de type matriciel.

Tout d'abord, nous avons tracé les grandes lignes de l'évolution formelle de ce Groupe École Supérieur de Commerce et défini les phases clefs d'investissement en technologie de l'information. Cette organisation matricielle a peu à peu décentralisé ses systèmes d'information formels dans le but d'avoir un système communicant, permettant plus d'efficacité et d'innovation.

Ensuite afin de déterminer les flux d'information et de communication au sein de la structure formelle et informelle, notre réflexion s'est appuyée sur la théorie positive de l'agence et la théorie des transactions.

A travers cette analyse nous avons remarqué l'importance qu'accordaient les clients et les partenaires à la performance du système d'information. Ce système est une représentation du pouvoir que l'interlocuteur détient dans son organisation, il est le gage de l'efficacité et du sérieux des coopérations engagées.

A leurs débuts, les systèmes d'information ont été conçus pour servir une double ligne hiérarchique (fonctionnelle et produit) de la structure matricielle. Maintenant la mise en oeuvre du système d'information/réseau permet de décentraliser de nombreuses tâches et de décloisonner certaines unités.

La mise en place d'un réseau d'information sophistiqué doit être considérée comme un outil, une solution technique face aux limites des technologies d'information utilisées précédemment dans le Groupe.

Cependant le concept réseau considéré n'est pas institué sur la base d'un projet organisationnel (cf. Jameux, 1992). Il renforce le modèle d'organisation matricielle établi. Il permet aux transactions informelles de se prolonger à travers le réseau télématique, et d'aider à la formalisation d'idées, de projets futurs. En fait le réseau d'information est un support au réseau de confiance existante. Son utilisation est liée à un apprentissage collectif, il doit s'inscrire dans le développement intérieur de l'individu.

L'organisation communicante ne peut s'accomplir qu'à travers la '*libération* (cf. Bouchaud, 1992) *des énergies individuelles*'.

Summary

Information Technology and Matrix Structures

The impact of the new technologies of information and communication on matrix structures is assessed. Will information systems in matrix organizations generate a new organizational pattern? Agency theory and transaction paradigms help us to understand different changes in formal and informal systems within matrix organizations. Motivation is required to create a new organizational pattern to accommodate IT. However, this same motivation can also reinforce the existing organizational structure.

The first part of this paper traces the evolution of matrix structures as they confront the new information technologies. The matrix structure is a specific multidimensional structure which can be defined as 'a structure within which an individual employee is controlled by a multiple hierarchical authority'. Within this structure, at least two axes can be drawn, representing the distribution of power between managerial staff in the different sectors of the organization.

Groupe Formagestion, a privately-funded higher education institution which has links with local industry as well as overseas contacts, is an example of a matrix structure. Groupe Formagestion has a matrix structure having a vertical axis which represents research and teaching departments, and a horizontal axis representing the various training departments. A policy of direct participation by objectives has been adopted. As a prestigious European business school, it places a high priority on investment in the new information and communication technologies, with an emphasis on developments in information distribution, service provision, publishing and hardware. The impact of technological investment on the internal information system is considered.

By 1972, Groupe Formagestion had been converted from a 'functional' organization with a hierarchical information system, where little attempt had been made to incorporate developments in new technology, to a matrix structure with a centralized information system. However, at this stage, there was still insufficient liaison between the different departments when it came to investing in new technology.

The second part of the paper looks at the development of information systems within the matrix structure—from the 'positive agency theory' to the 'transaction theory'.

The agency theory concerns the relationship between two, (or more) parties, one of whom is designated as the agent and acts on behalf of the other, designated as the principal. The relationship between the two parties is termed a 'contract'. The normative theory considers the optimal contracts required for the smooth functioning of the organization. The positive theory attempts to explain organizational behaviour on the basis of the agency theory. Analysis of the positive agency theory would also help us to understand the matrix structure, putting into perspective the relationships between different departments of the organization, as well as between different organizations. A clearer understanding of the parameters of organizational structure could be helpful in the implementation of new technology.

Transaction theory is also of particular importance in the analysis of matrix structures. The identification of appropriate management techniques is dependent on the context as well as the characteristics of the transaction being carried out. At Groupe Formagestion, for example, the context includes such factors as the size of the market, increasing international competition as a result of completion of the Single Market, and a loss of revenue which is directly related to taxation law.

Within an organizational framework, it is difficult for individuals to exploit fully the opportunities presented by information processing technologies. An organization confers the advantage of reliability by virtue of the hierarchical and structured environment in which decisions are communicated. At Groupe Formagestion, the information exchange network between lecturers and lecturer-managers relies on the exchange of articles and related work on common research topics.

An analysis of Groupe Formagestion has shown the importance to both clients and partners of the operation of an effective information system within a matrix structure. The existence of an organizational matrix will lead to the decentralization of departmental units, and of the distribution of tasks within these units. An information exchange network operating on these principles should be capable of providing technical solutions to problems requiring the implementation of new technology.

Références

A.F.I.T.E.P. (1992). Direction et contrôle de projet. **Actes de la 8e Convention Nationale de l'A.F.I.T.E.P.** (Association Française des ingénieurs et techniciens d'estimation, de planification et de projet), 1er et 2 octobre.

Berle, A. et Means, G. (1956). **The Modern Corporation and Private Property**. (2e édition) New York: McMillan.

Bienaymé, A. (1986). Compte rendu de l'ouvrage de O. Williamson: The Economic Institution of Capitalism (Ed. Free Press 1985), **Analyses de la Sedeis**, 51, mai.

Bompard, A. (1991). **Structures matricielles**, Mémoire de DEA en sciences de gestion, Programme doctoral de gestion Groupe ESC Lyon-IAE/Université Jean Moulin Lyon 3.

Bouchaud, J. (1992). La communication: système technique ou libération des énergies individuelles, **Brises**, 17, 13-17.

Breton, A. et Wintrobe, R. (1982). **The Logic of Bureaucratic Conduct.** Cambridge: Cambridge University Press.

Breton, A. et Wintrobe, R. (1986). Organizational Structure and Productivity, **American Economic Review**, 76(3), juin.

Charreaux,G. (1990). La théorie des transactions informelles: une synthèse, **Économies et sociétés**, Série sciences de gestion, 15, mai, 131-161.

Corey, E.R. et Star, S.H. (undated). **Organizational strategy: a Marketing Approach**. Boston, MA: Harvard University, Division of Research, Graduate School of Business Administration. 61-107.

Davis, S.M. et Lawrence, P.R., en collaboration avec Kolodny, M. (1977). **Matrix.** Reading, Mass: Addison-Wesley.

Egelhoff, W.G. (1988). **Organizing the Multinational Enterprise: an Information-Processing Perspective.** Cambridge, M.A.: Ballinger.

Galbraith, J.R. (1971). Matrix organization design, **Business Horizons**, 14(1), 29-40.

Guilloux, V. (1992). L'applicabilité en sciences de gestion du paradigme transactionnel, **Économies et sociétés**, Série sciences de gestion, 18, juillet, 177-198.

Guthmann, B. et Tardieu, H. (1991). **Le triangle stratégique: stratégie, structure et technologies de l'information.** Les éd. d'Organisation. p.58.

Harris, J.E., Wachter, M.L. et Williamson, O.E. (1975). Understanding the Employment Relation: the Analysis of Idiosyncratic Exchange, **Bell Journal of Economics**, 6(1), printemps, 250-278.

Jameux, C. (1992). Les systèmes d'information et de communication sont-ils porteurs d'un nouveau modèle d'organisation?, **Brises**, 17, 147-151.

Jensen, M.C. (1983). Organization Theory and Methodology, **Accounting Review**, 58, avril, 319-339.

Jensen, M.C. et Meckling, W.C. (1976). Theory of the Firm: Managerial Behavior, Agency Costs and Ownership Structure, **Journal of Financial Economics**, 3, octobre, 308.

Jensen, M.C. et Meckling, W.H. (1978). Can the Corporation Survive?, **Financial Analysts Journal**, janvier-février, 31-37.

Joyce, W.F. (1986). Matrix organization: A social experiment, **Academy of Management Journal**, 29(3), 536-561.

Kalika, M. (1988). **Structures d'entreprises: réalités, déterminants, performances**, Economica, gestion.

Kolodny, H.F. (1979). Evolution to a matrix organization, **Academy of Management Review**, 4(4), 543-553.

Martinet, A.C.; Charreaux, G.; Couret, A.; Joffre, P.; Koenig, G.; et Montmorillon, B. De (1987). **De nouvelles théories pour gérer l'entreprise.** Economica.

Mintzberg, H. (1990). **Le management, voyage au centre des organisations.** Montréal, Canada: Les Editions d'Organisation, et Paris: Agence d'ARC Inc.

Nalebuff, B. et Stiglitz, J.E. (1983). Prizes and Incentives: towards a General Theory of Compensation and Competition, **Bell Journal of**

Economics, 14(1), printemps.

Olivier, J.L. (1984). Systèmes d'information et planification, document **FNEGE**,71.

Peters T. et Waterman, R. (1982). **In search of excellence. Lessons from America's best run companies**. New York: Harper & Row.

Ross, S.A. (1973). The Economic Theory of Agency: The Principal's Problem, **American Economic Review**, 63(2), 134-139.

Smith, A. (1776). **The Wealth of Nations**, Traduction française de Germain Garnier, **La richesse des Nations**, Paris, 1843, t.2, p.401.

Stiglitz, J.E. (1975). Incentives, Risk, and Information: Notes towards a Theory of Hierarchy, **Bell Journal of Economics**, 6(2), automne, 552-579.

Williamson, O.E. (1985). **The Economic Institutions of Capitalism.** New York: Free Press.

Wissler, M. (1992). Peut-on parler d'une tendance au décloisonnement organisationnel?, **Papier de recherche**, 21, URA CNRS 1257/IAE-Université J. Moulin Lyon.

Wolff, M.F. (1982). Welcome to my matrix, **Research Management**, nov., 10-12.

Zaleznik, A. et Kets De Vries, M.F.R. (1975). **Power and Corporate Mind.** Boston: Houghton Mifflin Co.

The New Role of Information Technology in the International Division of Labor

Les Nouvelles Technologies de l'Information et la Division Internationale du Travail

Vijai P. Singh and William J. Haller
University Center for Social and Urban Research,
University of Pittsburgh,USA

Information innovations in different historical periods have influenced the capitalistic system of production, distribution and consumption. The continuous process technology in the mid-18th century, auto plant and factory control systems in the early 1900s, distant control of electrical transmissions in the 1920s and quality control in the 1930s are some of the examples in which information technology was pivotal in making these innovations possible (Hepworth, 1990, pp.2-5). The 20th century has witnessed a massive technological revolution in which information innovations and applications have grown dramatically. There are important implications of information technology (computers and telecommunications) for the economy in the forms of strategic decisions and actions by the major economic actors and institutions. As a case in point, volume of trade between nations is associated with the level of exchange of information between them (Jussawalla, 1989, pp.3-8).

The new international division of labor (NIDL) has marked a qualitative transformation of the global economy. At the head of this process are the technologies of transportation and communication which have made it possible to produce goods and services partially or completely just about anywhere in the world. The producer services, which include banking, insurance, engineering, accounting, legal expertise, data processing and communication, have enabled the decentralization of production and global mobility of capital.

The connection between the opportunities afforded by new technologies for transnational producer services and the global redistribution of manufacturing activities was drawn explicitly by Jones and Kierzkowski (1990, pp.42-43),

> The type of technological breakthrough and innovation that has characterized sectors such as telecommunications, transportation and financial services has had especially pronounced effects in reducing the costs of *international* service links.... The reduction in the cost of services generally has fostered increased fragmentation and division of labor in production; the greater relative cost reductions for services linking international operations have had a profound effect in stimulating the use of international markets at every stage of the production process.

Though Jones and Kierzkowski emphasize the possibility of ultimate gains for developing countries in general (via enhanced possibilities for participation in production for the world market), the empirical assertions of their model complement the NIDL perspective which emphasizes the exploitation of Third World labor forces. Regarding the effects of this qualitative shift in the world economy to a new international division of labor in the developed countries, recent industrial restructuring has been coupled with declining proportions of manufacturing employment in the old industrial regions. Closer examination of the roles of transnational producer services in the world economy enables a clearer understanding of the forces driving the ongoing reconfiguration of the international division of labor.

Information technology has revolutionized the access, efficiency and diversity of producer services. Without producer services, the transnational sourcing of production and the establishment of the international input and distribution networks for production and marketing would require a higher investment threshold, since the necessary preparatory research and logistical planning to transnationalize would have to be carried out by firms 'in-house' (i.e., on their own and largely from scratch). As illustrated by Williamson (1981) transaction costs are minimized by developing in-house capacities for routine functions, but in the case of non-routine functions costs are minimized, and effectiveness enhanced, when such services can be obtained by out-of-house contracting. Thus, international producer services can offer the specialized knowledge and experience necessary to lower the minimum investment threshold for the establishment of transnational production and distribution networks. But also, corporations' services which had been developed 'in-house' have been competing externally. As reported by the United Nations Conference on Trade and Development (United Nations, 1988, p.144),

> ...externalization of service production has taken place at two levels. First, in-house services have been increasingly replaced by the purchase of specialized services from other firms. Second, service operations provided within the firm have tended to be sold to outside clients, a process which usually leads to the establishment of externalized subsidiaries that then sell the service both back to the parent firm and on the open market.

This development should tend to both entrench and expand the international networks of fragmented production blocks by permitting more and more companies to take advantage of international market inequalities.

Producer services help the efficient use of various inputs in the production process. Foreign investment pushes demand for producer services to maximize efficiency in trade and manufacturing. Semyonov and Lewin-Epstein (1986) analyzed 45 developing countries from 1960 to 1980 and found that foreign investment led to the expansion of producer services, regardless of level of economic development and expansion of the manufacturing sector. Therefore, producer services in the developing countries as well have a strategic role as links in the international commodity chains facilitating the reconfiguration of the international division of labor.

Information technology promotes structural adjustments by helping to respond to demands for products, production efficiency, quality control, and capital mobility. Information technology is helping change the industry structure where new products are developed to gain competitive advantage. It has led to a growing integration of such financial services as banking, insurance and brokerage (Spero, 1985, p.128). The new telecommunications technologies allow centralized financial control over off-shore production facilities spread throughout the world. The faster communication infrastructure has enhanced the global mobility of capital. Information technology has not only made producer services more efficient but has also undermined the ability of national governments to exercise effective control on financial markets through various governmental regulations including monetary policies (Jussawalla, 1989, pp.12-14).

Communications technology, the introduction of the computer, the demand for specialized products, and global economic growth and the emergence of multinational and multi-product corporations have contributed to the growth of producer services. It is important to note that many large corporations are located in those cities that also happen to have concentrations of international banking and financial services, law and accounting. These places also have major research and development establishments where new technology products and management strategies are devised and tested (Noyelle, 1986, pp.150-151). Such centers are very few in number and command tremendous economic power nationally and internationally. These include New York, Tokyo and London, among others. These centers influence the flow of capital and technology owing to their concentration of corporate headquarters.

Information technology is essential in new product development and marketing, but its role is not yet fully recognized and understood in the development of new economy and global trade policies. Even though knowledge-based industries have shown a remarkable growth and knowledge-based jobs have transformed the occupational structure, it is only recently that some serious attention is given to the impact on the economy and society. Finally, information technology is no longer viewed as a costless resource (Krommenacker, 1989, pp.124-125; Hepworth, 1990, p.5). The long-term scenarios that guide the planning for industrial restructuring decisions cannot be successfully carried out without taking into account such elements as hardware, applications, communication, data and human resources (Sifonis, 1990, pp.253-259).

Just as advanced electronics brought the industrial revolution, transforming economy and society, the next revolution is spearheaded by information technology which has simplified the performance of routine tasks and provided efficient links within and between business organizations, locally and globally, for decision making. Kiechel (1993, p.39) has identified the following trends that have begun to transform the work place:

- The average company will become smaller, employing fewer people.
- The traditional hierarchical organizations will give way to a

variety of organizational forms, the network of specialists foremost among these.

- The vertical division of labor will be replaced by a horizontal division.
- The paradigm of doing business will shift from making a product to providing a service.
- Work itself will be redefined: constant learning, more high-order thinking.

The major change in the infrastructural technologies has come in the form of information technology, in which 'the computational infrastructure... ...takes over progressively more of the work that can be routinized—and ever more can, with the new technology—from guiding machines that make things to transmitting information within the organization or across its boundaries... ...flexible manufacturing, programs trading and point-of-purchase terminals wired into the supplier's factory' (Kiechel, 1993, p.39).

The impact of information technology on industrial organizations is reflected in the use of flexible production, streamlined organizational hierarchies, teamwork and the need for coordination between various sub-units within the organization. Transaction costs such as preparation of contracts, securing commitments, and monitoring are needed. In addition, the planning, information search, and communication for decision making are accomplished with a high level of efficiency, especially when hierarchy is reduced and vertical integration is enhanced (Gwerin-Calvery and Wildman, 1991, pp.22-30). The information technology helps in market research by helping assess shifts in the demand for the products, thus introducing a flexible production system and the efficient use of capital and labor (Michalski, 1989, p.13). The internalization of business services has created an environment that forces increased economic cooperation between nations (Krommenacker, 1989, pp.127-128).

In the computer network, telecommunications circuits are used to connect computers and terminals at different locations making flexible production possible. As Ogura (1989, p.xi) suggests, ' ...the development of computer control and information networks may lead to a more customized marketing of goods and services at lower costs. This may influence location of factories and sales offices'. Information technology is changing the competitive environment in which businesses contract out certain functions while maintaining quality control. It helps them become more cost effective, in developing and marketing customized products. Business organizations will become less hierarchical and more horizontal, in which 'hundreds of separate sites—stores—offices transmit information to a single headquarters where it is digested, decisions made, and directions, in turn, sent back to the sites which do not need to be in touch with one another' (Kiechel, 1993, p.41).

Business has always relied on the communication of information, but the specific forms of such communication and the ways in which business uses information has changed dramatically in recent years. The impact of the new information and telecommunications technologies on business is evident at all levels of economic organization: from computerized local area networks (LANs) which promote the efficiency of work groups at a single site, to global telecommunications networks which enable the global orchestration of dispersed production and distribution chains, facilitate investment between the world's financial markets, and permit the instantaneous transmission of raw data and knowledge-based products between (potentially) any choice of sites around the world. State-of-the-art information and communication technology has 'transformed telecommunications from the status of a simple cost, like buildings or energy, into a tool for defining the structure of a corporation and its relationship with suppliers and markets' (Mulgan, 1991, p.224).

The international distribution of comparative advantage in key producer services, particularly banking, contributes to the power of the economies of core nations in determining the distribution of roles in the international division of labor among both core and peripheral countries. As indicated by the United National Centre on Transnational Corporations, 'banking is only one part of the services sector—albeit one of the most important ones—and the services sector as a whole has become the single most important sector for foreign direct investment, both in terms of stocks and flows' (United Nations, 1987, p.60). In this context, banking tends to govern the distribution of scarce resources and their application. As stated by Jussawalla and Dworak, 'in modern market exchanges, financial intermediaries stand at the intersection of production and consumption and are the conduit through which information about these two most basic economic activities is exchanged, both intra-nationally and internationally' (Jussawalla, 1989, p.866).

Transnational banks (TNBs) heightened dramatically their role in the economies of less developed countries across the 1970s. 'From the early 1970s to the eruption of the debt crisis in 1982, transnational banks were the major suppliers of external financing to developing countries'

(United Nations, 1987, p.49). This intensification of TNB involvement in developing countries followed shortly on the heels of the early development of the Eurocurrency market in the 1960s when the banking industry first emerged into the international market as an arena of activity (United Nations, 1989, p.65). Though some TNBs are based in developing countries, the lion's share of the assets of TNBs operating from developing countries are held by offshore banking centers. Such sites are typically located in the Caribbean Basin, East Asia, and the Middle East. Moreover, these banks are owned mainly by firms represented among the top 100 banks for special benefits such as 'favorable taxation treatment, secrecy, lack of exchange controls and the near absence of regulation on international banking business' (United Nations, 1989, p.79). Including offshore financial centers, the relative share of developing countries' international banking assets held at about 20 per cent from 1975 to 1985, but the exclusion of offshore banking reduces the developing countries' share of international banking assets down to four or five percent over the same period (United Nations, 1989, p.79n). Thus, the developing countries remain excluded from developing international command and control centers of a stature which could parallel those of the core countries.

By the early 1980s the growth of foreign office and subsidiary networks ebbed among the largest 100 transnational banks, following their fast expansion during the 1970s. 'In 1985, the 100 largest TNBs had a foreign network of 4,660 offices. This represented an increase of only 147 offices from 1980' (United Nations, 1989, p.75). Nevertheless, the lower-tier TNBs appear to have continued the expansion of their networks. The United Nations Center on Transnational Corporations indicates that 'All Japanese banks...added some 354 offices to their foreign networks as against the 110 reported for the top banks only. Again, for the sample of the 100 largest banks, 32 additional foreign offices were opened in the United States between 1980 and 1985, whereas the total increase for all foreign banks was more than 200' (United Nations, 1989, p.75). Thus, the increasing internationalization of banking may well have continued across the 1980s even though the growth of the largest banks' networks of foreign offices dropped.

Though the expansion of the networks of the top 100 banks leveled off during the early to middle 1980s, the cast of corporate actors was reshuffled with the simultaneous relative decline of the American TNBs and a dramatic ascendance of the Japanese TNBs. By 1987 the Japanese had already secured their top position in international banking with 15 firms represented among the world's 20 largest banks (by assets) while the largest American bank was Citicorp, which then held the twenty-second position among world banks (*American Banker,* 1989, p.128). The significance of the emergence of the Japanese banks bears particular relevance for the international sourcing of manufacturing activities, not merely because of the general control over the distribution of scarce resources implied, but also because of the central role of banks in overseeing the direction and management of commodity chains. The salience of such networking is underlined by the case of the Japanese keiretsu (Gereffi and Hamilton, 1990, p.25):

> Each of the six intermarket business groups (Mitsubishi, Mitsu, Sanwa, Sumitomo, Fuyo, and DKB) is a network consisting of over 100 very large corporations, which are in turn linked through long-term subcontracting ties to thousands of small and medium-sized firms. Each network, including the subcontracting firms, encompasses many commodity chains spanning all major industrial sectors and contains a full set of financial firms, including a main bank.

The new telecommunications technologies facilitate the role of banking in the orchestration of international production and distribution networks which, in turn, contribute substantially to the total mix of factors which determine the continuing reconfiguration of the international division of labor.

The international banking system influences the pattern of the international division of labor not only through its control over the distribution of credit and capital, but also politically through the International Monetary Fund (IMF), which serves as an institution of mediation among TNBs, borrowing governments, and lending governments. The IMF also provides a 'multilateral front' to draw the brunt of public resentment for harsh lending terms away from the banks and governments which ultimately finance the loans (Gisselquist, 1981, p.27), and, furthermore, pressures the development policies of debtor governments.

But the banking sector, too, has felt the pressure of globalized competition. Banks have begun to lose control on the credit markets because information technology and governmental financial deregulations have enabled the insurance and brokerage firms to enter the credit market.

Information technology permits the efficient storage, retrieval, compilation, and analysis of information. Telecommunications technology has enabled the instantaneous off-site retrieval and transmission of both raw data and value-added information. A crucial feature of the recent trend in information and telecommunications technologies is the integration of these initially distinct lines of technology into a family of technological systems of information processing and transmission. As Dicken (1992, p.102) states, 'It is this quality of the convergence of two initially distinct technologies which is of the greatest importance for developments in today's (and tomorrow's) global economy'. Convergent information technology is a family of hardware and programming (i.e., software) technologies which is advancing very rapidly in terms of information processing speed. The convergent technology is also moving towards greater compatibility among separate technological products. This convergent technology has expanded the possibilities for more efficient economic organization both between and within firms by allowing rapid inter-firm transactions and by minimizing intra-firm response time to shifts in market trends. Furthermore, the accuracy of market assessment is enhanced by the amenability between the data collection and information retrieval tools of digital telecommunications and the analytic tools provided by computers running statistical programs.

The significance of information and telecommunications technology for coordinating economic activity dispersed worldwide is exemplified by the 'just-in-time' (JIT) production model in manufacturing. JIT signifies the accelerated feedback of market information into production planning to market goods optimally designed to capitalize on even the most fleeting market trends. Information technology is used at every step in the JIT cycle, from the automatic collection and compilation of sales data to the analysis and use of that data for product development and the modification of the production process to respond to current market demand. For knowledge-based economic activity, the impact of convergent technology is even more direct because global telecommunications systems themselves provide efficient delivery worldwide. The common denominator for the significance of information and telecommunications technologies for economic activity at the level of the firm is the cutting of minimum market response time in conjunction with the enhancement of the accuracy of the information on which such responses are based.

It is important to note that technological advancement in hardware serves to increase power (the speed and throughput of information processing and transmission) while improvements in software increase the efficiency of hardware utilization and ease of use. The goal of compatibility for systems development and integration can be promoted by improvements in either software or hardware.

A generalized understanding of the possible content of valued information transferred by telecommunications systems is necessary to comprehend the ways in which telecommunications technology has transformed the global economy. But also it is the capacities of the current telecommunications infrastructure and emerging telecommunications hardware technologies which set the boundaries for the ways in which information technology will affect business organizations and the regions worldwide where their activity is concentrated.

There are a number of telecommunications hardware technologies, such as fiber-optics and satellite-based transmission. The long-term discussions for worldwide digital connectivity standards, the Integrated Services Digital Network (ISDN), have determined that the technologies currently in use by the telephone companies should take the pre-eminent role in the future global digital telecommunications systems while other technologies will be employed for auxiliary roles in any standardized global network to be established. 'Although packet-switching and satellite providers may be less than happy with these conclusions, the overwhelming prevalence of telephone networks dictates that these networks form the basis for ISDN' (Stallings, 1992, p.5). Thus, the technological foundation for any standard worldwide digital telecommunications infrastructure which may be implemented will be based on the newer fiber-optic networks, which transmit digital signals. (The traditional metal wire technology which conveys analogue signals is, by contrast, much less efficient.) Dicken (1992) describes the capacity of the fiber-optic infrastructure under construction in the Pacific Basin region which is planned to be merely the first step in implementing a 'global digital highway.' According to Dicken (1992, pp.106-107), 'This will link the world's three major markets of North America, Western Europe and Japan, using a network of optical fiber cables capable of carrying 100,000 simultaneous messages'.

However, the plans for a single standardized telecommunications infrastructure remain problematic. The initial intentions for ISDN have already been undermined by the competing interests of the major corporate players and the smaller companies. As explained by Mulgan (1991, pp.39-41), the major corporations generally benefit by pursuing the monopolistic strategies of cultivating dependence on the technologies under their control while the smaller companies benefit by providing the technical means for users to circumvent such technological dominance established by the large corporate players. 'Initially conceived as a universal, standardized service, ISDN was instead marketed to target groups as one of a number of specialized services' (Mulgan, 1991, p.41). The consequences of telecommunications technology for societies and their economies may well differ depending on whether the plans for a standardized global network will be fulfilled or whether the development of the global digital telecommunications infrastructure will continue in an *ad hoc* fashion. 'The vision of the mosaic of competing customized networks stands in stark opposition to that of a global integrated network based on common standards' (Mulgan, 1991, p.46).

Though it may at first glance seem that the idea of a 'global digital highway' stands only to offer numerous services to most people, its implications for social and economic development will be mixed. Much of the literature on contemporary social and economic change which discusses the significance of telecommunications technology suggests that it carries far-reaching indirect effects across a much broader range of the labor market than merely the direct effects it has on the knowledge-based occupations.

The first major study to raise a warning about the negative consequences of the emerging global telecommunications infrastructure on the employment of less-skilled workers in the older industrialized countries was the project on the new international division of labor (NIDL) by Fröbel *et al.* (1980). The NIDL thesis predicted the siphoning off of low-skilled routine production jobs from the high-wage economies of the older industrialized countries to the low-wage economies of the newly industrialized and less developed countries. The emerging telecommunications infrastructure granted opportunities for minimizing production costs by enabling tight coordination of production sites dispersed globally to locations where the economic inequalities between countries could be exploited. The NIDL thesis, therefore, discussed 'structural' unemployment caused directly through the increased use of telecommunications technology by transnational corporations for the international organization of production. The employment trends of the older industrialized countries and the newly industrialized and less developed countries, however, have not conformed to the NIDL predictions and structural unemployment effects have proven to be more the exception than the rule (International Labour Organization, 1988; Fernández-Kelly, 1989; Dicken, 1992). As the European studies show, 'Over the long-term, employment gains tend to be concentrated in branches and companies that generate above average increases in labor productivity: conversely job losses tend to be greatest in industries and companies that do not innovate' (Michalski, 1989, p.14). However, the local protection for labor markets, which resulted not only from distance and geographical barriers but also from states' regulations, have been eroded partially as a result of the new telecommunications technologies (Dicken, 1992, pp.103-106, 365-366). The structure of labor force will shift in such a way that all types of industries will require workers who possess education and skills broadly applicable in the production of various goods and services. As the importance of specialists in the work place becomes more pronounced, greater coordination and cooperation will be required.

The worldwide trend in manufacturing and services is toward a global division of labor, superseding the international division of labor that characterized the organization of economic activity worldwide during the middle of the century. The highly competitive economic environment imposed by the consolidation of various sectors of multiple national- and local-level markets into a global market, made possible by the new information and telecommunications technologies, appears to have had a role in causing considerable *indirect* structural unemployment in the older industrialized countries. Interregional inequalities are exacerbated by the effects of telecommunications technologies, and

> [U]neven development tends to feed on itself. Those areas with the most advanced networks attract the most advanced sectors of manufacturing, finance or services which in turn do most to generate new demands for communication. As new global transoceanic fiber-optic networks are built...they tend further to enhance the relative weight of key hubs such as Tokyo, Singapore, Seoul, Hong Kong, London, New York, Chicago, and Los Angeles (Mulgan, 1991, p.47).

With the use of high technology in production and the shift of research and development from product development and innovations to applications, the advanced industrial nations are likely to benefit more than other nations. As Ogura observes (1989, p.xi), 'The tendency is to reduce raw materials input in manufacturing as a result of miniaturization of products and computerization of quality control procedures. Such a trend, if it continues for long, may upset the complementary trade patterns and suppliers of manufactured products'. The impact of information technology may be difficult to avoid, but for many nations, especially in the Third World, it does not seem all that positive. The fastest growth of information-related industries and the ease with which they can be linked with one another has already begun to create large multinational conglomerates which operate globally without much control.

If the national governments exercise controls on the free flow of information, they may discourage standardization of information technology and related systems. This undoubtedly will create a burdensome regulatory environment worldwide making open access more difficult and costly (Ogura, 1989, p.xi). For now, the internalization of production and mobility of capital are only marginally under the control of government. In spite of growing economic interdependence, many regions in industrialized countries and some developing countries are uncertain of their economic future because the growing density of economic networking globally increases competitive pressure in manufacturing and services.

The economic forces driving the trends towards faster and more powerful telecommunications systems are beyond the control of nations because they are manifest globally. The global structure and content of economic activity has already been transformed by the possibilities opened by the telecommunication infrastructure. Though the economic and social consequences of the global telecommunications infrastructure has, to date, been mixed, the movement towards higher capacity telecommunications systems and an even more tightly integrated global economy appears inevitable.

Résumé

Les Nouvelles Technologies de l'Information et la Division Internationale du Travail

L'influence des nouvelles technologies de l'information sur la division internationale du travail, sur les procédés de fabrication et sur les services commerciales est considérée, notamment sur la décentralisation de la production ainsi que sur la mobilité globale des capitaux. Les conséquences de ces derniers développements pour l'économie des pays développés et pour les pays en voie de développement sont notées. C'est l'utilisation optimale des capitaux et du main d'oeuvre qui détermine aujourd'hui la localisation industrielle.

Les nouvelles technologies de l'information ont transformé l'efficacité et la diversité des services commerciaux, en particulier, par la création des réseaux de diffusion transnationale et internationale destinés à la production et au marketing. Par suite du développement des ressources internes visant l'exécution des travaux de routine, les autres opérations étant contractées à l'extérieur, les coûts des transactions sont minimisés. Avec les nouvelles technologies, il y a une plus rapide évaluation de la demande par rapport aux produits, à la production efficace, à la contrôle de qualité et à la mobilité des capitaux. L'introduction d'une infrastructure de communication plus accélérée a également libéré les marchés de la contrôle nationale.

La convergence des technologies de l'information et des télécommunications a entraîné un temps accéléré de transaction et de production, ainsi qu'une réponse plus vite aux exigences du marché. Cependant, l'introduction d'une infrastructure de télécommunications normalisée (ISDN) reste toujours à l'état de projet. En même temps, il faut considérer les implications sociales et économiques d'un tel développement, par exemple, la formation technique insuffisante du main d'oeuvre des pays industrialisés.

Par le contrôle du crédit et du capital, ainsi que par l'intermédiaire du Fonds Monétaire International, la division internationale du travail se laisse influencer par le système bancaire international. Ce sont les établissements bancaires et les centres financiers qui s'efforcent de réaliser et de mettre à l'épreuve les nouveaux produits technologiques et les stratégies de l'implémentation. Les TNB (banques transnationales) ont entrepris le financement des projets en cours dans les pays en voie de développement, bien que ces institutions-là ne favorisent pas généralement les pays en dehors des îles Caraïbes, de l'Asie de l'Est et du Moyen-Orient. L'émergence des banques japonaises a contribué également en grande partie à la transformation du réseau de fabrication.

Il faut souligner les tendances suivantes:

- Les entreprises de plus petite taille.
- Les organisations hierarchiques traditionnelles cèdent la place à une diversité de formes organisationnelles.
- L'objectif de fabrication des produits remplacé par celui de fournir un service.
- La redéfinition du concept de 'travail' pour incorporer le

processus continu d'apprentissage et de décision.

L'implémentation des nouvelles technologies d'information dans les procédés de fabrication, ainsi que l'adaptation de la recherche et du développement envers les produits d'application est susceptible de favoriser les pays industrialisés plutôt que les pays en voie de développement. Le contrôle national de la diffusion de l'information aurait l'effet de créer un réseau d'accès restreint. L'introduction d'une infrastructure de télécommunications plus rapide a déjà transformé l'économie mondiale, tandis que la réalisation du projet de création d'un réseau de télécommunications intégré, est plus ou moins certain.

References

American Banker (1989). Top Numbers. New York.

Dicken, P. (1992). **Global Shift: The Internationalization of Economic Activity**. (Second Edition). New York: The Guilford Press.

Fernández Kelly, M.P. (1989). Broadening the Scope: Gender and International Economic Development. **Sociological Forum**, 4, 611-635.

Fröbel, F., Heinrichs, J., and Kreye, O. (1980). **The New International Division of Labour: Structural Unemployment in Industrialised Countries and Industrialisation in Developing Countries**. Translated by P. Burgess. Cambridge: Cambridge University Press.

Gereffi, G. and Hamilton, G.G. (1990). **The Social Economy of Global Capitalism: Modes of Incorporation in an Industrial World**. Second Draft of a paper presented at the American Sociological Association meetings. Washington, D.C., 11-15 August.

Gisselquist, D. (1981). **The Political Economics of International Bank Lending**. New York: Praeger Publishers.

Gwerin-Calvert, M.E. and Wildman, S.S. (1991). Information Technology and Vertical Integration: Evidence from Managing Sectors. In **Electronic Services Networks: A Business and Public Policy Challenge**, edited by M.E. Gwerin-Calvert and S.S. Wildman. New York: Praeger Publishers.

Hepworth, M.E. (1990). **Geography of the Information Economy**. New York: The Guilford Press.

International Labour Organization. Various years: 1972 through 1990/91. **Year Book of Labour Statistics**. Geneva: International Labour Office.

Jones, R.W. and Kierzkowski, H. (1990). The Role of Services in Production and International Trade: A Theoretical Framework. In **The Political Economy of International Trade**, edited by R.W. Jones and A.O. Krueger. Cambridge: Basil Blackwell.

Jussawalla, M. (1989). Overview of Thoughts Expressed on Information Technology and Economic Interdependence. In **Information Technology and Global Interdependence**, edited by M. Jussawalla, T. Okuma, and T. Araki. New York: Greenwood Press.

Kiechel, W. (1993). How We Will Work in the Year 2000. **Fortune**, May 17, 38-52.

Krommenacker, R.J. (1989). The Impact of Information Technology and Trade Interdependence. In **Information Technology and Global Interdependence**, edited by M. Jussawalla, T. Okuma, and T. Araki. New York: Greenwood Press.

Michalski, W. (1989). Advanced Information Technologies: Challenges and Opportunities. In **Information Technology and Global Interdependence**, edited by M. Jussawalla, T. Okuma, and T. Araki. New York: Greenwood Press.

Mulgan, G.G. (1991). **Communication and Control: Networks and the New Economies of Communication**. New York: The Guilford Press.

Noyelle, T.J. (1986). Advanced Services in the System of Cities. In **Local Economies in Transition: Policy Realities and Developmental Trends**, edited by E.M. Bergman. Durham: Duke University Press.

Ogura, K. (1989). Forward: Information Technologies and International Relations. In **Information Technology and Global Interdependence**, edited by M. Jussawalla, T. Okuma, and T. Araki. New York: Greenwood Press.

Semyonov, M. and Lewin-Epstein, N. (1986). Economic Development, Investment Dependence, and the Rise of Services in Less Developed Nations. **Social Forces**, 64, 582-598

Sifonis, J. (1990). The impact of Technology on Restructuring. In **Corporate Restructuring: A Guide to Creating the Premium-Valued Company**, edited by M.L. Rock and R.H. Rock. New York: McGraw-Hill Publishing Company.

Spero, J.E. (1985). Comment: U.S. Trade Policy and International Service Transactions. In **Managing the Service Economy: Prospects and Problems**, edited by R.P. Inman. New York: Cambridge University Press.

Stallings, W. (1992). **Advances in Integrated Services Digital Networks (ISDN) and Broadband ISDN**. Los Alamitos, CA: Institute of Electrical and Electronics Engineers Computer Society Press.

United Nations Centre on Transnational Corporations (1987). **Foreign Direct Investment, the Service Sector and International Banking**. Series A, No. 7. UNCTC Current Studies. New York: United Nations.

United Nations Conference on Trade and Development (1988). **Trade and Development Report**. New York: United Nations.

United Nations Conference on Trade and Development (1989). **Foreign Direct Investment, the Service Sector and International Banking**. Series A, No. 7. UNCTC Current Studies. New York: United Nations.

Williamson, O.E. (1981). The Economics of Organization: The Transaction Cost Approach. **American Journal of Sociology**, 87, 548-577.

Desktop Publishing: New Opportunities for Public Libraries

L'Edition Electronique: les Défis pour les Bibliothèques Publiques

Ian Hunter
Gateshead Libraries and Arts Service, UK

Introduction

My arguments in this paper assume certain principles fundamental to the sustenance of a national public library system: that access to knowledge, free at the point of delivery, is a basic right and a function of a national economy; that access to literature and information by the greatest number ultimately enhances economic performance; and that public libraries can serve to ease the impact of economic deprivation.

I respond as a practitioner to the current position of public libraries in the United Kingdom. I do hope, however, that what I have to say has wider significance.

My aims are:

- to review the role of the public library in the light of rapid developments taking place in the information media business.
- to examine key areas of opportunity for public libraries.
- to describe some of the desktop publishing work that has been undertaken by Gateshead Libraries and Arts Service in the UK.

If the role of public libraries is to store and facilitate access to books, then they are under threat on a global scale. New and not so new technologies are successfully competing with the book as carriers of knowledge and culture.

This can be illustrated in the field of fiction video sales set against the sales of novels. The novel is regarded by many as the core of the public library service but a survey of the figures suggests that it is in danger of being marginalized. Ignoring the big sellers by famous names, the average sale of a new hardback novel has fallen in the UK to about 600 copies (Morgan, 1993).

However, the market for 'fiction' videos is increasingly prosperous. They represent a lucrative bonus for film producers and a boost for retailers who can charge whatever they feel the market will bear, unlike booksellers whose prices are fixed by the net book agreement.

Some titles can be directly compared. For example, the video *JFK* sold over 400,000 whilst Penguin's tie-in, *On the trail of the Assassins*, sold 110,000 (Morgan, 1993).

Sell through video turnover in 1992 was £375m, whilst gross annual book sales have been running at about £1.4 billion. However, applied to fiction literature alone, the figures are much closer together with books only about 20 per cent ahead of their electronic competition (Morgan, 1993).

At such a rate, with video sales doubling each year, within three years two fiction videos will be sold for every one fiction book.

The domestic television is a key strategic instrument. Individuals are spending an increasing amount of time per day watching TV and this is likely to increase as new interactive formats, such as CD-I (Compact Disc Interactive) and cable networking through ISDN (Integrated Services Digital Network), become popular.

There is not only an exponential growth in electronic systems. In each year of the 1990s, more information will be printed than the total up to the start of the 20th century (Feenan and Dixon, 1992). Newspapers remain the key distributors, with the advertising market serving as a useful indicator of the enduring power of this medium which has been around for longer than public libraries. For example, throughout European countries in 1991, the press took an average of 65 per cent of all advertising set against radio's 5 per cent. Over 27 million national Sunday newspapers are sold throughout the UK when every public library is closed for business.

So what role can be played by publicly funded library services under much stress? As a key cog in a democratic society, how we can we benefit from and, in turn, provide benefits out of the information explosion? A good starting point would be to ask 'why bother?'. At a time of recession it is customary to view public libraries as a value added service, rather than a necessity. Maintenance takes priority over development.

It helps to return to principles, to look at the basic philosophy. In 1849, the report from the UK's Select Committee on Public Libraries, lamenting the lack of developments in comparison with other European countries and the United States, concluded that public libraries were there to 'foster and encourage...that love for literature and reverence for knowledge...for the great body of our people' (Great Britain, 1849). This was to be achieved through books, which is hardly surprising because the book was effectively the only medium available.

Today, the book and the building would appear absurd starting points to anyone wishing to pioneer access to knowledge for the 'great body of our people'. Without doubt, the book is a powerful and much loved medium that has a future, but it is no longer the exclusive purveyor of knowledge. It would seem that we have remembered the medium but forgotten the essential message. There are now many more forms of media which, in some cases, represent more appropriate means of facilitating access to knowledge to the widest public.

In the UK, the net expenditure on the public library service was £698.5m in 1991/92 with over 19,000 service points and nearly 30,000 staff employed. At least half of the population holds a library card. This indicates an important national facility, provided to satisfy a demand. However, as we approach the twenty-first century, it must never be allowed to become unimaginative, marginalized and archaic.

Public librarians embrace new technology to a far lesser extent than our academic librarian counterparts, yet there is no reason why students and academics should be deemed more appropriate users than the public at large.

The mixed progress has many causes. Three can be identified:

- *Governing bodies*: There is a marked lack of vision and funding in all sectors.
- *IT vendors*: There is little confidence in technologies that are sold to practitioners with considerable hyperbole on the basis of features rather than benefits.
- *Librarians*: The customary model of information management describes the assimilation, storage, organization and, finally, the retrieval of information. However, an additional node in the model should represent 'presentation'—information manufacture, or knowledge presented in the most appropriate form.

A fundamental role shift is required for public librarians, from passive storekeepers to publishers, healthily aware of the manifold needs of the public they serve.

Technological developments are inviting unprecedented opportunities for development and effective service delivery. These can be addressed in the following key themes:

- The capacity to gain new customers
- Secondary publishing
- Income generation

The capacity to gain new customers

Any publicly funded service should aim to reach all members of its intended audience. Those who do not currently use public library services can be functionally divided into the 'unwilling'—people disinclined to use the service for whatever reason—and the 'unable'—people disabled by the form in which the service is provided.

'The unwilling'

Having been bound to PCs over the last few years, with all of the paraphernalia associated with multi-functional computers—external drives, keyboards, mixed interfaces etc.—multimedia technology is at last available in the home. Riding on the success of CD-I, Sega and Nintendo, opportunities are being created for interactive multimedia information systems through domestic appliance-based technology—boxes with little physical resemblance to computers.

The games titles currently on sale quite consciously pitch at the mass market. They are unreservedly down market and spectacularly successful. CD-I marketeers talk of unskewering the 'couch potato' from his couch and creating a new family hearthside around the interactive television.

Those very same couch potatoes ought to be our target. In the UK, they comprise the 65 per cent who do not use the service in its current form for whatever reason. They are the great unwilling, who pay for the service through local taxes yet never visit the local library.

In Gateshead, we recognize the need for pragmatic service provision and are accordingly working with United Artists, our local Cable franchise, with a view to developing a community information channel. Currently we have a videotext-based community information system available on a multi-terminal network, and we will utilize this core information for the cable system. It is pragmatic to acknowledge the power of the TV as an effective device for information delivery.

Disabled people

Public libraries in the UK are statutorily compelled to provide access to their services for all in the community, regardless of abilities or disabilities. The 1964 Public Libraries Act refers to the need for libraries to 'reach the whole population', a statement unqualified by conditions of physical ability. We have 6 million registered disabled people in the UK alone, all of whom have a basic right to information.

Multimedia represents a major breakthrough in the field because the use of multisensory formats can compensate for particular forms of sensory impairment.

In Gateshead, we have developed CD-I as an information resource for disabled people. With most published information available only in print, millions are denied rightful access. The National Disability Information Project, a £3m initiative over three years by the British government's Department of Health was established to address this issue. Gateshead, one of 12 pilot projects, is probably the most innovative in exploring various technological methods of facilitating access.

Like many products not specifically designed for disabled people, CD-I has certain coincidental advantages. Apart from its multisensory capacity, its link to the domestic television affords benefits to those with mobility difficulties which are unavailable in, for example, PC-based multimedia systems stationed at points often remote from convenient access. Other advantages include the functional similarity between the navigational control on a CD-I handset and the arm mounted control on electric wheelchairs.

Our first disc, published in February 1993, is entitled *Into Work—employment opportunities for disabled people*. It is an informative product but our main interest was to see how the concept would be received and how effectively the medium performs.

The disc follows rigid design principles following consultation with groups such as the British Deaf Association, and includes British Sign Language in partial motion video form.

We are currently conducting strategic tests with various groups and individuals and so far the response has been extremely positive and encouraging. Most disabled people are acutely aware of denied access and quicker than most to see the enabling potential of technology. Some use quite sophisticated systems to help them achieve independent daily living.

We are currently working on our second disc, on health issues, and have other ideas in mind.

Electronic publishing enables information delivery in forms preferred by customers not currently using traditional services, from those who are unwilling to those who are unable for reasons of disability.

The more customers reached, the more cost effective the service and this must impact upon governing bodies when considering the economic viability and vitality of library services.

Secondary publishing

There are millions of organizations publishing printed information in diverse formats and it has been a traditional role of public libraries to assimilate and distribute such sources of knowledge.

This casts the librarian in the role of passive handler, accepting information in the form in which it is published and disseminating it in the same form. Some would see library services as rightly distinct from the publishing industry, each with different aims. However, a scan through the annual reports of international publishing companies would suggest that we are at least in the same field of business.

Examples include (Graham, 1993):

- CEP Communication 'is dedicated to helping people share knowledge and have access to a comprehensive range of information'
- News Corporation is 'committed to the generation and dissemination of information and ideas'
- Time Warner 'takes a responsibility...to lead in fighting for a healthier society, improving the education of our children, wiping out functional illiteracy, and opening up the marketplace of ideas to the widest diversity of human thought and experience'
- Wolters Kluwer's objective is 'to meet on a commercial basis...the requirement for information which should be appropriately classified, upgraded and updated'

Each of these mission statements would serve the public library movement, yet individual services would probably regard such bold philanthropy as incongruous in the light of impoverished resources.

Publishing may not appear to be the responsibility of libraries but desktop technologies, including video, printing and multimedia, have brought the capacity to all who have an interest in producing accessible information.

Desktop publishing has brought new opportunities. It is now possible to collate printed information, transcribe it and publish it in other formats that are more appropriate to their purpose.

For example, in Gateshead, using quite simple facilities—desktop scanners, optical character recognition software, Apple Macintosh PCs and laser writer printers—we take material published by a range of organizations, both large and small, and transcribe it into braille, large print, audio cassette, plain English or any other suitable format. We have 'handled' diverse data, from electricity bills, to art gallery guides, committee reports and tourist information. The public library service thus becomes a specialist publishing house complementing its traditional storage and retrieval functions. The information management model begins with assimilation and should not end with retrieval, but with presentation. Knowledge can be presented in forms that will reach the unable and tempt the unwilling.

As well as generating revenue, such projects render the service a key economic cog in a fair society dependent on effective communications.

Income generation

With electronic publishing skills and equipment 'in-house', it is possible for public libraries to offer training and bureau services with a view to income generation. For example, in Gateshead, we have helped a wide range of organizations to produce their own videos and other material including presentations using multimedia computer systems. This work fits quite clearly with our brief to facilitate access to knowledge, enabling its dissemination in mass media formats such as videos. The income subsequently generated helps the continuation of this work.

Apart from training and bureau work, there are opportunities for direct selling either by retailing published materials or selling 'digital space'. This can be illustrated by the hyperTour system in operation in Gateshead. Situated in the MetroCentre, the biggest indoor shopping mall in Europe, hyperTour is a heavily used tourist information system running on Apple Macintosh equipment installed in the tourist information bureau. It comprises text, colour stills and movies, presenting information on hotels and attractions in the area. Each colour image enhancement is 'for sale' on the database with the revenue sustaining the system. The principles of audio visual librarianship are carried forward into multimedia with tourists not seeing commercial advertising but visually enhanced information. For example, they see the beds in which they are to sleep that night, before confirming accommodation bookings.

In the area of direct sales, videos, CDs and computer games offer unique opportunities to bring people into library buildings if provided on an imaginative and commercial basis. Our own 'Sound Gallery' in Gateshead— a library of audio visual items and equipment for hire— has increased its turnover by 300 per cent in four years at a time when book issues have remained relatively stable. Managed commercially, it competes well against high street video rental stores but complements its entertainment stock with a range of more informative titles.

Conclusion

Gateshead Libraries and Arts Service is much like other public libraries in providing a traditional book lending and reference information service. We are conscious of our 'core' services, eager to protect them and proud of having one of the highest book issue ratios in the UK. Books are highly valued by our customers for many reasons and accordingly, we issue for loan about 2.5 million volumes per year.

However, the book is not an exclusive purveyor. People are usually the best carriers of knowledge and we value dedicated and enthusiastic individuals on our staff.

We try to make our service more cost effective and economically viable by targeting 'the whole population' within our community, including those who don't read books. To achieve this, our approach to information technology is based on a conviction that its true worth to a public service is not in administrative or housekeeping systems but in direct information delivery. Publishing is critical: video, multimedia, audio, paper—whatever the customer wants. The form is as important as the content.

Such services do not threaten the book, rather they boost issues by making the total service more accessible.

We have achieved much work through disparate funding sources and it is a constant challenge to maintain services. In the current uncertain political and economic situation, it is not clear how long we will be able to continue certain developments. To a great extent, matters are beyond our control.

However, I hope that I have demonstrated some of the practical ways in which libraries with a public to serve can take opportunities from electronic and desktop publishing that will enhance their standing and reinforce the necessity of the cultural and economic role they play.

Résumé

L'Edition Electronique: les Défis pour les Bibliothèques Publiques

Le rôle de la bibliothèque publique dans le contexte des développements récents dans les nouvelles technologies de l'information est évalué, relevant de nouveaux défis pour les bibliothèques publiques. Une analyse des procédés d'édition électronique à Gateshead Libraries and Arts Services au Royaume Uni est présentée.

Les formats de la nouvelle technologie remettent en cause le rôle traditionnel des bibliothèques publiques qui consistait à fournir les services de stockage et d'accès aux livres. C'est le cas pour les vidéos, par example, surtout pour les titres correspondant aux oeuvres d'imagination, pour la télévision, pour la communication interactive par réseau téléphonique (ISDN), etc. La croissance des systèmes électroniques ainsi que des médias est notée.

La redéfinition du rôle de la bibliothèque a pour but d'encourager l'exploitation de la croissance de l'information. Il y a lieu de reconnaître que le livre n'est plus le seul véhicule de l'information, bien que l'investissement dans le réseau de bibliothèques municipales au Royaume Uni indique l'importance de cette ressource. Pour éviter la marginalisation, les bibliothèques publiques devront revoir le développement des technologies de l'information afin d'évaluer les possibilités d'implémentation éventuelle. L'absence d'une stratégie et des fonds gouvernementaux, aussi bien que d'un modèle de la gestion de l'information est déplorée.

Parmi les initiatives futures de la bibliothèque publique: la recherche de la clientèle nouvelle; l'édition secondaire; et les nouvelles sources de revenu. Prochain développement: l'accès domestique au multimédia, qui offre plusieurs possibilités à la bibliothèque publique, tout comme l'ordinateur personnel. Gateshead Libraries a profité de la technologie du

CD-I (disque compact interactif) pour créer un service d'information communautaire à base de vidéotexte avec accès sur un système à plusieurs terminaux.

Le droit d'accès à l'information est imposé par la loi. Les bibliothèques publiques doivent mettre en place des initiatives pour garantir l'accès aux handicapés. Ces initiatives seront facilitées par les développements technologiques tels que le multimédia offrant des présentations diverses. Un tel projet— dans le cadre du National Disability Information Project— c'est la responsabilité de Gateshead Libraries, qui se charge de rechercher les voies technologiques pour l'accès des handicapés.

La bibliothèque publique doit s'adapter à la génération des informations sous des formes multiples, en maîtrisant la technologie de l'édition électronique et en participant aux réseaux de diffusion. A Gateshead, les informations diffusées par un grand nombre d'organisations sont transcrites en braille, par exemple, ou enregistrées sur cassette. L'édition électronique se voit comme une forme de présentation entre autres.

En utilisant les ressources de l'édition électronique, de la technologie et de l'expertise interne, la bibliothèque publique peut offrir les services de formation et de bureau. Gateshead Libraries est venu à l'aide des organisations voulant présenter des vidéos ou autre matériel, y compris les présentations multimédia. La vente des publications à base de diffusion électronique ou de l''espace digitale' est désormais possible. A titre d'exemple—le système hyperTour à Gateshead, système électronique d'information touristique dont les images en couleur se vendent à travers la base de données. Gateshead Libraries a crée une 'galerie de sons' ou audiovidéothèque comportant des vidéos, des CD et même des jeux d'ordinateur.

Malgré son rôle traditionnel de bibliothèque publique, avec ses services de prêt et de référence, Gateshead Libraries and Arts Service a fait l'effort de s'adapter aux nouvelles technologies de l'information afin de fournir à la communauté un service comportant l'information sous toutes les formes, y compris les présentations électroniques. En dépit des problèmes de financement, les efforts de modernisation et d'efficacité de la bibliothèque pourrait servir d'exemple.

References

Feenan, R. and Dixon,T.J. (1992). **Information and technology applications in commercial properties**. Macmillan.

Graham,G. (1993). Reporting the reports. **The Bookseller**, 25 June, 28.

Great Britain. (1849). **Select Committee on Public Libraries**. Report 1849. London: House of Commons.

Morgan, R. (1993). The primal screen. **The Independent**, 2 January, 27.

MEASURES OF ECONOMICS OF INFORMATION AND INFORMATION ECONOMICS

Les Mesures de l'Economie de l'Information et de l'Economie Informationnelle

Keynote Address

Discours-programme

José-Marie Griffiths
University of Tennessee, Knoxville, Tennessee, USA

Introduction

This paper presents a general framework for describing measures of economics of information and information economics.[1] It focuses primarily on information as an entity (or commodity) that is created, processed, communicated, and used. In particular, the framework of measures applies to information traditionally recorded in publications and other media, and to services and products that facilitate communication of the recorded information. The measures are not intended to address the role of information in improving the efficiency of markets or the information in the context of disequilibrium as briefly discussed by Lamberton (1994). To help describe the framework of measures, I will provide examples for scholarly journal publications and database search services—the former being an example of an information product and the latter a service, although the service results in a product in the form of printed outputs. Most of these examples are extracted from three books (Griffiths and King, 1990, 1991 and 1993a).

I wish to emphasize that in both of these examples, as well as in most information services and products we at this conference deal with, *information* is the economic entity of concern. However, economics of information are affected to an appreciable extent by the attributes of information, of media or technologies used, and of services or products. Many of the papers in this conference allude to the unusual nature of

1. My colleague Donald King contributed to this written version of my address to the Third International Information Research Conference.

information as an economic entity to which traditional properties of public, private, welfare, and merit goods do not easily apply. For example, information in books found in a publisher's inventory awaiting sale is somewhat like a private good, in that a copy sold depletes the stock of books and those who purchase it benefit from the purchase. However, the same book found in a public library is more akin to a public good, in that use does not deplete the stock (although it denies use to others for a period of time) and the information has a shared common good for the community served. One aspect of information services and products that is different from consumer services and products is that the consumer market usually involves several very similar sources of services or products provided by competitor companies. The decision to purchase an item or use a service depends on a choice among competing prices and other attributes, such as quality, reliability, ease of use, etc. However, the competitive sources of information are often not found in other like services or products, but rather in different sources of the information. For example, when deciding to subscribe to a journal, a scientist will consider not only price and amount and relevance of information found in the journal, but also whether the journal is available in a nearby library or from a colleague, or whether the information is available from other sources such as colleagues, conferences, books, and so on.

Definition of information

In this framework, I define information as 'recorded messages that convey meaning to both the creators and intended users of the messages'. Information *content* is the meaning of the information, and two *forms* of information include *format* (e.g., textual, numeric, graphic, etc.) and *structure* within the formats (e.g., language, syntax, semantics of textual information, expression of numeric information in equations, tables graphs, etc.). Information *medium* as used in the framework includes the ways in which information is 'packaged' or 'captured', such as paper-form, microform, electronic, magnetic, etc. Most information services and products are designed to process information or information media. Information processes are performed for the purposes of improving content (i.e., making it more accurate, precise, relevant, etc.), transforming from one form to another to make it more usable and useful (e.g., translating from one language to another, editing a text, aggregating or modeling data, etc.), describing or synthesizing information to provide intellectual logical access to it, and evaluating or analyzing information to assist end-users. Media processing is performed by information services to enhance communications and provide storage and physical access to information when needed. All of these processes 'add value' to information and affect the economics of information.

Generic economic measures

For each service or product, economics of information involve several types and levels of participants, including:

- information service or product *providers* such as creators, primary and secondary publishers, libraries, clearinghouses, vendors, etc.;
- information *users* such as students, teachers, professionals in the workplace (scientists, engineers, lawyers, medical practitioners, managers, sales staff, etc.), recreational readers (e.g., some public library users), etc.;
- user *organizations* (e.g., educational institutions, companies, government agencies, etc.) or *communities* (e.g., served by public libraries);
- aggregations of organizations or communities to *industries* or *sectors*; and
- *society* as a whole.

These participants are all affected to some degree by changes in the economics of services and products, and a framework of measures should include all their perspectives.

There are five generic economic measures that can be applied to each information service or product:

- *Inputs* are (1) the amount of resources applied to perform the service or provide the product and (2) the attributes of these resources.
- *Outputs* are the results of the resources applied to perform the service or provide the product, in terms of quantities of output and attributes of the service or product.
- *Usage* measures the amount of service or product use (or non-use) and factors that affect use (or non-use).
- *Outcomes* are measures of the consequences of use and non-use of a service or product.
- *Domain* measures involve descriptions of the service or

product environment or market, including the size and characteristics of the user community, inherent information needs and requirements, and other factors that might affect the economics of information.

Figure 1 presents more specific measures associated with these five types of generic measures.

Examples of information services and products discussed to this point involve what one might call direct services or products, in that they all serve users of the information. The economic measures above, particularly input and output, apply to indirect services and products as well. For example, in a library a number of operational functions are performed, such as collection development, acquisitions, catalog maintenance, etc., that might be considered indirect services. Also, support functions such as administration, finance and accounting, personnel, etc., are indirect services. Usage and outcome measures of indirect services involve the extent to which they are used and affect direct services. I will say more about indirect services later.

Input measures

The types of resources applied to perform a service or provide a product include staff, equipment and systems, facilities (and furniture, etc.), information, supplies, and so on. The amount of these resources can be measured by the amount of time of staff and equipment, size of facilities, amount of information applied, amount of supplies used (e.g., reams of paper), etc. One economic measure common to these resources is expenditures measured in monetary units. Attributes of staff include their knowledge and skills developed from education, training, and experience. Attributes of equipment include quality, reliability, readability, etc.; attributes of facilities include ambience, temperature and climate control, etc. Attributes of information applied include accuracy, precision, comprehensiveness, etc. Resources applied to journal publishing include editors, redactors, printers, administration and other support, etc.; computers, character readers, presses, etc.; space required for all the publication activities; information (manuscripts) provided by authors; and paper, wrapping, postage, etc. Resources used in database search services include searchers and support staff; equipment and systems such as PCs (or terminals), search software, vendor services, photocopiers, etc.; and information such as the databases and entries provided by vendors.

Figure 1: Conceptual Framework: Generic Measures

PARTICIPANTS	SPECIFIC ECONOMIC MEASURES
Information Service or Product Provider	Inputs (Resources) • Amount of resources • Cost of resources • Attributes of resources Outputs (Products/Services) • Amount of output • Attributes of output » Price » Quality » Timeliness » Availability » Accessibility
Information User (Actual and Potential)	Usage • Amount of use and non-use • Factors affecting use and non-use » Purpose of use » Alternative sources of information » Importance of attributes of output » Satisfaction with attributes of output » Awareness » Ease of use » Cost of use
Organization/Market/ Community Served Industry/Sector Society	Outcomes (Consequences of Use and Non-Use) • Time saved • Improved productivity • Improved quality of work • Improved timeliness of work • Achieving organization/community goals Domain • Number of persons in community served • Number of persons who use a service of product • Characteristics of users and non-users • Characteristics of community or organization served • Inherent information needs and requirements

Output measures

Output measures include the amount of services performed or products produced by the provider, and their attributes such as price, quality, timeliness, availability, accessibility, and so on. Output quantities of scholarly journal publishing could include number of pages, articles, issues, and subscriptions (and/or separate copies of articles distributed). In fact, estimates of total publishing costs are dependent on all these measures. Attributes include quality and comprehensiveness of articles, readability of type fonts, quality of citations, and so on. Output quantities of database search services might include number of user requests filled, number of searches (queries) performed, number of databases searched or number of items identified (or presented, if screening is performed). Attributes of search services include quality of searches (e.g., recall and precision), timeliness of response, availability of search service (e.g., hours service is provided), and accessibility (e.g., distance to the service and whether telephone requests are accepted).

Usage measures

Usage measures include amount of use (and non-use) and factors that affect use and non-use of information services and products. Amount of use can be greater than output measures. For example, a journal subscription can be read many times by a subscriber or it might be shared by colleagues, an article can be photocopied and given to a colleague, and a library subscription can involve hundreds of uses involving many users. Similarly, usage of information from search outputs might extend beyond the number of searches or items identified and read.

Factors found to affect use (or non-use) include the purposes for which information is used. Purposes of use can be categorized in many ways, but type of work (e.g., management, research, legal work, operations, etc.) and activities (e.g., making decisions, performing laboratory experiments, preparing legal briefs, examining new lighting systems, etc.) for which the information is used seem to discriminate amount of usage fairly well. Also, usage varies with users' disciplines. Some specialties in disciplines can be very narrow, thereby limiting the amount of use of publications, database searching, and other services and products that are subject-related.

One of the most important factors affecting the use of information services and products is the availability of alternative sources of information. As I mentioned above, this factor is somewhat different for information than for consumer products, in that the choices for information services and products are not, for the most part, among competing brands, but rather among entirely different ways of obtaining the information. When asked where they would obtain information read in an article, if the article were not available, some said they would not seek the information and others said they already knew it. Most said they would seek the information from colleagues, consultants, other types of documents, etc. These sources tend to be much more expensive to obtain than the journal source of information. More is said about alternative sources later. On the other hand, alternative sources of database searching are found to be more 'competitive' with searches performed by library staffs.

When asked what alternatives might be used for their most recent search (if library search services were not available), about one-eighth indicated that the searches would not be done. About one-half would be performed by the requesting professionals, with the remaining searches by someone on the staff (12 per cent), a broker (11 per cent), another external library (12 per cent), or by contacting someone else for the information (2 per cent). On average, the cost of the alternatives is about twice the cost of using library services, although in some instances the difference in cost is not great. Generally, reasons given for using the library search services are that they are considered better, faster, and less expensive than the alternative sources. More is said later about the effects of such attributes on the extent to which the service is used.

Other important factors related to the extent of use of information services and products are the importance of and satisfaction with attributes of the services. Price is clearly an important attribute of information services and products. Other attributes of scholarly journals found to be important include relevance of articles to work, whether or not articles are refereed, currency of reported information, emphasis on theory or methods, typestyle, and so on (see for example Charles River Associates, 1979; Institute of Physics, 1976). Studies do not always show price to be the most important attribute. In fact, subscribers express willingness to pay more for certain attributes. Attributes of particular importance to database search services include relevance of output to users' information needs, number of references in search output, timeliness of response, and remote access to service (i.e., telephone or e-mail requests). As I will show later, the extent of use of the service is related to the level of satisfaction with such attributes.

Lack of awareness is often found to inhibit the amount of use of information services or products. Professionals are sometimes unaware of relevant scholarly journals, and while database search services are designed to identify needed articles, some professionals are even unaware of database search services. For example, in 21 organizations for which King Research performed in-depth studies (Griffiths and King, 1993a), we found that more than one-fifth of the professionals were unaware of these services and one-third of them indicated they would be likely to use the service now that they are aware of it. Many information services have even lower levels of awareness.

Other factors related to the extent of use are ease and cost of use of services or products. Ease of use is going to become a highly relevant factor for journals as they become more available through electronic media. Users may resist in-depth reading of articles at workstations in much the same way they have with microform readers. Ease of use is less important for database search services than for many other services, although interaction between the user and searcher can be important. Cost of use is a very important factor and is part of the 'price' paid by users. Typically, journal readers 'pay' an average of nearly 100 hours per year in acquiring the reading journals. About 10 per cent of this time is spent in acquiring articles (i.e., identifying, locating, and obtaining them). Later I will show that such time has an appreciable effect on the sources used to obtain journal articles. The literature contains many examples of how library use declines as distance (measured in time) to them increases. This obeys the typical price-demand relationship of consumer products. The principal reason given by users as to why they delegate database searching to intermediaries is the time it would take for them to search themselves.[2] They average about 15 minutes requesting database searches compared with hours of their time needed for searching themselves.

Outcome measures

Outcome measures describe the consequences of information service or product use and non-use. For professionals, outcomes can be described

---

2. Users have also said that competent database searchers can often perform searches *better* than they themsleves can.

in terms of how use affects their work in terms of saving time; improving productivity, quality, and timeliness of work; and helping achieve their organizations' goals. Similar outcomes can also be measured for public library use (Griffiths and King, 1990; Griffiths and King 1993b).

Both national surveys (King et al, 1981; Griffiths et al, 1991) and surveys of professionals in organizations (Griffiths and King, 1993a) have shown that information read in journals results in savings (in labor time or other resources) to the readers or their colleagues of about $300[3] per reading.[4] About 44 per cent of journal readings are said to affect the quality of the primary activity for which the article was read, and 19 per cent of readings affect the timeliness of this work. Reading is also found to improve decisions, result in new ideas, and help guide future work. Several indicators of productivity are found to be positively correlated with amount of reading, and professionals whose achievements have been recognized through awards and other means read journals significantly more than others. Information identified through database search services also has a significant effect on such outcomes. Clearly, if there were no journals, the cost to obtain the information found in them would be significantly greater than the time now spent acquiring and reading articles (roughly 100 hours) plus the other costs involved. For database search services, the additional cost is estimated to be $138 per search over the current costs.

Domain measures

Domain measures describe the community or market served by information services or products. Such measures can include the number of persons in the potential population, such as all scientists in a discipline for a scholarly journal or all professionals in an organization for database search services. These measures might also include the number who subscribed to or read a journal article, or the number who used database search services in an organization. Sometimes it is useful to know the characteristics of the user population—such as work roles, educational

---

3. Unless otherwise noted, monetary amounts are given in US dollars.
4. Only about one-fourth of the readings result in such savings, and most of the savings used in the calculation of this average are derived from less than 2 per cent of the readings.

backgrounds, year of experience, and so on—that can have an effect on information service or product use. For example, managers are more likely to subscribe to and use trade journals than professionals engaged in research, but the reverse is true of scholarly journals and use of database search services. Older professionals are more likely to use database search services than younger ones (because the latter search for themselves more frequently). Scientists in academic institutions use database search services far less than those found in companies and government agencies. Organizational cultures also affect the extent to which time is spent reading and services such as database searching are used. The new emphasis on 'learning organizations' is likely to affect such use. Other organizational characteristics of importance might include the number of sites and their geographic proximity, organization structure, type of product sold, and so on.

I have described five generic types of economic measures—service or product *inputs* and *outputs*, *usage*, *outcomes*, and *domain*—and I have presented some examples of observations my colleagues and I have made regarding these measures for journals and database search services. These economic measures, while interesting, convey little meaning on their own and provide little use for decision-making. For these measures to be useful, one must develop relationships and comparisons among them. Below I will provide a description of such relationships, with examples.

Derived economic measures

There are five types of relationships among economic measures derived from the five types previously described (see Figure 2). These include:

- Service or product *performance measures* are relationships between input and output measures.
- *Effectiveness measures* are relationships between outputs and usage.
- *Cost-effectiveness measures* are relationships between inputs and usage.
- *Impact measures* relate usage and outcomes, usage and domain measures, and outcomes and domain measures.
- *Cost-benefit measures* compare any of the economic measures observed for two alternatives.

***Figure 2**: Conceptual Framework: Relationships among Measures*

PARTICIPANTS	SPECIFIC ECONOMIC MEASURES	RELATIONSHIPS AMONG MEASURES
Information Service or Product Provider	Inputs (Resources) • Amount of resources • Cost of resources • Attributes of resources Outputs (Products/Services) • Amount of output • Attributes of output » Price » Quality » Timeliness » Availability » Accessibility	Performance Effectiveness Cost-Effectiveness Cost-Benefit
Information User (Actual and Potential)	Usage • Amount of use and non-use • Factors affecting use and non-use » Purpose of use » Alternative sources of information » Importance of attributes of output » Satisfaction with attributes of output » Awareness » Ease of use » Cost of use	
Organization/Market/ Community Served Industry/Sector Society	Outcomes (Consequences of Use and Non-Use) • Time saved • Improved productivity • Improved quality of work • Improved timeliness of work • Achieving organization/ community goals Domain • Number of persons in community served • Number of persons who use a service of product • Characteristics of users and non-users • Characteristics of community or organization served • Inherent information needs and requirements	Impact

More extensive examples of these derived measures are given in the three books mentioned previously.

Performance measures

The two most common economic performance measures are productivity and unit costs. Productivity is the ratio of output to input, where output is the quantity and input is measured by number of staff hours or cost required to perform a service or provide a product. Productivity of database search services is typically found to be about 10 searches per hour for quick look-up searching and 0.5 searches per hour for in-depth searching.[5] Productivity measured by units per hour is useful for determining how well staff perform a service or provide a product. Also, for budgeting and planning, if one has an estimate of the trend of the number of units or transactions likely in the future, the productivity ratio can be used to estimate the amount of staff time required to produce that number of transactions. For example, a forecast of 1,000 in-depth searches would require about 2,000 hours of staff time. Raw productivity measures should be considered in light of the input and output attributes as well. For example, a database searcher with experience and subject knowledge should be more productive than a person without these attributes. Furthermore, such a searcher should produce higher quality searches.

Productivity measured in units produced per dollar convey little meaning to either journal publishing or database search services (e.g., 0.006 searches per dollar for database searching). However, unit costs convey substantial meaning for both. Unit cost is the ratio of input cost to output quantity. For example, the unit cost of a typical scholarly journal subscription is about $150 where total costs[6] are about $250,000. Typical unit costs of database search services are $16 per search for quick look-up searching and $160 per search for in-depth searching. Unit cost measures are also useful for budgeting and planning in that future costs can be estimated from them. They also provide a very useful reality check.

---

5. A search is defined here as a user request which may involve any number of queries to one or more databases.
6. Total costs for these calculations include the allocation of all indirect costs associated with journal publishing and library operations and their support functions.

Often, unit costs decrease as the amount of services performed or products provided increases. This phenomenon is termed economies of scale. Economies of scale are principally due to spreading large fixed costs (those costs incurred regardless of the number of units produced) across increased quantities of output.[7] Both journal publishing and database search services exhibit such economies of scale. For journal publishing fixed costs include the large cost of starting a new journal and pre-run costs associated with editing, composition, graphics, page masters, and so on. For database searching the fixed costs involve equipment, special reference materials, and so on. Variable costs are those that vary with each unit output. Variable costs for journal publishing, known as runoff, include subscription maintenance, printing, binding, wrapping, mailing and distribution costs, and so on. These costs vary largely by the number of issues per year, number of pages per issue, and copies printed per issue (i.e., number of subscriptions). Typically, fixed costs might account for 60 per cent of total costs, variable costs for about 32 per cent, and other costs for about 8 per cent. The total and unit costs for journals are depicted in Figures 3 and 4. One aspect of economies of scale caused by spreading large fixed costs is that the average costs approach the average variable cost (i.e., the runoff and distribution costs for journal publishing). For any service or product one would like to have average or unit costs close to the variable costs. The output quantity at which average costs come close to this amount is referred to as a 'critical mass'. This relationship between input cost and output quantity is very important in determining whether certain services or operational activities should be centralized or decentralized. For example, if several library branches each operate at output quantities below the critical mass, but the combined total is above the critical mass, then centralization of a service should be seriously considered.

Another important economic relationship involves marginal cost, which is the difference in cost from one level of output to the next higher level, divided by the corresponding difference in output quantities. Sometimes the marginal cost will decline and then increase as the number of units increases. I will talk again about this measure when discussing

7. Economies of scale are also achieved through volume discounts for purchases, the inherent production-like nature of some activities, and the ability to avoid having to spread special staff capabilities across unrelated activities.

Figure 3*: Total costs of journal publishing*

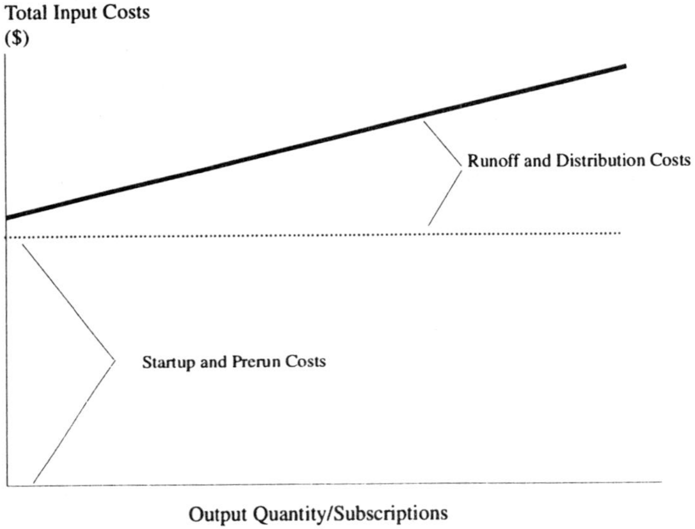

Figure 4*: Unit costs of journal publishing*

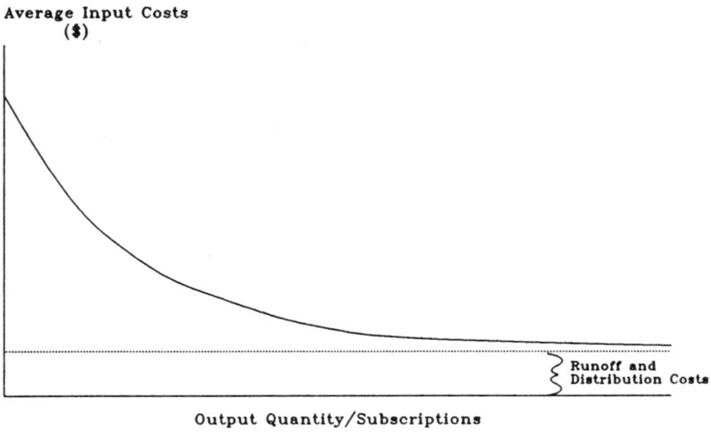

effectiveness.

I mentioned above that input and output measures can be applied to indirect services associated with operational and support functions. Thus, performance measures can be derived for indirect services as well. Furthermore, performance measures can be applied to specific resources such as staffing, equipment and systems, and space.

Effectiveness measures

Effectiveness is derived from the output and usage measures. One relationship is the number of readings per subscription for journal publications. Studies by King Research (King et al, 1981; King and Roderer, 1978; Griffiths and King, 1993a; King and Roderer, 1981) show that this factor influences the decision to subscribe to a journal or obtain articles from alternative sources. The more articles read from a journal the more likely one will subscribe.[8] However, higher subscription prices result in fewer subscriptions because the breakeven point of subscription price versus cost of alternatives increases. This relationship is shown in Figure 5, in which output price plus user acquisition cost is plotted for two prices ($80 and $120) across number of readings from a journal. Also, the cost to use a library copy as an alternative to subscription is plotted by number of readings (recognizing that several readings may occur for each visit or use of the journal). With a journal price of $80 the breakeven point is at 10 readings of the journal (i.e., it is less expensive to use the library for fewer than 10 readings and less expensive to subscribe above that number). At a subscription price of $120 the breakeven point is about 15 readings.

An important question is how many readers are likely to read the journal at various levels. An example of this is also given in Figure 5. Here it is shown that 500 individuals have fewer than 10 readings, 2,500 have fewer than 15 readings, and the total number of potential readers is about 4,000. If the journal price is $80, there would be an expected 3,500

---

8. The average number of readings per personal journal subscription is 14.1, versus 5.8 from library copies, 8.2 from shared office collections, and 5.7 from other sources. These are average readings per journal per professional per year. When all professionals are included, the averages are still 14.1 readings per journal from personal subscriptions, 102 from library copies and 33 from shared office collections.

Figure 5*: Journal price and demand relationship (output versus usage)*

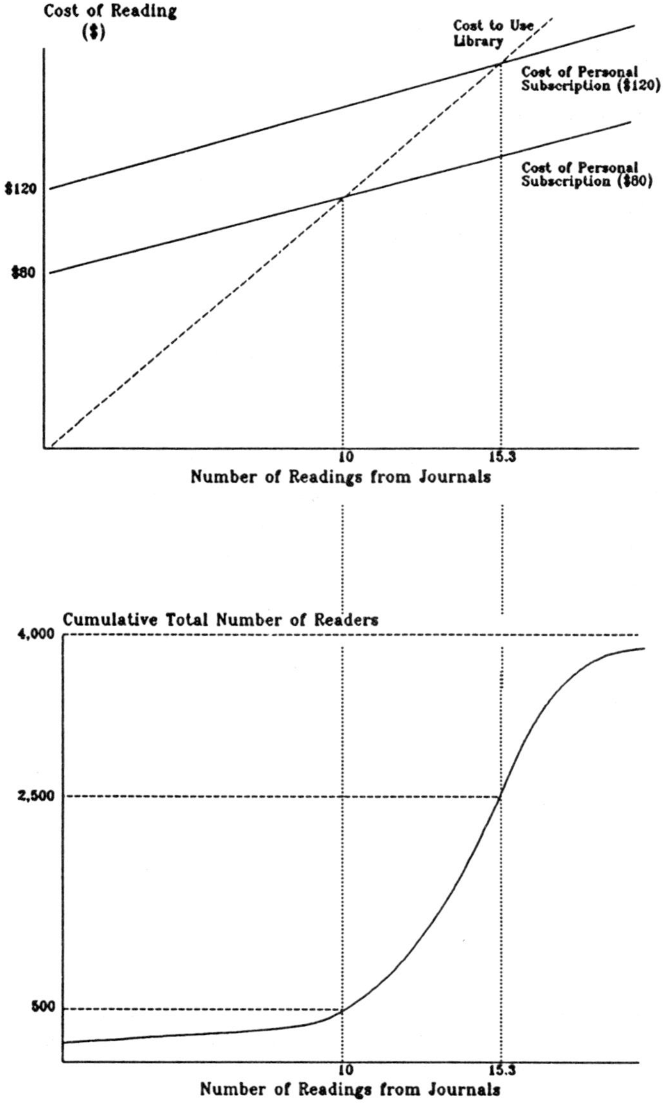

subscribers yielding a revenue of $280,000; if the price is $120, the expected number of subscribers is 1,500 for a revenue of $180,000.[9] If the journal's fixed cost is $120,000 and the variable cost is about $35 per subscription, the total cost at the $80 price is $242,500 and the total cost at the $120 price is $172,500. Thus, with this distribution of readings there would be higher net revenue from the $80 price than from the $120 price (i.e., $37,500 versus $7,500 profit). The point is that availability and cost of alternatives largely dictate demand. One study (Charles River Associates, 1979) showed that factors explaining physicists' probability of subscribing to their most important journal are ranked as follows:

- availability of the journal in the physicist's most frequently used library,
- convenience of location of this library,
- subscription price,
- proportion of articles read for current awareness,
- whether the journal is an association journal, and
- out-of-pocket expenditures on STI services.

These results seem to reinforce the hypothetical relationship given above.

Berg (1972), Braunstein (1977), and others have taken a more traditional economic approach to relating outputs and usage (i.e., price and demand). In these instances, marginal demand is determined as a function of price and marginal costs are plotted to determine a price which achieves optimum net revenue.

Other economic relationships between output and usage include amount of use as a function of output attributes. Price and demand is one such relationship, and journal attributes and resultant likely number of subscriptions are listed above. Another example is the relationship between the number of database searches requested and level of user satisfaction with search attributes (see for example, Figure 6 in which satisfaction with relevance of search output is compared with number of searches requested per year). In this example, users who indicate they

9. Note that revenue could be considered a derived effectiveness measure of output (quantity sold) times price paid (a usage factor).

are very satisfied average 6.15 search requests per year; this amount drops to 0.45 requests when users are very dissatisfied.

I mentioned earlier that users are willing to pay not only for information, but also for attributes of services or products. This phenomenon is depicted in Figure 7, in which the price users are willing to pay for search

Figure 6: *Relationship between number of searches performed and satisfaction with relevance of search output to users' information needs*

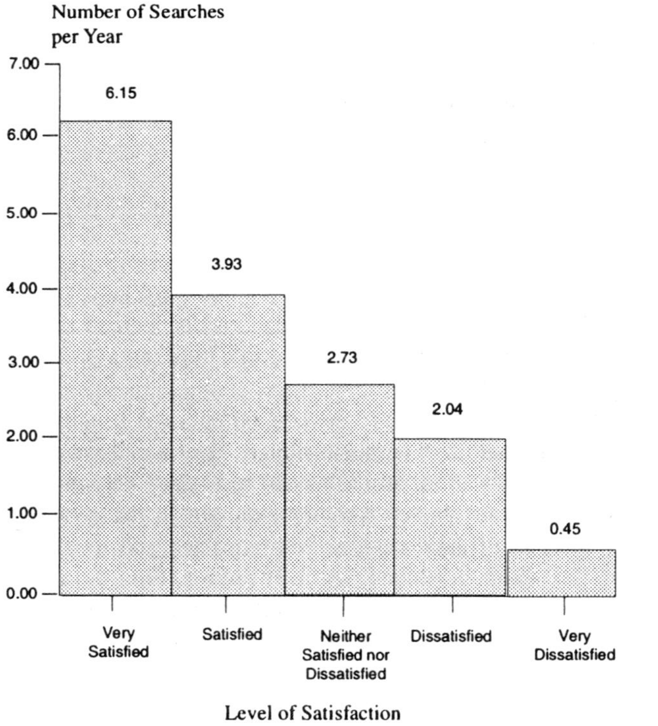

Source: *Special Libraries: Increasing the Information Edge*. José-Marie Griffiths and Donald W. King. Washington, D.C., Special Libraries Association, 1993.

relevance and response time[10] is compared over three levels of these two attributes. If relevance of output is high and response is within a day of the time promised, users are willing to pay $290. However, as the response time increases to 1 to 3 days, and over 3 days, the price users are willing to pay decreases to $225 and $140, respectively. At a response time of one day, the price users are willing to pay decreases substantially as relevance decreases to medium relevance ($170) and low relevance ($50). With low relevance and slow response, users are willing to pay only about $15 for a database search. The model used for this economic relationship is conjoint measurement, discussed by Johnson (1974) and described by Griffiths and King (1991).

Cost-effectiveness measures

Cost-effectiveness measures are derived from input costs and usage. Examples include publication cost per reading of journal articles (or entire journals). Typical publications costs per reading are in the $3 to $10 range. Service cost per database search request has been given above. Service cost per identified item read is about $4 (or about $10 including allocation of all indirect costs). Another kind of cost-effectiveness measure of interest is the ratio of what users pay in terms of their time to the cost of the service or product (or vice versa). For example, journal article readers pay (in their time) about 4 to 12 times the journal publication costs. Cost to libraries to provide access to journal articles is about one-fourth the cost to readers. Cost to users for using database search services and reading information provided is more than three times the cost to a library to provide the service (including all indirect costs allocated). These ratios show that users 'value' information provided by a service or product much more than the cost of the service or product.

Other cost-effectiveness measures include service cost necessary to achieve different levels of user satisfaction with attributes; service cost compared with cost of alternative sources of information (e.g., about 2 to 1 for database search services); service cost necessary to achieve higher levels of service awareness; comparison of service costs involving different purposes of use; and so on.

---

10. Response time is amount of time beyond the time promised (or negotiated).

***Figure 7:** Relative trade-off value to user of online search relevance and turnaround time*

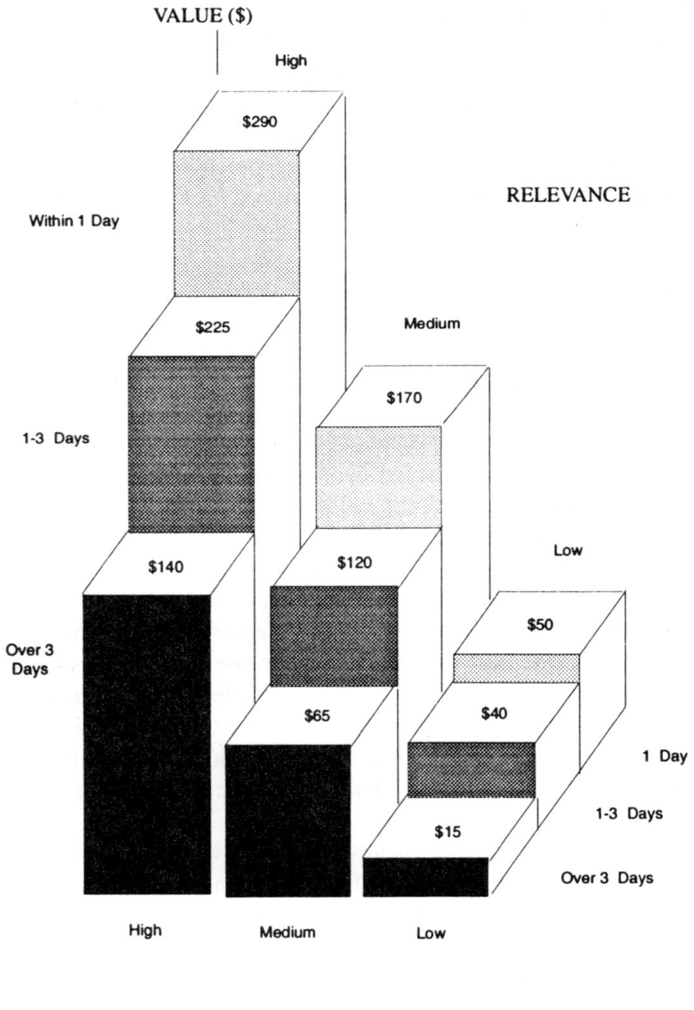

Source: *Special Libraries: Increasing the Information Edge.* José-Marie Griffiths and Donald W. King. Washington, D.C., Special Libraries Association, 1993.

Impact measures

Impact measures are derived from relationships among usage, outcome, and domain measures. Examples of impact measures are the proportion of readings of journal articles that achieve favorable (or unfavorable) outcomes (i.e., measures of outcome divided by usage). The proportion of journal article readings that achieve savings is about one-fourth, and the average savings (across all readings) is $310 per reading. Average cost for acquiring and reading journal articles is about $37 per reading, so one impact measure is that average savings is 8.4 times the average cost to users to acquire and read articles (a form of return-on-investment in information found in journals). Similar ratios are observed for database search services, since reading costs dominate user-related cost (i.e., the cost of time spent by users requesting searches is only about $9 per request). Other impact measures are the proportion of the community served who use a service or product (i.e., amount of usage per person in the community or proportion of all database searches that are performed by the search service). The proportion of professionals in companies and government agencies who request database search services has been estimated to be 17 per cent, the average number of searches (across all professionals) is 0.8 searches per professional, and about 38 per cent of all database searches are performed by library search specialists (compared with 38 per cent done by the professionals themselves and the rest delegated to subordinates or search specialists within the users' units).

Cost-benefit measures

One can compare any of the measures mentioned above (i.e., input, output, usage, performance, effectiveness, cost-effectiveness, and impact measures) for a current service or product with alternatives. Comparisons in terms of each of these measures are either favorable or unfavorable. For example, a journal publisher may wish to compare current paper-based journal subscriptions with electronic alternative distribution. Examples of potential results from the publisher's perspective might be lower input costs, fewer articles published (because of author preference for publication medium) at a higher price, less demand (but, perhaps, higher revenue resulting from higher price plus additional revenue from separates not previously received from copyright royalties), fewer readings per article (from lower awareness), and so on. Each favorable or unfavorable comparison is, respectively, a benefit or a cost measure as used in this framework. This way of measuring 'costs' and 'benefits' is discussed by Bickner (1983), where he gives a sound argument for analyzing 'costs' and 'benefits' through comparisons between alternatives such as providing a service or not, increasing price of journals from $80 to $120, providing a service at one level of quality or another level, and so on.[11]

Each alternative can be compared in terms of each level of measure and categorized as to whether they are unfavorable ('cost') or favorable ('benefit'). Examples of 'cost' and 'benefit' measures include:

- The example above of increasing journal prices from $80 to $120 hypothetically shows that publishing costs decrease from $242,500 to $172,500, which is a 'benefit' of $70,000. However, revenue decreases from $280,000 to $180,000, which is a 'cost' of $100,000. The net cost-benefit, therefore, is minus $30,000. There undoubtedly would be additional 'costs' in that lower demand would probably result in less reading (thereby losing favorable outcomes) and reading articles from other sources would cost users more.
- One type of benefit is that services or products costs users far less than alternative sources would. Such savings might be considered a value derived from use. (Some economists could argue that this is a measure of 'worth', rather than 'value' (Machlup, 1979)). For example, the cost to users of not having a database search service available is about $270 per search (i.e., it would cost them about $270 more to use the least expensive alternative than it now costs them), or about $570 per user per year. The quality and timeliness of searching is perceived by users to be worse using the alternatives.

Economic cost and benefit analysis can be performed by developing cost and benefit ledgers with all relevant economic measures in order to provide a comprehensive basis for decision-making.

It is important to recognize that there are interactive effects that must

11. I put quotes around 'costs' and 'benefits' because 'costs' used in this context do not necessarily mean expenditures of money, and 'benefits' might well involve expenditures of money. For example, an alternative to a service might cost less, which would be a 'benefit', but achieve lower quality or timeliness of response, which would be a 'cost'.

be taken into account in this framework (see Figure 8). Changes in output attributes (e.g., price of journals) should affect usage, which in turn affects input costs (and revenue) and outcomes from use of the services or products. As another example, a database search service might decide to train searchers (or use an improved search vendor). In addition to increasing input costs for training, such a change may improve search output quality and timeliness; result in more requests, which in turn increases total service cost (but, perhaps, a lower cost per search resulting from economies of scale); and lead to greater positive outcomes. If net cost and benefit is measured by average search cost less average savings (or derived value), economies of scale might result in improved net cost and benefit even though total costs increase because of interaction.

Information economics

I think of information economics as dealing with macro economics, such as how information contributes to the GNP (initially envisioned by Machlup (1962) and expanded upon or measured later by Bell (1973), Porat (Porat and Rubin, 1977), Rubin (Rubin and Huber, 1986), and others in Europe, Japan, and elsewhere (Rubin, 1990)). Also, several studies have shown a positive correlation between expenditures for information-related resources and corporate profits (see for example, Hayes and Erickson, 1982; Braunstein, 1985; Koenig and Gans, 1975; Jonscher, 1983; Terleckyj, 1984). I believe one could also aggregate the outcomes observed in organizations across organizations and sectors to obtain indicators of information economics.

Summary

I have presented a framework of economic measures that my colleagues and I have found to be useful for performing economic analysis and evaluation of information services and products. We have applied this framework to a wide range of services and products, including an entire range of library services, traditional and electronic publishing, CD-ROM products, document delivery services, information analysis centers (IACs), government-sponsored clearinghouse services, records management services, census information, materials property data, copyright formalities, knowledge-based systems, and standard data reference services and products. I recognize that there are many other economic

***Figure 8:** Conceptual Framework: Interaction*

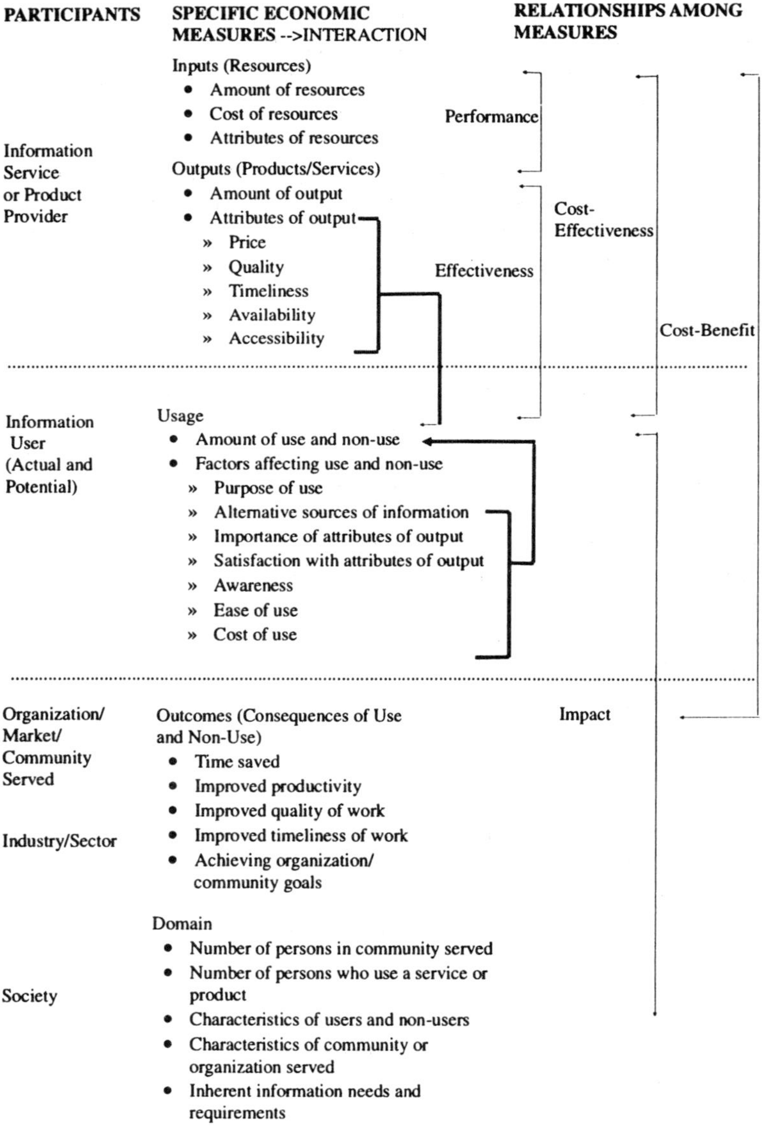

measures and models to which the framework here does not apply. However, for many information services and products it has worked well.

I believe that one glaring weakness in economic measures is the lack of derived measures relating input, output, usage, and outcomes. Ideally, it would be desirable to have a situation where, for example, a library director could make a decision concerning input resources and know, with some degree of confidence, the consequences of the decision on output (quantities and attributes), usage, and outcomes on the community served. This might be possible some day if library associations would collect reasonably standard measures of input, output, usage, outcomes, and domains served, and collect these measures in such a way that the relationships between measures could be developed and modelled. I hope our framework serves as a modest step in that direction.

Résumé

Discours-programme

Un mécanisme est présenté pour l'évaluation des mesures de l'économie de l'information et de l'économie informationnelle. Les mesures s'appliquent également à l'information enregistrée sous les formes traditionnelles et à la méthodologie de sa diffusion. L'information est définie comme un produit commercial, dont la création, le traitement, la communication et l'utilisation sont décrites. Une distinction est faite entre l'information 'privée' et l'information 'publique', ainsi qu'entre les différents types d'utilisateurs et les niveaux d'utilisation.

Cinq mesures économiques génériques sont énumérées: la mesure des entrées (ressources) et des sorties (résultats d'utilisation des ressources); de l'utilisation; des conséquences d'utilisation ou de non-utilisation; et de domaine (description de l'environnement du service ou du produit, description du marché).

Il est possible de dériver cinq types de relations entre les mesures économiques génériques décrites ci-dessus. Ces mesures économiques dérivées comportent: mesure de la performance du service ou du produit (relations entre les mesures d'entrée et de sortie); mesure de l'efficacité (relations entre sorties et usage); mesure de coûts et d'efficacité (relations entre entrées et usage); mesures d'impact (mesures dérivées des relations entre les mesures d'usage, de sortie, et de domaine); mesures coûts-bénéfices (comparaison entre les mesures soulignées ci-dessus).

Le mécanisme de mesures présenté peut s'appliquer dans le contexte de l'évaluation des services et des produits de l'information, y compris les services de bibliothèque, l'édition traditionnelle et électronique et le CD-ROM. Il faut pourtant remarquer le défaut de mesures par rapport aux relations entre les entrées, les sorties, l'utilisation et les conséquences de l'utilisation. L'importance de la standardisation des mesures des entrées, des sorties, de l'utilisation, des conséquences d'utilisation et des domaines pour le développement d'un modèle des relations entre les différentes mesures est soulignée.

References

Bell, D. (1973). **The Coming of Post-Industrial Society**. New York: Basic Books.

Berg, S.V. (1972). An Economic Analysis of the Demand for Scientific Journals. **Journal of the American Society for Information Science**, 23(1), January-February, 23-29.

Bickner, R.E. (1983). Concepts of Economic Cost. In **Key Papers in the Economics of Information Systems**, edited by D.W. King, N.K. Roderer, and H.A. Olsen. White Plains, NY: Knowledge Industry Publications, Inc. for the American Society for Information Science.

Braunstein, Y.M. (1977). An Economic Rationale for Page and Submission Charges by Academic Journals. **Journal of the American Society for Information Science**, 28(6), November.

Braunstein, Y.M. (1985). Information as a Factor of Production: Substitutability and Productivity. **Information Society**, 3(3), 261-273.

Charles River Associates, Inc. (1979). **Development of a Model of the Demand for Scientific and Technical Information Services**. Prepared for the National Science Foundation, April.

Griffiths, J.-M. and King, D.W. (1990). **Keys to Success: Performance Indicators for Public Libraries**. London: HMSO. [Available in the United States from Unipub, 4611 F Assembly Drive, Lanham, MD 20706; 1-800-274-4888.]

Griffiths, J.-M. and King, D.W. (1991). **A Manual on the Evaluation**

of Information Centers and Services. (AGARDograph No. 310). Neuilly sur Seine, France: AGARD. [Available in the United States from American Institute of Aeronautics and Astronautics, Technical Information Service, 555 West 57th Street, Suite 1200, New York, NY 10019.]

Griffiths, J.-M., King, D.W., Williams, M.E., Carroll, B.C., and Sheetz, C. (1991). **Description of Scientific and Technical Information in the United States: Current Status and Trends** (2 vols.). Prepared for the National Science Foundation by the University of Tennessee, July.

Griffiths, J.-M. and King, D.W. (1993a). **Special Libraries: Increasing the Information Edge**. Washington, D.C.: Special Libraries Association.

Griffiths, J.-M. and King, D.W. (1993 b). Libraries: The Undiscovered National Resource. **Information Policy Briefings**, 2. London: The British Library, Research and Development Department.

Hayes, R.M. and Erickson, T. (1982). Added Value as a Function of Purchases of Information Services. **Information Society**, 1(4), 307-338.

Institute of Physics. (1976). **Author/Subscriber Survey**. Bristol, England: Institute of Physics.

Johnson, R.M. (1974). Trade-off Analysis of Consumer Values. **Journal of Marketing Research**, 11, May, 121-127.

Jonscher, C. (1983). Information Resources and Economic Productivity. **Information Economics and Policy**, 1(1), 13-35.

King, D.W. and Roderer, N.K. (1978). **Systems Analysis of Scientific and Technical Communication in the United States: The Electronic Alternative to Communication Through Paper-Based Journals**. Prepared for National Science Foundation by King Research, Inc., Knoxville, TN, May.

King, D.W. and Roderer, N.K. (1981). **The AIP Journal System: Relationship of Price, Page Charges, Demand, Cost and Income**. Prepared for American Institute of Physics by King Research, Inc., Knoxville, TN, July.

King, D.W., McDonald, D.D., and Roderer, N.K. (1981). **Scientific Journals in the United States: Their Production, Use, and Economics**. Stroudsburg, PA: Hutchinson Ross Publishing Company.

Koenig, M.E.D. and Gans, D.J. (1975). The Productivity of Research Effort in the U.S. Pharmaceutical Industry. **Research Policy**, 4(4), October, 331-349.

Lamberton, D. (1994). Information and Organization: Questions and Clues. Paper submitted to this Conference.

Machlup, F. (1962). **The Production and Distribution of Knowledge in the United States**. Princeton: Princeton University Press.

Machlup, F. (1979). Uses, Value and Benefits of Knowledge. In **Knowledge: Creation, Definition, Utilization**. Newbury Park, CA: Sage Publications, Inc..

Porat, M.U. and Rubin, M.R. (1977). **The Information Economy** (9 vols.). Washington, DC: U.S. Department of Commerce, Government Printing Office.

Rubin, M.R. and Huber, M.T. (1986). **The Knowledge Industry in the United States, 1960-1980**. Princeton: Princeton University Press.

Rubin, M.R. (1990). The Size and Shape of the Information Economy: An Historical Overview. In **Information: A Strategy for Economic Growth**. Washington, DC: Special Libraries Association.

Terleckyj, N.E. (1984). A Growth Model of the U.S. Communication Industry, 1948-1980. In **Communication and Information Economics: New Perspectives** edited by M. Jussawalla and H. Ebenfield. New York: North-Holland.

The Impact of Information on Development: Results of a Preliminary Investigation

L'Impact de l'Information sur le Développement: Résultats d'une Investigation Préliminaire

Michel J. Menou
CIDEGI, Gentilly, France

Acknowledgement

The work presented in the first three sections below was accomplished as a collective effort in the framework of the project 'Assessment indicators for the impact of information on development', sponsored by the Information Science and Systems Division of the International Development Research Centre (IDRC) of Canada, whose initiative and support are gratefully acknowledged. The results presented could not have been achieved without the contribution of all those who participated in the project, to whom we are no less indebted. They are listed in the footnotes.

The project

Background

For several decades, institutions in developing countries and development assistance agencies have supported the development of information infrastructures in developing countries. This has encompassed the establishment or strengthening of all kinds of information services at all levels, facilitating access to the world's information resources, education and training of information specialists and users, and elaboration of information policies and plans.

For the majority of the developing countries, these efforts have resulted in a steady growth in the provision of information services. At the same time, some serious questioning has arisen from all sides regarding the relevance, appropriateness and sustainability of the services offered. The extent to which they contribute to the empowerment of people and the accountability of the institutions concerned are subjects of controversy and concern (see for instance Sturges et al, 1991).

The assessment of these efforts and the related information services has, up to now, mainly relied upon measures of input or immediate output. Figures about the size, growth and use of databases tell little, if anything, however, about the ultimate benefits for the users and their constituencies. Many are wondering whether there is a link between investments in information systems and services and the achievement of specific development goals. The only answer so far consists in the repetition, under various formulations, of the axiom 'Information is the most critical resource for, and plays a fundamental role in, development'. This assertion, although it may sound like common sense, is still not supported by any systematic body of evidence, in spite of the fact that Saracevic (1980) pointed out this deficiency more than ten years ago.

Unless a more convincing answer can be provided, it will be quite difficult to justify a high level of priority for information related programmes and win for them a share of scarce resources when competing with other endeavours whose relationship to development is better recognized, if not established.

The problem

The above summarized considerations led the Information Sciences and Systems Division of IDRC to recognize that a long-term effort was required in order to establish tangible criteria by which the relevance of information for development can be measured (Stone, 1992).

The challenge is twofold. There is a need to clarify, as far as possible, what factors are involved in the process by which information use is turned into, and perceived as, a lasting benefit by the various stake-holders in development. There is a further need to identify meaningful parameters, or indicators, both qualitative and quantitative, by which the benefits can be assessed, and to propose practical procedures by which the relevant data may be gathered and the assessments implemented.

The fuzziness of both key concepts in the problem statement—information and development—does certainly not make the task easier. For the former, it was felt more appropriate not to limit it to any particular institution or activity but rather to consider all steps and functions in the information cycle. For the latter, apart from the requirement that any particular perspective be specified beforehand when discussing benefits in a given situation, it is unlikely that a commonly agreed definition could be formulated. It is therefore preferable to rely upon the perception of each constituency under investigation that it has reached a stage where it is in a better position to cope with the challenges it faces.

An attempt at producing some acceptable answers to the problem through the usual 'quick and dirty' project would have been understandable, but clearly foolish. IDRC recognized instead that a long term effort and a stepwise approach were necessary. The initial project was meant to produce as systematic and comprehensive an overview as possible of what is to be monitored and how, when considering the impact of information on development. The theme may otherwise be stated as, 'What is the contribution of information activities to development and how can it be assessed?'. There was, however, no intention to provide a complete or final answer to the many problems raised by this question, since this can only result from the cumulation of the results of empirical studies in the field. However, a basic framework is required for such studies to be undertaken on common ground later on. The goal of the project was thus to try to develop an initial workable framework towards this end.

From the inception it was anticipated that the output of this project would be used as a basis for a number of action-research projects which IDRC, and, it is hoped, other organizations, would undertake in order to validate the selected approaches and gather the related evidence. In addition to this second phase, it was hoped that the project could set the pace for sustained research efforts, both theoretical and empirical, in order to elucidate the trade-offs between information and development. The focus of the project was clearly on developing countries. However, its subject is obviously relevant to societies at different levels of development. Apart from the differences in the provision of material resources, one may well wonder, in the perspective of the information age, which country is not a developing one.

Design and implementation

The project was implemented in two successive steps. The first was a computer conference which ran from April to November 1992. The second was a three-day post-computer conference workshop, which took place in Nairobi at the beginning of March 1993.

An uninhibited and thorough brainstorming over a sufficiently long period of time was felt necessary in order to review all aspects of the problem and formulate practical approaches. In view of the time constraints and geographic scatter of those who were likely to contribute to such a debate, conventional methods would not have allowed for the required level and duration of interaction. In spite of the fact that it excluded a number of potential participants without appropriate access to telecommunication facilities, a computer conference appeared to offer the most suitable mechanism.

On the basis of its previous involvement in similar endeavours, the COSY computer conferencing system of the University of Guelph, Canada, was selected by IDRC as the facility for holding the conference. COSY offers a variety of inter-related functions such as structured conferencing, report editing, electronic mail, small group discussion and real time conversation.

IDRC selected 15 specialists on the basis of their previous work on related issues to form, in a purely personal capacity, the core group of participants.[1] As far as possible, the composition of the core group represented all sectors—private, government and academic—and all regions. Although the computer conference was closed in order to ensure continuity, a number of public announcements were made, encouraging all those interested to provide comments. Messages received from 18 external contributors were in fact included, or reported on, in the conference. In addition, IDRC identified a group of 15 specialists, who for various reasons could not participate in the computer conference, but formed a consultative panel. They received the summaries of the transaction and commented upon them.

The computer conference began with a face-to-face meeting which facilitated better personal acquaintance among the participants and established the required group dynamics. It also allowed the participants to review the scope, objectives, agenda and procedures of the conference and provided them with basic training in the use of the COSY computer conferencing system. The conference was structured in 10 discrete topics which were intended to be dealt with in sequence. A duration of five

1. Participants in the computer conference are listed in the appendix at the end of this paper.

months had been initially envisaged but an extension of two months was later decided on in order to compensate for the relatively slow start during the first months. A total of 387 messages were posted, about half of which were commented upon. Considerable person-to-person interaction also occurred through electronic mail. Four summaries of the transactions were produced at various intervals as a means of summarizing the proceedings and providing guidance to the further discussions. Towards the end of the conference a preliminary report was produced and submitted to the participants in print and electronic form. The computer conference was subjected to an independent evaluation (Thorngate, 1993). The latter concluded that it compared favourably with traditional meetings in terms of participation and interaction, but allowed for much deeper and constructive discussions, while it proved far more cost-effective. It is planned to submit the evaluation report to a specialized journal for publication.

The post-computer conference had been designed as a distinct process, although directly linked with the first part of the project. Its main purpose was to define criteria for the identification of indicators and to formulate plans for their field testing in developing countries. The participants selected by IDRC included five of the participants in the computer conference, seven senior professionals (all but one from developing countries, with a broad experience in the planning and management of information systems), two IDRC officers and one IDRC consultant acting as facilitator.[2] The size of the group was deliberately kept small with a view to ensuring the best possible conditions for maximum interaction and intensive group work. All participants received in advance the summaries and the preliminary report of the computer conference. The workshop was residential and lasted for three and a half days. After an initial presentation, the participants split into two working groups which prepared in parallel a framework for conducting impact assessments. Their discussions were based on one case study common to the two groups and one particular to each. The case studies were intended as a means of providing a practical background, to help focus on real life application as opposed to general considerations. They were not, however, to form the main subject of the discussions. On the

2. The participants in the post-computer conference workshop are listed in the appendix at the end of this paper.

third day, the two groups assembled in plenary in order to synthesize their findings and discuss them. The rapporteurs later produced a report for each working group and a combined report (*Post-computer conference workshop*, 1993).

The results

The final report of the project is due to be published for general distribution by IDRC. The internal documents produced in the course of the computer conference (*Assessment Indicators*, 1992-3) and the workshop may be released by IDRC upon request to individual researchers who would wish to undertake related studies. The following presentation can hardly do justice to the many points considered. It should also be emphasized that the project, and more specifically the computer conference, was intended to be a preliminary investigation. Even though it considered all possible facets of the relationship between information and development, which, in addition to the title, may generate excessive expectations, there was no intention, nor would it have been possible or desirable, to produce original results about the positive role of information in development, and even less actual measures, beyond a comprehensive and articulated framework, description of critical issues and identification of a number of hypotheses.

General considerations

One of the first questions which the project had to deal with was whether it is desirable—and possible—to assess the impact of information at a high level of aggregation, such as national benefits. Even though the issue is often referred to and attempts were eventually made in this direction, the participants were of the opinion that a narrower scope was required where specific constituencies and selected problems are considered. The latter may be selected by referring to the major development challenges, as they are commonly recognized, e.g. food security, conservation of natural resources, women's participation, etc. We feel, however, that exploring the nature of aggregate benefits at the national level and the ways and means by which they could be traced is worth trying.

The concept of information also required some preliminary discussions. They stressed the need to stick as far as possible to one state of information—commodity, activity or contents—when considering its impact. Due emphasis was also placed on the coexistence of formal and informal information channels and resources. The latter play a far more important role in developing countries. The built-in equation between information and the formal information sector, which tends to dominate the analysis of information activities and the move towards an information society in the industrialized countries, should thus at least be reconsidered. It was also stressed that the raw information embedded in natural resources represents a huge reservoir of potentially high financial value for the developing countries whose utilization would be worth considering (see for instance Vogel, 1991).

A great deal of the discussion centred around socio-cultural factors. The overall cultural traditions and the particular conditions of each group of stake-holders in any development issue have far reaching consequences on the perception and use of information. These factors may, in particular, induce behaviours which an outside observer, particularly if educated in the North, would call 'irrational', failing to recognize that there is no one single rationality, or 'normal' way of thinking and acting (see for instance the challenging paper by Magoroh Maruyama (1974)). This led to the recommendation to build the impact assessment exercises with a bottom up approach, on the one hand, and to include, as Taylor (1991) himself had envisaged, culture as one of the basic parameters in the description of the Information Use Environments (IUEs), on the other hand. The power games and hidden agendas of the various constituencies, in particular politicians and community leaders, were also stressed as a risk of 'noise' or misinterpretation, since they induce dual systems of logic and appraisal of benefits.

In the participants' view, most statements of information policy(ies) or justifications of information programmes did not go beyond the established cliché and could hardly provide any clue as to the benefits which could be subjected to empirical research. The deficiencies in the information infrastructures and the services they provide may bias both the design of impact studies and the feedback from the groups investigated. In addition to including the non-formal information sector in the studies, due attention is to be paid to ways in which this limitation can be overcome, e.g. by seeking respondents' appraisal of 'the best possible' information provision and their indications as to how the latter could work in practice. It was also felt that the idiosyncrasies of the information professionals have to come into the picture at some point, to the extent they may lead to a particular perception of the value of information and thus an interpretation and follow-up of the results of an impact assessment which may differ from those of the other stake-holders.

The participants felt that this area could benefit considerably from the methods and findings of similar endeavours which have investigated the impact on development of other types of investments and activities, whether hard, such as transport or telecommunications, mixed, such as tourism, or soft, such as science and technology or, more specifically, education. The conditions of the project did not allow for fully exploring these avenues.

Benefits

Three broad classes of impact may need to be distinguished:

- those that are both measurable and quantifiable, such as cost and time savings
- those that are measurable but not quantifiable, such as increased quality
- those that are neither measurable nor quantifiable, such as new insights, learning, etc.

One may make a further distinction between direct benefits, which are an immediate consequence of the use of information according to the purpose for which it was sought, and indirect benefits, which are not specifically related to the problem at hand. In each category, the benefits may be: immediate, when they occur in the short term as some sort of mechanical effect of the use of information; delayed, when both their direct and indirect effects are more diffuse and take more time to appear; or potential, when they require other conditions to be fulfilled in order to concretize. The tracing and presentation of benefits according to this categorization would require what may be called an effect mapping.

Focusing only on the effect of information used on demand would not do justice to a major characteristic of information which is its versatility. It can apply to a variety of problems or situations over time. This and some of the models which have emerged in development science (see for instance Srivanasan, 1977), led to the highlighting of access to information as an important facet of the problem, if not a more important one than the success of its use, which is much dependent on externalities and structural or institutional changes. To the extent that the situation in developing countries is widely considered as one of 'information poverty', it is also tempting to consider more specifically the issue of equality of access as a key aspect of the problem. Furthermore, if equality of access to essential facilities and opportunities—such as educational or medical facilities, opportunities for employment or creation of enterprises, etc.—is being measured, this would almost unavoidably imply the measurement of the channels of information leading to them. However, following the point made by Neelameghan (1981), the participants recognized that equality of access does not ensure equal benefit to everyone, since the use of information is directly dependent on its appropriateness, which itself is related to many factors. Improvements in the equality of access, in particular for disadvantaged groups, and in the appropriateness of information may thus be regarded as equally important issues as direct benefits derived from its use.

Strong emphasis was placed upon the need to assess benefits in conjunction with cost: firstly because the provision of information always has a cost; secondly because its access and use also have a cost, which is often overlooked; thirdly, and more importantly, because one would otherwise tend to consider the potential benefits of information as an absolute justification, regardless of cost, and thus jeopardize the whole exercise. This led the participants to consider at some length the applicability of cost-benefit analysis (CBA) to information activities. It was recognized that information can produce both quantitative and qualitative benefits, which may themselves be recurring or non-recurring, just as it involves costs which may themselves be recurring or non-recurring, fixed or variable, quantifiable or not. CBA should be regarded as a methodology and a means. Furthermore, the final appraisal or decision will take into account not only economic aspects but also social and political ones. A noticeable difference between information activities and projects and those related to more material endeavours lies in the fact that the returns are both more diffuse and longer to accrue, hence the need to use lower discount rates.

It further appeared that the closer one is to the bottom of the pyramid in Maslow's hierarchy of social needs (1968)—often the situation in developing countries—the more difficult it becomes to rely upon a CBA framework to explain, defend and justify expenditures and benefits associated with information. On the basis of an adaptation of Maslow's hierarchy which had been proposed earlier by Horton (1983), the participants examined the possible conditions of applying CBA. Although these models are quite helpful, they are not exempt from a cultural bias and should thus be applied with caution, possibly by neutralizing the built-in hierarchy till one has been validated by the constituencies concerned. The Common Pool Resources (CPR) model proposed by Ostrom (1990) was considered as one possible alternative to CBA in view of its original treatment of norms and discount rates, its dynamic nature and the importance it places upon the stake-holders' perceptions and participation.

Beyond the discussion of appropriate frameworks, due consideration was given to the various kinds of benefits which may result from information use within organizations, as well as for constituencies, whether formally or informally organized. Two cases, the operation of a Rural Community Resource Centre and a cost-benefit analysis of an information project in the health sector, were examined at some length.

Assessment methods

In selecting and organizing indicators, one should ensure that data collection and analysis are as easy and simple as possible, that the interpretation of indicators is straightforward, that the indicators point to benefits which are recognized by the constituencies concerned, and that the resulting conclusions will be intelligible, if not appealing, to those who are going to act upon them. One should also make sure that the set of indicators responds to the needs of their various user groups, among whom policy-makers and technical decision-makers are critical. The purpose for which the indicators are going to be used should also be considered. This may be evaluating the performance of the information cycle in relation to a set of objectives or concerns, planning the development of services or activities, or justifying a proposal. Any benefit may be conceptually translated into several definitions which can themselves be operationalized by a variety of measures. For instance, 'reduced uncertainty about the information needs of the community' may be translated as 'monitored demand', which can itself be traced by 'average number of records of requests', or 'distribution of requests by topics'.

Most studies and projects in the information field take a narrowly specialist view, focusing on the particular technical aspects of the function under consideration. The picture of the initial situation, the environment and the related information functions is often quite limited if it exists at all. Related facts and data are eventually gathered and presented according to methods and reference frameworks which are peculiar to each study and thus prevent consolidation. The construction of a 'natural history' in the information field may thus be regarded as a fundamental requirement. This would in turn call for a systematic description of the Information Use Environments, based upon minimum standards, which would cover seven sets of data: population, settings, culture, problems, perceived solutions, problem-solving processes, available information sources.

Another striking fact is that constituencies hardly recognize information as a subject in its own right, separate from the activities for which it is sought and used. Using the latter as the guide in impact assessment may be quite difficult since many different factors intervene over time, whose relative role could be hard to differentiate. It would thus seem appropriate to concentrate on well-focused issues which are amenable to the various critical incident methods, and to decompose them into a nested hierarchy of objectives and related activities, by which a sequence of simple events may be traced and analyzed.

The systematic collection of anecdotes was regarded as a promising avenue, provided they can be precisely categorized according to their formal characteristics and the types of IUEs they refer to. One should further be able to determine their reliability, significance and position in the existing body of evidence on the basis of objective criteria. Assuming a body of properly calibrated anecdotes is available, statistical analysis methods may be tried in order to extract a common set of variables.

Finally, when considering information as a commodity, it seems quite obvious that the observation of market trends on both the supply and demand sides may point to some key aspects of information value and benefits, at least in the formal information sector. When feasible, introducing a fee in existing or new services may be a direct way to impact assessment. To a lesser extent, market studies may also offer a viable alternative.

Preliminary framework

Three series of working assumptions were formulated which, it is believed, must underpin all efforts at developing indicators for the assessment of information activities and projects. They deal with the nature of information, its role and the concept and functions of indicators. These assumptions are not intended as comprehensive, definitive or uniquely valid. Rather they remind us of the basic need for a clear definition of the points of view from which any impact assessment is attempted.

Furthermore, strong emphasis was placed upon the fact that the assessment of the impact of information cannot be a self-contained, isolated and one-time exercise. On the contrary, it should be an ongoing process, built into project formulation, not added as an afterthought, and should be beneficiary/ user driven. The target audiences who will use the results of the assessment should be clearly identified from the inception, bearing in mind that not all the indicators will apply in any given situation. Five main categories of potential audiences were identified among the many different groups which could potentially be interested in the results of an impact assessment exercise:

- decision-makers,
- information managers,
- information and information system users,
- the community at large,
- donors or funding agencies in general.

Information managers should be interested in all categories of indicators. All audience groups should be interested in the impact indicators. The particular perception of, and idiosyncrasies about, the critical issues and the benefits resulting from information should be determined for each audience, in order to be able to devise relevant indicators and include them as far as possible in the assessment exercise. Once the analysis has been completed, the results should be checked against these requirements and repackaged as appropriate for an effective communication to each particular group.

The following list of prerequisites, which should be met before undertaking an impact assessment exercise, was developed. It is not necessarily exhaustive.

1. Define user community;

2. Define the development issue(s) and/or programme(s) to which the relevant information activity(ies) or project(s) are contributing;

3. Set up standard guidelines for collecting, analyzing, interpreting and presenting anecdotes and other data;

4. Identify the main patterns of operation of the global information life cycle and the factors which influence its effectiveness for the user community and issue under consideration.

5. Describe the Information Use Environments (IUEs) of the selected user community(ies);

6. Identify the target audiences for the results of the assessment and describe their IUEs;

7. Assemble baseline data.

After the prerequisites have been met, it is necessary to work collaboratively with representatives of the beneficiary groups (both decision-makers and end-users) in order to determine the perceived and/or expected benefits of information activities and products. The identification of the factors to be included in the framework, from the point of view of the provision of information, should follow the steps tentatively presented below:

1. Identify which primary objectives are being served (economic, social, political, etc.);
2. Develop a nested hierarchy of objectives/outcomes:
   a. Define outputs and establish input requirements;
   b. Specify other factors that influence the outcomes;
3. At each level of the hierarchy, identify critical factors which are either informational in nature or information dependent;
4. Define the indicators in the framework which would show that the information provision and use are secured or improved.

In some instances, e.g. when the provision of information seems to be grossly inadequate or relies heavily upon informal channels, a similar process may need to be followed from the perspective of information needs and behaviour. Its result may either be combined with the results of the former or replace them.

On the basis of the work previously done by Griffiths and King, especially their latest book (1993), complemented by the results of the computer conference and the discussions at the post-conference workshop, the overall structure of a model for the assessment of the impact of information can be tentatively outlined. The model, which is shown in Figure 1, contains four major components:

- the object(s) of assessment and assessment perspectives;
- generic types of assessment measures;
- derived measures or indicators;
- interactions and externalities.

Generic types of assessment measures include inputs, outputs, usage, outcomes and domain measures. The measures, taken by themselves, convey little information and therefore a more detailed assessment can be achieved through the development of derived measures or indicators for assessment. The framework shows five types of assessment indicators: performance, effectiveness, cost-effectiveness, cost-benefit and

***Figure 1**: Conceptual Model for Measures: Interaction and Externalities*

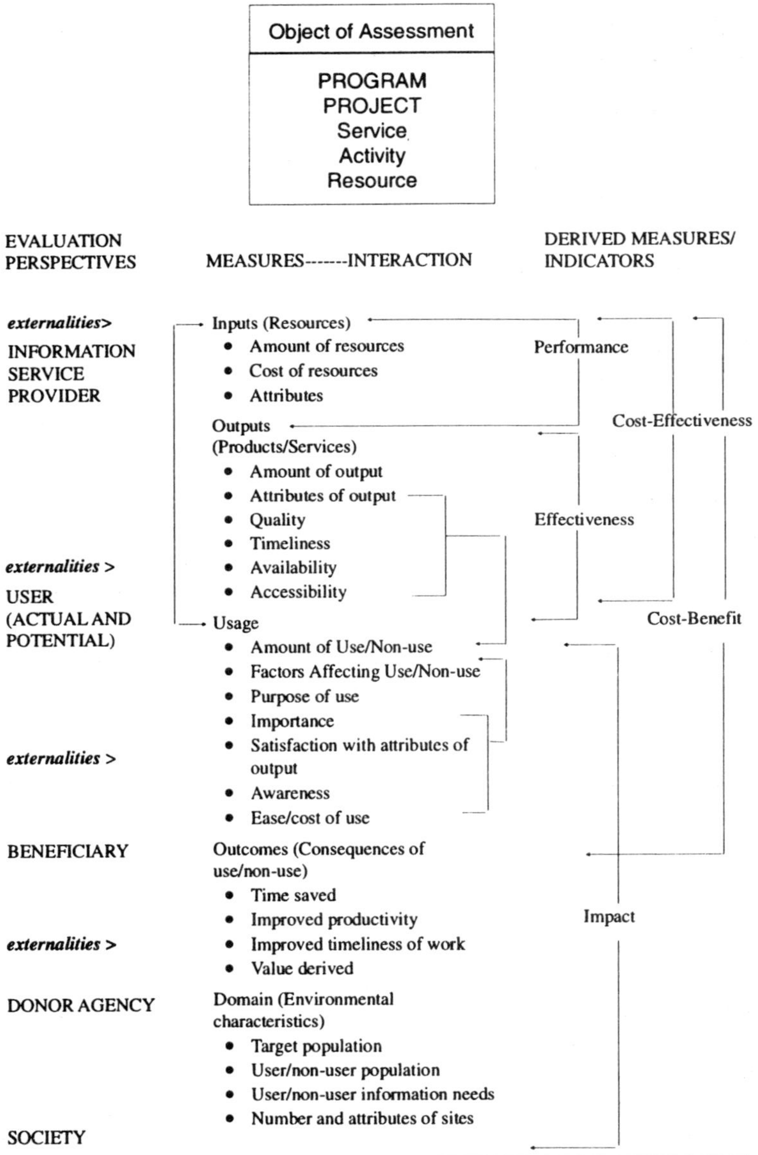

impact indicators. Changes in performance or output attributes should affect usage. Increased usage requires increased inputs to produce increased outputs. Also, changes in conditions that affect usage will also affect input and output requirements. Thus, there is an interactive affect or feedback mechanism built into the framework. Other extraneous factors or externalities also affect the measurements at all levels. Externalities are beyond the control of the assessor but play an increasingly important part in outcomes as the measurement moves from the top part of the model to the bottom.

Information activities and projects are established upon an existing information infrastructure and draw upon its components for nurture and support throughout their lifetime. The following input categories should be considered:

- human factors;
- information and communications technologies;
- systems and processes;
- financial aspects;
- plant capacity;
- external links and distribution;
- policy and environment;
- users.

For each category a tentative and illustrative list was produced of the main characteristic features, about sixty in total, which would need to be depicted by means of appropriate indicators.

An initial list of five major general categories of benefits, or expected outcomes was further devised, recognizing that additional ones might be required. These were political, economic, social, cultural and technological benefits. The benefit areas should further be divided into two subcategories, quantifiable and non-quantifiable, or quantitative and qualitative.

A basic input-output matrix was tentatively developed which seems to offer a suitable canvas for identifying the interactions between the resource and benefit categories. A stepwise approach was also devised in order to trace and weight them according to a five point scale:

1. Weak–correlation–
2. Below Average
3. Average
4. Above average
5. Strong

Figure 2 shows how the matrix may be filled in as a result of this iterative process. It must be emphasized that the marks in the matrix cells are only illustrative, and by no means prescriptive.

It is only after this framework has been tested in the field that it will be possible to judge its effectiveness. We feel that it offers in any case the kind of starting point which the project was aiming at.

Future activities

As previously mentioned, this project is a first step in a long term effort. The participants in both the computer conference and the workshop were asked to make suggestions as to which activities should be undertaken, in addition to the field tests which IDRC had indicated from the inception that it will carry out. At the time of writing, although there is a general agreement in principle about the validity of the proposals, only a few of them have been decided upon and their implementation is under preparation.

Field tests

IDRC will include in a number of its new information projects an impact assessment component. At least three such exercises are likely to take place in the near future in different regions. Each will obviously be tailored to the particular scope of the project concerned and the constituencies it serves. However, the use of a common methodology and joint monitoring is likely to facilitate the consolidation of the results.

It is hoped that other national and international organizations will also consider undertaking impact assessments in conjunction with their respective projects. Several have already indicated their interest in doing so.

These tests are clearly required in order to evaluate the effectiveness and validity of the tentative framework which was developed by the project. Until empirical results are available about both the process and the relevance of the assessments, further discussion, even though it could be enlightening and is certainly welcome, is likely to remain quite artificial and inconclusive.

Figure 2

INPUT FACTOR AREAS	MAJOR OUTPUT BENEFIT AREAS									
	POLITICAL		ECONOMIC		SOCIAL		CULTURAL		TECHNO-LOGICAL	
	Quant	Qual	Quant	Qual	Quant	Qual	Quant	Qual	Quant	Qual
Human factors	3		3			3		4		
Information & communication technologies									4	
Systems & processes			2	3	3	3	2	3		
Financial aspects			5	2						
Plant capacity			3	4					5	4
External linkages & distribution		4	1	2	2	1	2	3		
Policy & environment	4	5	3	3	3	2	2	3	3	3
Users			4	2	5	2	5	3	3	3

Consolidation

Because of the specificity of each field study, the availability of results of a more general value will depend on the number of studies which it will be possible to implement within the shortest possible time. Hence the need for widely disseminating the findings of the project and facilitating their further application.

This may call for the production of guidelines for defining, collecting, analyzing, interpreting and presenting anecdotes and other data which are required, especially by organizations in developing countries, for eventual impact assessments as well as for their own strategic management.

It would also be helpful to produce, even before the first field tests have been implemented, an expanded version of the criteria and framework, providing examples and more detailed guidance for the design of impact assessment studies, and also for presenting their results to the various target audiences.

One of the most intriguing conclusions of the project was the realization that very little attention has been paid so far to cost-benefit aspects when designing information projects in developing countries, except for large scale programmes such as those related to telecommunications infrastructures. Consequently, IDRC has decided on the preparation of a practical handbook for the cost-benefit analysis of information projects, as a first step toward the possible elimination of this drawback.

Supporting research effort

A number of issues have been raised in the course of the project which could generate a wealth of theoretical and applied research.

For instance, the conditions required for information systems and services to achieve sustainability and the eventual limits of this concept were highlighted as one of the topics worth attention. Another serious question, which the computer conference was only able to allude to, is the role of information as a commodity, as opposed to a resource, and the conditions under which the developing countries could profit from the income generated by information sales as an end or intermediate product both on the internal and international markets.

Among the many issues of a more theoretical nature which emerged, one may cite, for instance:

- What is the appropriate level of aggregation when identifying IUEs or problem areas in order to keep into account all relevant externalities without making the system too complex?
- Are the characteristics of particular IUEs homogeneous across countries or are they changed as a result of the geo-political,

socio-economic or cultural features of the countries?

- Are the benefits perceived by the information professions identical to those perceived by the constituencies they serve?
- Do the benefits derived from supporting the immediate provision of information differ from those resulting from the building of information infrastructures and can the two sets combine?
- Are benefits occurring in the short-, medium- and long-term similar, and do short-term benefits cumulate to form longer term ones?
- Are global benefits, e.g. those of large groups, the sum of benefits of small groups or do they have a distinctive nature?
- What criteria could be used in order to determine or trace causality among a set of complex factors?
- What criteria could be used in order to determine whether a factor is primarily informational in nature, information dependent or not affected by information?
- What is the nature and degree of information dependence of the critical issues commonly pointed at by the development indicators?

The project also stressed that very little is known about the total information cycle in the constituencies for which information projects are undertaken. In most instances the analysis of the initial situation is limited to the technical appraisal of the input and output of information directly linked to the proposed system, hence the need to systematize the accumulation of baseline data. Many descriptive studies, which constitute the core of the literature on information in developing countries, are partial and methodologically inconsistent, with the result that comparisons and consolidation are difficult to carry out (Box, 1993).

Research on issues related to information and development in general, and on impact issues in particular, has up to now shown a number of limitations:

- it is marginal compared to the mainstream research focusing on IT development, new storage and retrieval techniques, multimedia, etc.;
- it is scattered among many institutions;
- it is not supported by effective communication;
- its visibility is minimal;
- it does not attract appropriate funding;

- it is mainly implemented in academic institutions of the North.

The developing countries have now built up a capacity for research in information science, but have not yet gained enough experience and visibility and lack the human and material resources required to sustain research programmes.

The institutional weakness and low visibility of this segment of the information science research front may make it extremely difficult for isolated research teams, both in the South and in the North, to mobilize the resources required to develop related research programmes.

The establishment of a group in an appropriate format, e.g. network, consortium, coalition, etc., would allow practical steps to be taken towards overcoming these limitations. Creating standing links among the relevant schools and research teams in Library and Information Science and other related fields will help to:

- build up a critical mass,
- ensure proper interaction,
- facilitate the dissemination of results,
- enhance the visibility of this segment of the field,
- streamline two-way cooperation,
- strengthen the capabilities of the schools in the South,
- facilitate the design and implementation of joint or comparative research projects,
- allow research to focus on topics related to the impact of information,
- help individual schools or the whole group to obtain the required support,
- facilitate the cross-fertilization of education and research.

IDRC is currently considering a project which would help the institutions concerned to determine the possible role and activities of such a group and eventually to establish it.

A tentative model

After the close of the computer conference, we proceeded on our own to explore some of the ideas expressed during the project, especially the notion of appropriateness. This led us to outline a tentative model which is briefly presented below. It should be regarded at this stage as an hypothesis.

The states and processes of information

Examining the impact of information on development and possible ways to assess it inevitably brings into the picture the perennial drawback constituted by the absence of a decent definition of information and an established theory of information. Recent literature seems to evidence a renewal of interest in this question.

Many efforts are directed at refining Shannon and Weaver's theory (see for instance Cole, 1993) and incorporating into it some additional parameters which, by way of simplification, may be coined as 'intelligence factors'. One of the latest examples is Hayes' introduction of a syntactic measure (1993). However, these models are geared to the analysis of discrete transactions, either single or iterative, of single messages exchanged between a single pair, sender and recipient. Even in the most simple situation, any human is in fact exposed to, or using, a plurality of channels conveying a plurality of messages. For example, I may check the time from my watch, from the car's clock and from the radio; assuming they do not give exactly the same time, which is quite likely, how do I decide which is correct, and how much does it matter, depending on the nature of my next commitment?

Other attractive metaphors are mentioned or tried from time to time. One of them stems from the many analogies between information and energy, which Stonier (1991) recently reminded us of. Another is based on the similarities between information and capital (Ribault, 1993).

The term 'information' embodies a wide range of concepts and phenomena, of which Belkin (1978) provided a most useful review. They relate to both processes and material states, which are closely inter-related and may often come into play in any situation. The fact that they are inextricably interwoven is no excuse for not pursuing their differentiation and definition, even if these are only tentative and temporary. Remaining alert about what type of information one is dealing with at any stage appears to be a basic requirement for effective reasoning.

The processes refer to the transformation and transportation of information. They may be regarded as including six main categories:

- Acquisition
- Material, or physical, processing
- Intellectual processing
- Transmission
- Utilization

- Assimilation

Information as an 'object' may be differentiated according to its source, or store, as suggested by Ruben (1992). We would rather consider four instead of his three orders:

- The raw information existing in nature but yet to be discovered
- The information existing in the environment, consisting of messages or stimuli which are intelligible but waiting to be perceived and interpreted (also called raw data)
- The information configured by individuals
- The information configured by groups or social systems.

There might soon be a need for a fifth order, the artificial information contained in computer systems for collective use.

Information as an 'object' may further be categorized according to its various 'states', which can be:

- A product
- What is carried in a channel, including by extension the channel itself, as for instance in 'electronic information'
- The contents

All processes, sources and states constantly interact and are interdependent, but they are distinct and do not have the same 'value'.

The core

Constant in the examination of the nature and role of information, from whatever perspective, is the recognition that it operates only when it 'makes sense', that is, it either fits with pre-existing meanings, or even can be integrated with them, and thus possibly transform them. Asking mothers to report incidents such as blood in the urine of their children, in order to monitor the spread of bilharziosis, when they instead regard the lack of blood as abnormal, is one among many examples of the basic requirement for meaning. We feel that this should further lead us to recognize that it is only in the 'contents' state that the essential value of information may be discovered.

The contents state is made of successive layers:

- semantic
- syntactic
- paradigmatic

All three contribute to the construction of meaning. However, from the example above, it is clear that in the absence of a supportive paradigm, a message recognized only at the semantic and syntactic level will have no effect. The stock of paradigms is not static, even though it may evolve only slowly. Also, it is not isolated, but permanently confronted with incoming information-contents that it has to process and organize.

We therefore feel that the value of information can best be assessed as contents through the changes occurring in its core, the stock of paradigms, or if one prefers, the stock of 'cognitive maps', available to individuals and groups. The more diversified and comprehensive this stock, the more it is able to interpret new information or generate appropriate meanings leading to adapted actions, the more effective it is, and the more value the information-contents accrues.

The dimensions

Should this premise be accepted, then comes the question of suitable ways to characterize a stock of paradigms and its evolution. Trying to impose pre-conceived yardsticks may be fraught with ethnocentric biases. It seems more appropriate to derive the measures from the properties which emerge from actual observations and are recognized as significant and distinct by the various groups being investigated. However, it may be helpful to refer from the start to a number of dimensions which *a priori* appear to be useful pointers to the characteristics of a given stock of paradigms.

We have tentatively identified seven dimensions, on the basis of those particular aspects of appropriate information which are often mentioned in the literature and/or we had the opportunity to observe:

- Informal—Formal: the existence, or otherwise, of an identified formal source for the paradigms
- Endogenous—Exogenous: whether or not the paradigms originated from within the group
- Resident—Circulating: whether the paradigms remain unsaid or are exposed to open discussion
- Unconscious—Conscious: the degree to which the paradigms are grounded in structured justifications
- Ancient—Recent: the length of time the paradigms have lasted
- Stable—Changing: the possibility of the paradigms being adapted, or not, as a result of experience,
- Multi-purpose—Single purpose: the range of events that can be supported by the paradigms.

These dimensions should be seen as axes along which the paradigms can be positioned. Although it is possible that some paradigms fully fit at any one end of an axis, the more likely situation is that they take an intermediate position, being more formal than informal, more circulating than resident, etc. The relative position could be depicted by using, for instance, a scale of 1 to 10, where 1 would represent a fully informal paradigmatic stock, 5 an equally informal and formal paradigmatic stock, and 10 a fully formal paradigmatic stock, etc. A 'traditional' stock of paradigms could hypothetically be characterized as being fully informal, endogenous, resident, unconscious, ancient, stable and multi-purpose. This implies no value judgement. Conversely, a flexible and responsive paradigmatic stock may be *a priori* depicted as one which would concentrate in the area along the axes which is more congenial to the problem at hand, or in general terms evenly distributed around the median position. Considering, for example, the adoption of a new cultural practice, an appropriate stock of paradigms would need to be more on the formal, exogenous, circulating, conscious, recent, changing and single purpose side.

Using these dimensions, one may be able to draw maps similar to the chart of a field of vision. The differences between the paradigmatic stocks of two groups confronted with a particular problem, or the evolution of the paradigmatic stock of a single group over time, in conjunction with an improved supply of information, for instance, could then be visualized and assessed. A theoretical example is shown in Figure 3 where we tentatively mapped the paradigmatic stock of two groups—farmers and extension workers—involved in a given problem such as the preservation of water resources in a Sahel village.

Not all the dimensions may be relevant in any particular context. It may prove appropriate to consider other dimensions. We feel nevertheless that the proposed seven dimensions are in fact the most critical ones with regard to the ability of information to leave a community in a better position to cope with the challenges of its existence.

It should also be emphasized that attempts at 'measuring' information-contents, or any other state, as a discrete entity cannot go without a parallel effort at characterizing the individuals or groups who are using it and possibly measuring their most critical traits. Hence the importance of the description of the Information Use Environments which was stressed above.

Two traits may be regarded as especially important according to Lamberton (1993):

Figure 3

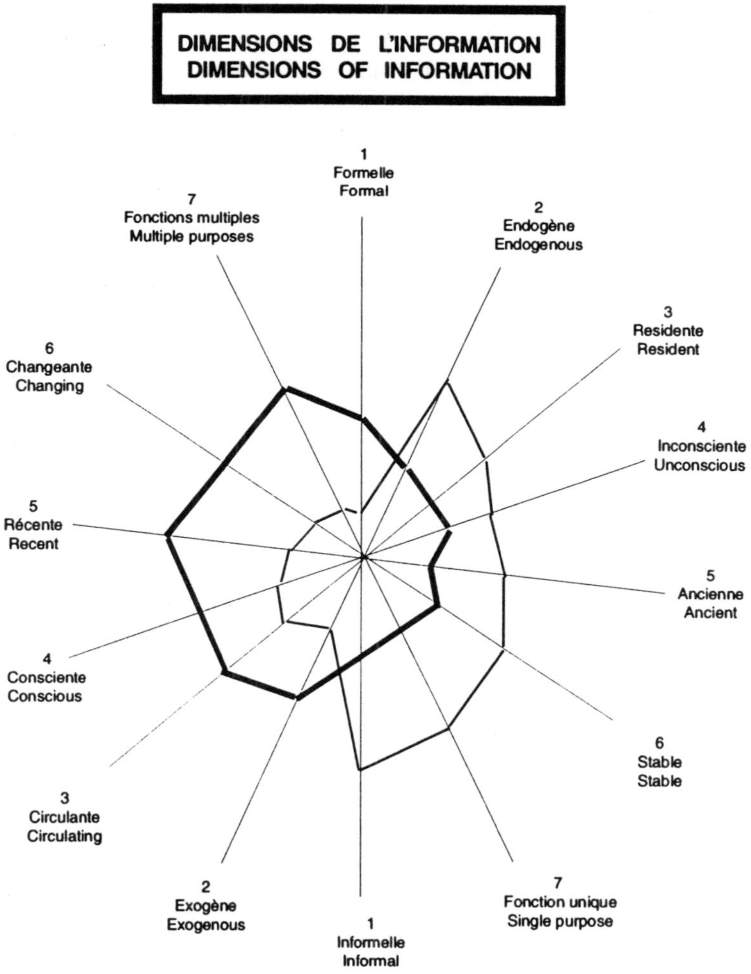
DIMENSIONS DE L'INFORMATION
DIMENSIONS OF INFORMATION
1
Formelle
Formal
2
Endogène
Endogenous
3
Residente
Resident
4
Inconsciente
Unconscious
5
Ancienne
Ancient
6
Stable
Stable
7
Fonction unique
Single purpose
1
Informelle
Informal
2
Exogène
Exogenous
3
Circulante
Circulating
4
Consciente
Conscious
5
Récente
Recent
6
Changeante
Changing
7
Fonctions multiples
Multiple purposes

- Readiness, which is the willingness and ability to act upon the problem
- Capability, which is the talent to turn action into effective results

These traits are obviously dependent on the complex interaction of a wealth of factors. But they also suppose the existence of paradigms which can support them. In the absence of those traits, the availability of information-contents would make no difference, as we have plenty of evidence with regard to the protection of the environment, prevention of AIDS and the like. The timely provision of accurate and relevant information to the highly educated professionals who flourish in today's large and complex organizations seems, on the contrary, to breed more and more failures, to the point that one may wonder if the law of entropy should not be complemented by a law of 'idiotropy'.[3]

Measuring the core

Empirical research is required in order to determine whether:

- the model can indeed be applied
- objective, or non-biased, measures of these dimensions can be performed, and
- the resulting maps allow for meaningful interpretations in the eyes both of the groups under study and of the investigator.

We hope that a first attempt may be made in the framework of a research project soon to be initiated in Africa. Appropriate procedures and protocols for fact finding can only be devised when this takes place, but it may be useful to give some indications about the main constraints and likely approaches.

One would have to identify in the first place the groups to be studied, whose IUEs should then be described. The groups should then be segmented and sampled as appropriate. One would then proceed with the subjects to the identification of a specific problem, which is regarded as critical, and should be defined as precisely as possible, using when

3. Which may read 'In a complex environment, the larger the number of people involved in the decision-making process, and the higher their level of education and professional qualification, the more the average decision is likely to be stupid'. This was our tribute to N. Parkinson.

appropriate a nested hierarchy in order to reduce it to discrete components. Examples of problems could include 'Defending crops against baboons', or 'Availability of welfare programmes for single mothers to support the education of their children'.

The next step would be to identify, in cooperation with the sample group, the critical factors associated with the solution of the problem. Then, the more important ones may be selected, if there are too many and/or some are closely connected. One would have to further list the information which is related to each factor. At this stage, one would be in a position to move into the analysis of the paradigms which are called upon in order to interpret this information. This is obviously quite a difficult exercise, in which one should limit as far as possible, if not avoid, interference from the observer. Semi-directive interviews, with neutral questions leading the respondents to state the attributes attached to each unit of information and sources, may perhaps be a solution. For instance, a statement such as 'The extension agent is seldom available' may be clarified by such questions as 'How often is he/she in the village?', 'Is he/she aware of your problems?', 'Is he/she doing some fact finding for the administration when you ask for information?', in order to find out whether the original statement refers to availability, lack of familiarity with the group, interference from the administration or any combination of the these. The paradigms behind each unit of information will hopefully emerge in the course of the fact finding with also possibly some of their attributes.

One would then have to run a second series of interviews in order to position the paradigms along the axes of the dimensions. Here again extreme care should be taken not to bias the answers and their interpretation. During this process, new dimensions may become apparent. The investigator will also be in a position, either from the original replies or from subsidiary questions, to determine the relative importance and significance of the various dimensions. This discussion may also help single out the most critical factors, and/or a selection of the most relevant paradigms. It would then be possible to tentatively draw the maps for single paradigms and, when appropriate and feasible, a combined map, based for instance on mean values on each axis.

The resulting picture could be validated by constructing stories similar to those from which the initial information was gathered, relying upon paradigms with the same dimensions as those found, or on the contrary antithetical ones, and analyzing the feedback of the respondents when they hear these stories. If the behaviour and information reported in the story are judged valid, where the same dimensions are implied, or else invalid, one may assume that the mapping is correct. Group discussions of the findings or the simple observation of relevant cases may also be considered as means of validation.

Single investigations are not likely to yield decisive results because of the risk of misinterpretation and other interference. It would be advisable to repeat them at regular intervals over some time, as a further means of verification. More distant observations would probably be even more interesting by evidencing possible changes in the paradigmatic stock and the related information use and behaviour.

Conclusion

Bearing in mind that this project was intended as an initial step, we feel that it has indeed accomplished a lot. Some critics will obviously feel that the various issues were unevenly discussed, some possibly omitted, others in need of further elaboration and a number not really new, also that too many directions are pointed at. Others may recognize that the comprehensive and uninhibited coverage of the trade-offs between information and development and avenues for their investigation offers in itself a renewed outlook. We hope that many specialists will find in the results of this project a range of ideas worth exploring as well as the inspiration and challenge for embarking on this endeavour.

Résumé

L'Impact de l'Information sur le Développement: Résultats d'une Investigation Préliminaire

La justification des efforts accomplis au cours des dernières décennies en vue de renforcer les infrastructures et services d'information dans les pays en développement tient dans l'affirmation selon laquelle 'l'information est une ressource essentielle pour le développement'. L'importance très relative accordée à l'information dans beaucoup de pays en développement suggère que la relation entre les investissements dans le domaine de l'information et la réalisation d'objectifs de développement particuliers est loin d'être évidente.

Le Centre de Recherche pour le Développement International (CRDI) du Canada a entrepris un projet afin d'analyser ce dilemme troublant et préparer le chemin à de futures activités qui permettraient d'apprécier de manière systématique les bénéfices liés à l'information. Le projet a consisté en une conférence informatique qui s'est déroulée d'avril à novembre 1992, suivie d'un atelier international. Un groupe de 15 spécialistes a constitué le noyau principal de la conférence informatique, qui a également bénéficié des apports de nombreux contributeurs externes. Son but était d'explorer le contenu et les modalités possibles de l'évaluation de l'impact de l'information et d'en discuter tous les aspects conceptuels et pratiques. L'atelier, auquel ont pris part cinq des participants à la conférence informatique et sept décideurs, responsables de programmes d'information, a élaboré un premier canevas pour la réalisation d'études d'impact, à partir du rapport préliminaire de la conférence informatique.

Les principaux résultats du projet sont présentés, notamment en ce qui concerne les facteurs de base, les approches d'une mesure de l'impact de l'information, tant d'un point de vue qualitatif que quantitatif, et les méthodes d'analyse proposées. Une version préliminaire d'un modèle qui permettrait de représenter et mesurer la valeur de l'information est également présentée. Il resulte de l'interprétation personnelle par l'auteur de certains résultats de la conférence informatique.

Les perspectives pour la poursuite de recherches dans ce domaine sont esquissées. Parmi les thèmes de recherche conceptuels et pratiques sont comprises: les conditions de développement des systèmes et des services d'information; le rôle de l'information en 'produit commercial'; la vente des produits de l'information; l'établissement des caractéristiques des environnements d'utilisateurs d'information; les bienfaits confiés aux réseaux d'information par l'existence des systèmes de support; le cycle d'approvisionnement de l'information.

L'impact de la recherche dans l'information sur la productivité des pays en voie de développement est étudié. L'absence des ressources humaines et du matériel dans ces pays est notée, ainsi que la faiblesse institutionnelle dans le secteur de la recherche. L'établissement d'un réseau d'organisations ayant l'objectif de poursuivre la recherche dans la science de l'information est proposé.

References

Assessment indicators for the impact of information on development. (1992-93). Ottawa, Canada: IDRC. Restricted distribution.
Problem statement. February 1992, 1 p.
Preliminary outline. Michel J. Menou. February 1992, 11 p.
Summary of transactions 6 April-6 July 1992. Michel J. Menou. July 1992, 14 p.
Summary of transactions 7 July-9 September 1992. Michel J. Menou. September 1992, 17 p.
Summary of transactions 10 September-6 October 1992. Michel J. Menou. October 1992, 1 p.
Summary of transactions 7 October-20 November 1992. Michel J. Menou. December 1992, 7 p.
Complete record of all contributions to the computer conference 4 April-8 August 1992. August 1992, 147 p.
Complete record of all contributions to the computer conference 8 August-8 November 1992. December 1992, 95 p.
Preliminary Report of an International Computer Conference. Michel J. Menou. January 1993, 93 p.

Belkin, N.J. (1978). Information concepts for information science. **Journal of Documentation**, 34(1), 55-85.

Box, L. de la Rive. (1993). Troubled waters, bridges and information professionals: A Dutch perspective. In **European Association of Development Research and Training Institutes (EADI), Development policy, research and information: Isolation or interaction?** Bergen: DERAP-Chr. Michelsen Institute.

Cole, C. (1993). Shannon revisited: Information in terms of uncertainty. **Journal of the American Society for Information Science**, 44(4), 204-211.

Griffiths, J-M and King, D.W. (1993). **Special Libraries: Increasing the information edge**. Washington D.C.: Special Libraries Association.

Hayes, R.M. (1993). Measurement of information. **Information Processing and Management**, 29(1) 1-11.

Horton, F.W., Jr. (1983). Information literacy versus computer literacy. **Bulletin of the American Society for Information Science**, 9(4), April, 14-16.

Lamberton, D. (1993). Private communication. See also his contribution to this volume.

Maruyama, M. (1974). Endogenous research vs. delusions of relevance and expertise among exogenous academics, **Human Organization**, 33(3), 318-322.

Maslow, A.H. (1968). **Toward a psychology of being**. 2nd ed. New York: Van Nostrand Rheingold.

Neelameghan, A. (1981). Some issues in information transfer: A Third World perspective, **IFLA Journal**, 7(1), 8-18.

Ostrom, E. (1990). **Governing the commons: The evolution of institutions for collective action**. Cambridge, UK: Cambridge University Press.

Post-computer conference workshop on Assessment Indicators for the Impact of Information on Development, Nairobi, Kenya, March 1-3, 1993. Ottawa, Canada: IDRC. Restricted distribution.
Report of Working Group 1, Prepared by Forest Woody Horton, Jr., Rapporteur. March 1993, 16 p.
Report of Working Group 2, Prepared by José-Marie Griffiths, Rapporteur. April 1993, 16 p. 8p
Integrated Report of Working Groups 1 & 2, Prepared by José-Marie Griffiths and Forest Woody Horton, Jr. April 1993, 24 p.

Ribault, T. (1993). **Economie de l'information: Approche patrimoniale**. Paris: A jour.

Ruben, B.D. (1992). The communication-information relationship in system-theoric perspective. **Journal of the American Society for Information Science**, 43(1), 15-27.

Saracevic, T. (1980). Perception of the needs for scientific and technical information in less developed countries, **Journal of Documentation**, 36(3), 214-267.

Srivanasan, T.N. (1977). Poverty: Some measurements problems. In **Proceedings, 41st session**. New Delhi: International Statistical Institute. (World Bank Reprint n77).

Stone, M.B. (1992). Documentation for development: A view from the North. In **European Association of Development Research and Train-**

ing Institutes (EADI), Strengthening cooperation in documentation for development: A seminar on networking with special emphasis on NGOs. Paris, 3-6 September 1991. Bergen: DERAP-Chr. Michelsen Institute.

Stonier, T. (1991). Towards a new theory of information. **Journal of Information Science**, 17(5), 257-263.

Sturges, P., Mchombu, K. and Neill, R. (1991). The indigenous knowledge base in African development, **Social Intelligence**, 1(3), 213-237.

Taylor, R.S. (1991). Information Use Environments. In **Progress in Communication Sciences**, Vol. 10, edited by B. Dervin and M.J. Voigt. ABLEX Publishing Corp.

Thorngate, W. (1993). **Evaluation of an International Computer Conference on Assessment indicators for the impact of information on development**. (Draft). Department of Psychology, Carleton University. Ottawa, Canada, IDRC, February. Restricted distribution.

Vogel, J. (1991). The intellectual property of natural and artificial information, **CIRCIT Newsletter**, Melbourne, Australia. 3(5), July, 7.

Appendix

Participants in the whole computer conference: Dr. T. Carbo Bearman, Dean and Professor, SLIS, University of Pittsburgh; Dr. J.B. Black, Chief Librarian, University of Guelph; Mr. J. Cubillo, Regional Adviser, CLADES, UN/CEPAL; Prof. S. Ferguson, DLS, University of the West Indies; Dr. J-M Griffiths, Director, Centre for Information Studies, GSLIS, University of Tennessee; Dr. F.W. Horton Jr., President, Information Management Press Inc.; Dr. M.J. Menou (Moderator); Mr. E. Molino, Centro de Estudos Electricas de Mexico.

Participants in the initial meeting and some aspects of the discussions ("*" participated only in the initial meeting): Mr. A.A. Briquet de Lemos, Consultant, Retired Head of Publications Department, University of Brasilia; *Dr. C. Burk, Jr., IMTC Canada; Prof. B. Cronin, Dean, SLIS, Indiana University; Dr. Y. Nusseir, Director, ICSC, Royal Scientific Society of Jordan; *Mr. J. Salmona, Director General, Data for Development; Dr. R. Samarajiva, Dep. of Communication, Ohio State University; *Mr. R.A. Vitro, Director, Global Business Development, Information Industry Association;

Members of the Consultative Panel: Dr. W.O. Aiyepeku, Director, ARCIS, University of Ibadan; Fr. P. Cariola, s.j., Director, CIDE; Dr. G. Deschatelets, EBSI, Université de Montréal; Mr. N. Hanna, World Bank; Prof. F. W. Lancaster, GSLIS, University of Illinois at Urbana Champaign; Dr. R. Mansell, Head, CICT-SPRU, University of Sussex; Mr. K. Mchombu, DLIS, University of Botswana; Mrs. A-M. Prat, CONICYT, Chile; Prof. T.

Saracevic, SCILS, Rutgers; Prof. P. Simmons, Associate Director, SLAIS, University of British Columbia; Dr. K. Stroetmann, GMD; Prof. R.S. Taylor, Professor emeritus, SIS, Syracuse University; Mr. A. Vespry, LRDC, Asian Institute of Technology; Ms. N.M. Wildgoose, Director General, PCPC, Canada National Defence Headquarters.

External contributors: Mr. R. Aubrac; Mrs. J. Carrie; Mrs. E. Cockburn; Dr. H. Cummings; Dr. M. Dahmane; Prof. M. Dosa; Dr. A.G. Dyer; Dr. O. Ganley; Dr. J.N. Gathegi; Prof. P. Havard-Williams; Mr. S. Heikinnen; Ms. M. Logelin; Dr. I. Miles; Mr. R. Neill; Mr. J.S. Parker; Mr. E. Schiefelbein; Prof. V. Slamecka; Mrs. S. Weaver-Wozniak.

The participants in the post-computer conference workshop were: Dr. Wilson O. Aiyepeku, Director, Africa Regional Centre for Information Sciences, University of Ibadan; The Honourable Betty Bigombe, Minister of State, Prime Minister's Office, Uganda; Dr. Cecil Blake, IDRC, Regional Office for Eastern and Southern Africa; Ms. Carol Collins, Information Resources Manager, CARICOM Secretariat; Mr. Julio Cubillo*; Mrs. Nathalie Dussoulier Director General, Institut National de l'Information Scientifique et Technique; Professor Stephney Ferguson*; Dr. José-Marie Griffiths*; Dr. L. J. Haravu, Manager, Library and Documentation Services, International Crops Research Institute for the SemiArid Tropics; Dr. Forest Woody Horton*; Mr. Kingo Mchombu, Lecturer, DLIS, University of Botswana; Dr. Michel J. Menou *; Mrs. Martha B. Stone, Director General, Information Sciences and Systems Division, IDRC; Mr. Paul McConnell, Director, Program coordination and development, Information Sciences and Systems Division, IDRC; Dr. Louis Vagianos, IDRC consultant. (Those who also participated in the computer conference are identified by an asterisk.)

A Commodity, but What Kind of Commodity?

Le 'Bien Informationnel': Evolution d'une Terminologie Exacte de l'Information

Michael Heine
Department of Information and Library Management, University of Northumbria at Newcastle, UK

Introduction

The discipline we call 'economics' has had a significant impact on the area of human activity we call 'information management'. We have only to think of such concepts as 'diminishing returns', 'costing', 'cost-benefit', 'economies of scale' or 'pricing policy' to make this point and appreciate that contribution. Yet significant as they appear to be, such contributions touch only obliquely the matter that concerns us above all: the nature of information itself, and its role in maintaining and fostering human society.

In this paper, I would like to attempt, possibly rashly, to review some of the thinking that may surround this matter. No doubt any excursion of an information manager into economics will turn out to be as inviting of the criticism of economists as the excursions of the latter into information management.[1] However, 'trans-border dataflow' is part of the small-talk of the 1990s, so I shall try to smuggle in these ideas under the umbrella of trans-disciplinary idea-flow, and see if I can get away with it!

1. This may seem an intemperate criticism. Yet so often in the writings of economists on information, the approach has been to see information as an entity serving only to support economic decision-making. See Stigler (1961) for example. Information as an entity having a wider behavioural remit, including a cultural one, surely needs a wider treatment.

More specifically, what I shall attempt is a brief review of this topic under four headings addressing:

- problems in interpreting 'information' as a commodity;
- the contribution of economic 'high rhetoric' to our understanding of this commodity;
- the contribution of econometrics to such understanding;
- the contribution of management techniques to it.

The conclusions offered will be tentative. For the relationships of interest: those between information, individual value-frames and social control, are both complicated and not easily observable. They are also usually unique or at best imperfectly replicable, even if—as we all know—information itself is readily replicable.

The concept of commodity, and the interpretation of information in terms of this concept

'Commodities' are customarily defined as 'tradeable entities'. The implicit assumption appears to be that commodities are traded through a price mechanism, rather than by barter, but where one wishes to be explicit on this point one can refer to 'priced commodities' (Kar and Siddiqui, 1989). 'Information', for its part, is increasingly referred to as a commodity (see for example: Broadbent, 1984; Crawford, 1989; Graham, 1987; Halliday, 1991; Harris, 1985; Hawkins, 1987; Killen, 1988; Morch, 1989; National Science Foundation, 1982; Nielen, 1985).

What could be simpler? It all seems cut-and-dried. Yet doubts seem to remain. For in referring to 'information' what exactly does one mean? Is it the physical carrier, such as the paper document, the fax, the full-text record stored on a hard-disc or tape, the CD-ROM disc, the fiche, or the sound-wave in an auditorium? Or is it the *construction* on what is embedded in those carriers by the human user? For it is a well-rehearsed point that meaning or informativeness is only latent in text, graphics, icons, sounds, etc. The cognitive action of people in interpreting such entities, in the light of their own needs and experience at that time, is what should more properly be called informing. Text, for example, is clearly only that: inert marks on paper or papyrus or a VDU screen, or scratchings on a rock; not information. However, its recognized capacity to change the human mind seems amply to justify our term 'information source'.

Of related concern is the unsatisfactoriness of price as a measure of value. A cheerful, robust economist might claim that when prices are market-determined, they express perceptions of commodity value. And yet there is variability in what individuals will pay for something, presumably expressing variability in perceived value. At least in part: 'capacity to pay' is another variable here. So price and value are not the same thing, even though a classical writer such as Marshall (1920) sees them as being measured by a common unit.[2] Therefore an economics of information—as also any economics of commodities—must recognize 'value' as an independent construct.

There is also the additional point that information units *provide services*, as well as *store information sources*. If we are to talk about tradeables, then we should certainly include such services as those that:

1. identify information sources using databases of sources;
2. extract parts from sources (thinking perhaps of the service we call 'reference librarianship');
3. create and maintain information source databases;
4. create or edit individual information sources;
5. provide cognition-driven interpretations or transcriptions of sources;
6. train users to search databases, etc.

All such services can be priced. Indeed, they seem increasingly to be priced. They can also be traded. (The host-system DataStar was recently purchased by DIALOG.) Are they therefore 'commodities'?

And even if we were, arbitrarily,to restrict our definition of informational commodity to 'physical objects', how workable would that distinction be, in any case? For is the transmission of a 'soft' document between a document collection (such as one maintained by a national library) and a manufacturing firm to be thought of as: (1) a service; or (2) the provision of an object? Is a drug-addict in receipt of a leaflet on his or her affliction in receipt of a service, or a good? Is a CD-ROM a 'good' when it is wrapped in brown paper, but a 'service' when it's put into a reader?

Lastly here, as an additional problem in definition, there is the question of *the extent of data-reduction that should be recognized.* A classical economist might refer to 'the price of tons of steel' without demur, i.e.

---

2. See his discussion of 'consumers' surplus' in Chapter 6: ' ... the satisfaction which [a person] gets from ... purchase, generally *exceeds* that which he gives up in paying its price' [my italics]. Clearly a common measure is assumed, but with what justification?

see little point in distinguishing one ton of steel from another. The justification for that particular level of data-reduction would be seen in the indifference of consumers to different loaves. But one online search is usually not like another, nor is the usage of the results of a search the same from one situation to another. Nor is one information source like another. So just how much data-reduction should we support, therefore, in defining our commodities? We have a non-trivial problem on our hands.

Questions such as these suggest that limited returns attach to our having the term 'commodity'. It is a concept with little to offer. It may be useful purely in language terms as a four-syllable shorthand for the seven-syllable 'tradeable good or service' (in English), and we shall continue to use it here for just that reason. But there appears to be little depth to it. Indeed, William of Occam—wielding his famous razor—would probably have looked askance at it.

The contribution of the 'high rhetoric' of economics

Much of the thinking in classical economics appears to have a rhetorical flavour. Classical economists liked (and still do) to talk of 'loaves of bread' or 'cans of beans', or 'cars', and the prices of same. Substitutability and elasticity theories blossomed on this basis. And yet although the appearance of what was said was simple and comfortable, it can be argued that the very usage of such language was deeply dishonest. The complexities involved in: (1) different people holding different values for individual commodities at different times; and (2) the dependency of demand for commodities in general on information itself (e.g. 'satisficing' [sic] or other behaviour responding to limitations of information, following H. Simon, J. Marschak and others; or simply adaptive behaviour responsive to information supply, e.g. advertising), point to artificiality in what was said.[3] The language may have been simple, but the conceptualization carried by that language was simplistic. Convincing proof of this is evident in: (1) the recognized lack of predictive power of

3. But it is not just arbitrariness in system definition that is the problem. Perhaps the real problems in economics lie in the inherent difficulty of *isolating* systems for study. A bomb-calorimeter in a physics laboratory is in reasonable isolation from its surroundings. A firm's market-research department is not.

present-day macro-economics, and (2) the existence of controversies between economists, weaknesses which perhaps led George Bernard Shaw to utter his exasperated comment that if all the economists of the World were put in a line, they wouldn't reach a conclusion.[4]

The somewhat limited returns offered by classical economic rhetoric can be illustrated by discussion of such concepts as price, externality, excludability, non-rivalrous consumption and the public/private goods distinction. A brief attempt at a discussion of these concepts, as they apply to information commodities, is as follows.

Price

This is perhaps straightforward, except insofar as the price may be imposed by the usual various mechanisms. (See for example Schwuchow et al, 1979 .) For example, pricing may be by subscription, as for the Bath University 'BIDS' service in the UK; unit-pricing, as instanced by British Library DSC coupons, or fines for overdue returns; or for quotas of a commodity, where for example a database host might permit 20 searches for a given fee. Alternatively, the pricing mechanism may be exercised (i.e. the cost of the commodity recovered) forcefully by taxation—when, curiously, the commodity is known as 'free', although in fact freedom to choose is then actually denied the consumer; or perhaps by top-slicing of budgetary headings for expenditures not dedicated to information supply, as in the top-slicing of faculty budgets in universities to support library operations. All such mechanisms would seem to control the demand for commodities in one way or another. We surely need empirical research on the effect of such controls on the demand for informational commodities.

What would be equally valuable would be analysis of information value by 'coloured money', where sensitivity in the user's perception of value in the service rendered is expressed by each commodity having several prices: a red price, a blue price, a green price, etc., and where society pays its members quotas of each money-type. (One could have different interest rates for each money type, also.) Fanciful—yes, but at

4. It is a separate point that economics itself can be portrayed as social activity (rather than solely a knowledge-discipline) which influences society. This view, which labelled economics as 'rhetoric' was put forward by McCloskey (1983) and Klamer (1984), and was reviewed by Gerrard (1990). It is not seen as relevant here except insofar as the notion of rhetoric was also used by these writers.

least in theoretical terms it forces the point that human values are expressible in different ways. I may have seen a reference to this device in the literature, but cannot recall it here.

Externality

A commodity may, or may not, possess 'externalities' (e.g. Coase, 1960; *Of bees and lighthouses*, 1991). By this term, one refers, rhetorically, to the benefits that acquisition of the commodity gives other people.[5] The benefits may be intended or not, may be anticipated or not, and may arise through negotiation between parties or not.

An example of an informational externality might be the increased life-expectancy of children due to dissemination of information on a new malaria vaccine; or an increase in social unrest due to the dissemination of information as to a new set of social values such as the 'politically correct' movement from the US. In the former case we would see the externality as beneficial. In the latter case we might see the externality as either beneficial or disbeneficial. Controversy may prevail! Information disseminated by TV may reduce the integrity of the family, and/or reduce national wealth by diverting self-development away from education and towards entertainment. The nature and extent of any such externalities is a matter for debate, as also are questions as to whether the externalities are beneficial or disbeneficial.

Excludability

'Excludability' in a commodity refers to the existence of restrictions on the benefits of use of that commodity. If, again rhetorically, I purchase a pair of hedgeclippers, I could clip only my side of a hedge between my garden and my neighbour's. I have control over that decision. I can, in other words, influence the *externalities* of that commodity. In information commodity terms, excludability has the support of the law through the concept of 'intellectual property', as in national systems supporting ownership in text ('copyright'), or in registered designs and trademarks. In each of these cases, excludability is declared publicly. Ownership that also confers excludability, but which is not declared publicly, exists in unpublished forms as in-house research reports, archives, MI5 tapes, etc.

---

5. I am aware that several other speakers at this conference, e.g. J.-M. Griffiths or M. Menou, have used this term differently, namely as a synonym for 'external influencing factor', i.e. as a determinant rather than effect.

The existence of national patents systems also confers a right to exclude others from the usage of a commodity, namely an invention. However, although the invention is described using an informational entity, namely the patent specification, that which is excluded is not an informational entity. Rather, it is usage or manufacture or selling of the invention.[6]

Non-rivalrous consumption

This is another recognized feature of commodities. 'Rivalrous' consumption of a commodity is one that has an effect on the consumption of the same commodity by others; 'non-rivalrous' consumption does not have such an effect. The favoured, classical example of non-rivalrous consumption is 'clean air' (if there is any of it left). One is tempted to label informational commodities as non-rivalrous. If user A searches MEDLINE to obtain some references, he or she doesn't prevent—or influence—user B's searching of MEDLINE. If the search software is 'single-user', then user B may be temporarily inconvenienced only. A book borrowed from a public library by one person can also be borrowed by other persons.

This also, at first glance, might seem to be convincing, useful, classical rhetoric. But it ignores the communication channel that can exist between user A and user B. User A can inform user B that the search led to no result, inhibiting usage by user B. Or user A could pass on the results, by voice, e-mail or diskette, say, to user B, again affecting (increasing or inhibiting) usage by user B. People simply do not behave independently. The simple dichotomy put forward is thus too simple: seductive, but unduly influenced by unsatisfactory system delimitation.

Inappropriate simplification is also evident when we consider the limitations on the consumer to consume. If an information worker or end-user uses one information source, he or she cannot at the same time be using another source. Whether the two sources are ostensibly in competition or not is not in question. The fact of limited capacity for attention—and action—by the individual would seem to determine rivalry between sources, irrespective of whether the sources are similar or not.

---

6. For clarification of this point, I would like to acknowledge J.L. Coujard.

An interim conclusion is that the high-table of economics should ponder more.

Public goods and private goods

Economists appear to conceive of public goods (national defence, river-cleaning, street lighting, light-houses, state education) as commodities that are both non-rivalrous and non-excludable.[7] One cannot NOT benefit from them, it is claimed, whether one wishes to or not! Arguments that defence budgets produce social disbenefits such as distortion to the national manufacturing base, or that street lighting contributes to global warming, presumably fall on deaf ears. But that apart, are information sources and services public goods? All of them? Just some of them? A national library maintains the nation's literary treasures. Ergo, its services are a public good. But what if it won't make its treasures accessible to all? What if its services are only weakly influenced by the needs of its end-users? (It might, for example, provide only an OPAC for in-house users, or provide a public OPAC but not permit remote libraries to generate interlibrary-loan requests directly from it.) An archive of governmental papers is also a public good, it would seem. But if there is a 30-year rule on access to the papers, and if weeding of papers is to be done by 'wise men' rather than publicly-agreed criteria... ?

But apart from the difficulty of establishing the status of a commodity as a public good or not, a much more fundamental question appears to be: is the distinction one that is worth pursuing? For since Coase's classic paper, thinking about public and private goods has become clearer, so much so that the distinction between the two now seems to be superficial. Coase's contribution was that the rights to the benefits and disbenefits of a commodity *can* be exercised through the marketplace. To talk of a 'public good' is then seen, post Coase, as a smokescreen preventing this insight. Lighthouses can, in principle, be paid for directly by those who benefit most immediately from them: the ship-owners. To label something heavily as a public good is really implicitly to presume that strong governmental control, whether from left or right, is a necessity. There are other ways of looking at things. So here some political insight can be gained from economic argument.

---

7. Musgrave and Musgrave (1984) define 'social goods' as those for which the consumption is 'non-rival'. The examples offered include 'a bridge which is not crowded'.

There are clearly many other factors to be discussed. 'Ownership' for one: who 'owns' Stendhal's works? Not in the narrow 'copyright law' sense, but in the sense that the information he released to the world is held by many. 'Delayed value' is another: ideas met in one's early childhood (e.g. 'Beethoven is good') may have appeared meaningless then, but assumed meaning later in life. Or 'synergy' as between our processing of different informational commodities might be another.

But at the end of the day, tantalizing though such questions appear, they are the conversation of the high table. At the low table, where we sit with our CD-ROM towers and recorders, our work-stations, fax-machines, host-system manuals and user-survey data askew, one wants a more immediate reality.

The contribution of econometrics

Another group of economists, even more reductionist than those at the high table, are the econometricians. The visions they offer can be attractive. The language used is precise, even if the operationalizations of concepts put forward are sometimes naive.[8] The host meta-language used, mathematics, is of known, though not always provable, consistency. Best of all, testable predictions are offered. Although one might have passing doubts as to the exclusion of some subtle system-control variables (variables referred to as 'political' and 'personality' variables), the closeness of the methods used to scientific methods can calm one's fears.

One such contribution was that of the Nobel prize-winner Jan Tinbergen, who argued that economic policy instruments should equal, in number, the system performance measures being optimized (see for example Tinbergen, 1967). So that, for example, if a government wished both to minimize inflation and maximize employment, two independent controls would be needed, such as central bank control of interest rates, and statutory wage control. Tinbergen seems to have been primarily interested in government policies towards education in Third World

8. The idea that the social value of a public good can be seen as the 'sum' of values held by individuals is surely naive: for even if individuals can be persuaded to express value-judgements on a numeric scale, who is to say that a simple scalar sum of such scores is a meaningful representation of the scores taken as a set?

nations, but by analogy, one could try to relate his findings to information commodities. So that if, for example, a government wished to see both the amount spent by manufacturing firms on in-house R&D increased, and also the amount of information import to firms via licensed manufacturing increased, then two policy instruments would be needed. The latter might involve various combinations of tax concessions or reduced VAT payments, for firms supporting in-house R&D or manufacturing under licence. And, as another example, if a university librarian wished both: (1) to maximize the 'document exposure' for a book collection (the number of hours per year the books are in the hands of the readers); and (2) to maximize 'book issues per reader', then Tinbergen's thinking would support the view that two policy instruments would be needed, e.g. a loans policy and a duplication policy.

Another intriguing econometric finding was offered by Hayes and Erickson (1982). Here, a Cobb-Douglas model was applied to data on the amount of 'added-value' for 50 US manufacturing firms, era 1967. Here, value-added was treated as a dependent variable, the chosen predicting variables being purchases of information services, labour, capital, and other services. In their words:

> Our results show that there is a demonstrable relationship between increased added value (and therefore profitability) and investment in information resources. Beyond that, the evidence suggests that manufacturing industry is using far less than the optimal amount of information resources than should be optimal.

There are several other regression analyses relating to the influence on information system performance of selected resource variables, for example the work of Young (1972) carried out at Edinburgh University on UK public libraries, showing the dominance of the supply variable over public library demand; that of Goddard (1973)—using a Cobb-Douglas approach—on public library issues for Indiana libraries, showing the potential for economies of scale in those public libraries; and the work on the Beverley Hills community, by Newhouse and Alexander (1972) for the RAND Corporation, showing for example the dominant influence on public library demand of the variable 'the presence of a child in the household'.

There are, of course, other studies in information science where the interplay of supply and demand is studied in formal terms. Some are pre-mathematical, such as Taylor's attempt (1982) to structure information processes within value-added 'life cycles' of information; others are more reductionist, e.g. the contributions of Braunstein (1985) and Sengupta (1982), or the intriguing writings of agricultural economists on 'the value of non-use' (see for example Larson, 1992).

It can be argued that to label such studies as 'econometric' is arbitrary, however. They could equally be termed 'studies to support policy-making', or 'social science studies'. But however one may term them, their attractiveness is that they do furnish falsifiable conclusions. We are not just talking of users dancing on the point of a pin.

The contribution of management-led analyses

Our last call, a brief one, will be on the literature of management. The literature on cost-effectiveness/cost-benefit analysis is now large. One significant part of it from our point of view as information managers is that dealing with the economic impact of research—if one accepts that 'research' is activity which generates information sources. Here, the value of the commodity we are discussing—the information source, and its delivery services—can be assessed by a variety of methods: before/after comparisons, case-studies and control-group approaches (Hornschild and Meyer-Krahmer, 1992). A more historic and very arbitrary reference could be Gillespie et al (1985). The literature here seems to be eclectic, borrowing from econometrics, management thinking, policy-analysis and even bibliometrics. Perhaps this is really where the real action needs to be? We don't pretend to do other than mark it, here.

Conclusions

Some generalizations which emerge from this discussion are as follows:

1. Since 'information' is not observable, it will often be preferable to refer in more concrete terms to 'information sources', 'information services' and related activities. The first two notions can, however, conveniently be grouped to define 'information commodity', even though no great theoretical insights are gained by this grouping.

2. Information commodities generate non-trivial problems in regard to the value placed on them by commodity users; and the extent of data-reduction that should be recognized in defining them.

3. The high-rhetoric of economics, with its concerns for 'externalities', 'excludabilities of benefit', 'non-rivalrous consumption' and 'public/private good' distinctions, etc., appears to have little to offer of practical application in information management. More careful attention to pre-mathematical conceptualization would appear to be desirable, if genuine rigour in approach is to be aimed at.
4. Some significantly useful methods and findings applicable to information management appear nevertheless to have been generated via econometric thinking. For example, there are the policy-related conclusions of Tinbergen, and the conclusions on economies of scale in investment in information commodities offered by those applying the Cobb-Douglas model to manufacturing industry (Hayes) or public libraries (Goddard).
5. The contributions of those applying management-centred techniques to specific problems, only briefly indicated here, may prove to be the most useful of all.

Acknowledgements
I am grateful to J. L. Coujard, W. Schwuchow and other colleagues for helpful criticisms used in revising this paper.

Résumé

Le 'Bien Informationnel': Evolution d'une Terminologie Exacte de l'Information

Le développement des nouvelles technologies de l'information a obligé les informaticiens de faire des tentatives pour comprendre les concepts de l'économie. Cependant, des concepts tels que la 'loi des rendements décroissants', l''analyse coûts-bénéfices', les 'économies d'échelle' s'adaptent mal à l'information. L'intégration des deux domaines a mis en valeur les problèmes de l'interprétation de l'information en 'produit commercial' en soulignant la contribution des domaines de l'économie, de l'économétrie et de la gestion.

Pour définir l'information en 'produit commercial', il faut l'établissement d'un mécanisme des prix. Il faut reconnaître ici que le statut commercial de l'information est nettement associé à son conditionnement physique, que ce soit en papier, en télécopie, en disque ou en fiche ainsi qu' à l'interprétation de cette information par l'utilisateur.

De plus, les départements de l'information fournissent des services d'information (tels les services de bases de données) aussi bien que l'information toute courte. Ces services seront redéfinis ici en 'produits commerciaux' bien que ce ne sont pas des entités physiques.

C'est à la terminologie de l'économie que l'on fait appel pour comprendre les relations entre ce domaine et celui de l'information. Les concepts suivants sont discutés: les mécanismes des prix; l' 'externalité' (c'est-à-dire les bénéfices de l'information acquise); l' 'excludabilité' (les réserves apportées sur l'utilisation de l'information, comme par exemple dans le cas de la 'propriété intellectuelle'); la 'consommation' de l'information, que ce soit pour des objectifs qui compromettent les droits des autres utilisateurs ou non, (par exemple, la recheche en ligne); la distinction est faite entre les 'biens publics' et les 'bien privés' en ce qui concerne les services et les produits de l'information.

Dans l'étude de la performance des systèmes d'information, les analyses de régression tracent les variables de l'offre et de la demande par rapport aux bibliothèques publiques. Pourtant, la question se pose du rôle de l'économétrie dans la recherche de la science de l'information. Une tentative d'évaluation se fait des coûts et des bénéfices des recherches dans ce domaine: dans ce contexte, la valeur du 'produit de l'information' est analysée par des méthodes différentes, y compris les monographies et les comparaisons de contrôle.

L'information ne constitue pas un phénomène observable, ce qui présente des difficultés en ce qui concerne l'interprétation de ce concept comme 'produit commercial', ainsi que l'établissement de sa valeur auprès de l'utilisateur. D'ailleurs, les concepts introduits dans l'informatique par une étude du domaine de l'économie ne semblent pas toujours pertinents pour les applications pratiques de l'informatique. Des concepts de l'économétrie (tels que les économies d'échelle pour l'investissement dans les produits d'information, ainsi que les implications de la philosophie de Tinbergen) sont présentés en aide utile à la recherche d'informatique. La contribution des techniques de gestion à la solution des problèmes particuliers doit être reconnue.

References

Braunstein, Y.M. (1985). Information as a factor in production. **Information Society**, 3(3), 261-273.

Broadbent, M. (1984). Information management and educational pluralism. **Education for Information**, 2(3), Sept, 209-227.

Coase, R.H. (1960). The problem of social cost. **Journal of Law and Economics**, 3, Oct, 1-44.

Crawford, M. (1989). Information as a commodity. **Aslib Information**, 17(2), Feb, 42-43

Gerrard, B. (1990). On matters methodological in economics. **Journal of Economic Surveys**, 4(2), 197-219

Gillespie, K.N. et al (1985). Cost-benefit and cost-effectiveness analyses of magnetic resonance imaging. **International Journal of Technology Assessment in Health Care**, 1(3), 537-550.

Goddard, H.C. (1973). Analysis of social production functions: the public library. **Public Finance Quarterly**, 1(2), 191-204.

Graham, J.D. (1987). Information: a leveraged commodity. **National Online Meeting, 1987: Proceedings**. Learned Information, 133-136.

Halliday, J. (1991). Fee or free: a new perspective on the economics of information. **Canadian Library Journal**, 48(5), 327-332.

Harris, S.C. (1985). The integration of the information and communication functions, and the marketing of the resulting products. **Information Services and Use**, 5(6), 313-322.

Hawkins, D.T. (1987). The commodity nature of information. **Online**, 11(1), Jan, 67-70.

Hayes, R.M. and Erickson, T. (1982). Added value as a function of purchases of information services. **Information Society**, 1(4), 307-338.

Hornschild, K. and Meyer-Krahmer, F. (1992).**Evaluation of economic effects: relevance and impacts of EC-programmes promoting industrial R&D with special emphasis on small and medium sized enterprises (pilot methodological study)**. Commission of the European Community: DG Science, Research and Development.

Kar, D.C. and Siddiqui, A.M. (1989). Information and information products: a priced commodity. **Infomediary**, 3(1), Sept, 15-19.

Killen, D. (1988). Information, calculating the cost of a new commodity. **Australian Library Journal**, 37(1), Feb, 46-56.

Klamer, A. (1984). **The new classical macroeconomics**. Brighton: Wheatsheaf.

Larson, D.M. (1992). Can nonuse value be measured from observable behavior. **American Journal of Agricultural Economics**, 74(5), December, 1114-1120.

Marshall, A. (1920). **Principles of economics**. 8th edition, Macmillan.

McCloskey, D.N. (1983). The rhetoric of economics. **Journal of Economic Literature**, 21, 481-517.

Morch, F. (1989). Information as a commodity. In **Information and Innovation: Proceedings of the 7th Nordic Conference for Information and Documentation**, pp.193-208.

Musgrave, R.A. and Musgrave, P.B. (1984). **Public finance in theory and practice**. 4th edition. McGraw-Hill.

National Science Foundation (1982). Division of Information Science and Technology: **Working Group on the Current Status of the Interface between Information Science and Economics** [1979/1980]. Report no. NSF-82-63.

Newhouse, J.P and Alexander, A.J. (1972). **An economic analysis of public library service, prepared for the City of Beverley Hills**. RAND Corporation, Feb, (RAND Report R-848-BH).

Nielen, G.C. (1985). [Is information a marketable commodity?] **Bibliotheek en Samenleving**, 13(3) Mar, 99-101.

Of bees and lighthouses (1991). **The Economist**, 318(7695), 23 Feb.

Schwuchow, W. et al. (1979). **Finanzierung und Preisgestaltung in Information und Dokumentation**. 175pp.

Sengupta, J.K. (1982). Informetric analysis of dynamic decision rules in applied economic models: a selctive survey. **International Journal of Systems Science (GB)**, 13(9), 939-959.

Stigler, G.J. (1961. The economics of information. **Journal of Political Economy**, 69(3), 213-225.

Taylor, R.S. (1982). Value-added processes in the information life cycle. **Journal of the American Society for Information Science**, 33(5), 341-346.

Tinbergen, J. (1967). **Economic policy: Principles and Design**. North-Holland. [See, for example, his Section 3.31].

Young, R. (1972). An exploratory analysis of demand for the public library lending service. **Applied Economics**, 5, 119-132.

Approche Analytique du Coût de l'Appui Documentaire dans un Etablissement de Recherche

An Analytical Approach to the Costing of Documentary Support in a Research Establishment

Jean-François Giovannetti et Alain Glarmet
Service central de l'information scientifique et technique,
CIRAD, Montpellier, France

Le CIRAD est une enterprise de recherche spécialisée dans le domaine de l'agronomie pour le développement rural des zones chaudes et tropicales. Elle dispose d'environ 1000 scientifiques (agronomes, vétérinaires, généticiens, chimistes, économistes, etc.) dont les équipes sont réparties dans 90 pays.

Le CIRAD a développé, pour ses équipes expatriées travaillant en coopération avec les systèmes nationaux de recherche agricole, un service d'appui documentaire personnalisé par diffusion sélective de l'information (DSI). Chaque scientifique reçoit individuellement, une fois par mois, la liste des références dans le domaine de ses centres d'intérêt propre. L'itinéraire technique de production de ces DSI repose sur des interrogations en ligne de plusieurs bases de données, suivies d'un télédéchargement et d'un reformatage permettant une homogénéisation de l'information et un envoi des références bibliographiques, en général sur disquette.

Cet itinéraire technique de production de ces DSI permet une évaluation fine du coût de ce service et permet, par extrapolation, d'apprécier la valeur économique de l'alimentation en information documentaire d'un organisme de recherche.

Le CIRAD, centre de coopération internationale en recherche agronomique pour le développement, est un organisme scientifique spécialisée en agriculture des régions tropicales et subtropicales. Sous la forme d'un établissement public, il est né en 1984 de la fusion d'instituts de recherche en sciences agronomiques, vétérinaires, forestières et agroalimentaires des régions chaudes. Sa mission: contribuer au développement de ces régions par des recherches, des réalisations expérimentales, la formation, l'information scientifique et technique.

Il emploie 1800 personnes, dont 900 cadres, qui interviennent dans une cinquantaine de pays. Son budget s'élève à près de 1 milliard de francs, dont plus de la moitié provient de fonds publics.

Le CIRAD comprend sept départements de recherche:

- cultures annuelles (CIRAD-CA)
- cultures pérennes CIRAD-CP)
- productions fruitières et horticoles (CIRAD-FLHOR)
- élevage et médecine vétérinaire (CIRAD-EMVT)
- forêts (CIRAD-Forêt)
- systèmes agroalimentaires et ruraux (CIRAD-SAR)
- gestion, recherche, documentation et appui technique (CIRAD-GERDAT)

Le CIRAD travaille dans ses propres centres de recherche, au sein de structures nationales de recherche agronomique des pays partenaires, ou en appui à des opérations de développement.

Le contexte

En tant qu'organisme de recherche en coopération, une large partie de son personnel travaille en expatriation.

En 1992, sur 907 cadres, 471 travaillaient en France métropolitaine. Le reste du personnel se répartissait comme suite: Afrique et océan Indien (259), DOM-TOM (88), Asie Océanie (43), Amérique latine (40), autres zones (6).

Ces chercheurs expatriés sont, la plupart du temps, mis à disposition des structures nationales de recherche agronomique de ces pays du Sud. Dans ce contexte, ils ne bénéficient pas d'un métabolisme de base documentaire suffisant en raison de la relative faiblesse des structures institutionnelles qui les accueillent. C'est pourquoi le Service Central d'Information Scientifique et Technique (SCIST) du CIRAD a développé depuis 1988 un programme particulier d'appui documentaire intégré par Diffusion Sélective de l'Information (DSI).

L'appui documentaire intégré par DSI au CIRAD

Ce service s'est développé depuis 1988. Il consiste à fournir individuellement les références bibliographiques pertinentes à la thématique de recherche des équipes de scientifiques, couplées à la possibilité pour ces derniers de commander les documents qu'ils jugent intéressants.

Itinéraire technique de production

Pour réaliser ces DSI, le CIRAD est connecté en ligne aux principaux serveurs internationaux de bases de données bibliographiques ou factuelles dans le domaine de l'agronomie. Chaque profil fait l'objet d'une équation de recherche sur au moins trois bases de données différentes. Un programme spécifique gère un pointeur correspondant pour chaque base à la derniére référence entrée sur la base lors de la derniére interrogation. Toute nouvelle recherche s'effectue donc sur la couche supérieure de mise à jour. Les références bibliographiques pertinentes sont ensuite télédéchargées, les doubles sont éliminés, puis enfin les structures de données sont homogénéisées en un format bibliographique commun. L'utilisateur peut recevoir, soit un produit papier, soit un fichier ASCII importable dans Texto (ajout piloté), ou micro CDS/ISIS, et livré sur disquette ou dans une boîte aux lettres électronique.

Depuis plus d'un an, certains profils sont envoyés par courrier électronique X400 à des équipes de chercheurs au Brésil et à la Réunion à travers le réseau DOMPAC.

Evolution du produit

Depuis sa mise en place, le Service a traité 614 thèmes de profils pour 809 utilisateurs dans 54 pays. Actuellement, ce service est fourni à 617 utilisateurs (468 thèmes de profils) dans 52 pays. La Figure 1 illustre l'évolution du service depuis sa mise en place.

Approche économique du service des DSI

Nous avons élaboré une approche analytique des coûts à travers 6 postes distincts: le coût des références bibliographiques, le coût du temps machine, le temps documentaliste, le matériel mis à disposition, les frais généraux et enfin les frais indirects.

Figure 1: Graphique sur l'évolution du service DSI depuis sa mise en place

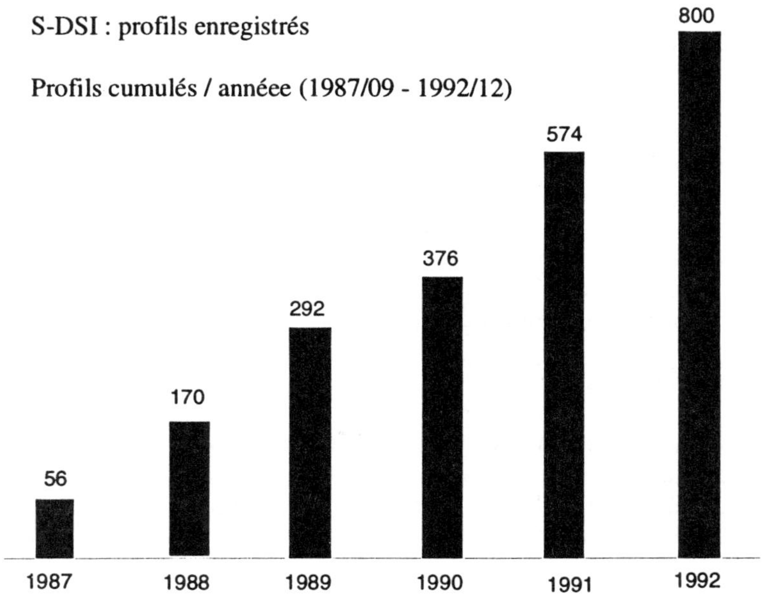

Les coûts des références bibliographiques

Leur coût dépend des royalties réglées au serveur et des coûts de télécommunications. Si les derniers coûts dépendent, de façon proportionnelle, à la durée de la connexion et au volume des données échangées, les premiers coûts sont variables d'une base ou d'un serveur à l'autre, selon des modalités très hétérogènes.

Nous avons, à titre d'exemple, parmi les nombreuses opérations assurées, essayé de déterminer ce coût sur un lot de 7433 références achetées à Dialog, sur un mois complet, en mars 1993.

La facture correspondant a cette opération a été de 1.17 $ par référence, soit 6,44 F la référence.

Les coûts de télécommunications sont calculés, pour 7433 références sur la base de 33 h 34 mn et 7793 segments de 1 kilo octets, soit respectivement, pour une référence 0,024 F et 0,084 F, soit environ 0,1 F/référence au total.

Le coût du temps machine

Au CIRAD, la comptabilité mise en place par l'informatique gère les comptes des utilisateurs accrédités auprès du service informatique. Ce calcul se fait sur la base du temps de connexion et d'utilisation de la mémoire centrale (CPU) et du volume de l'espace disque occupé, selon un protocole très proche de ce que pratiquent les grands centres de calculs universitaires, comme le CNUSC par exemple sur Montpellier. Sur le même fichier télédéchargé de Dialog 7433 références le coût de retraitement d'une référence a été de 0,804 F.

Temps documentalistes

Le calcul a été effectué sur la base du coût moyen des salaires chargés des cadres du service en 1992 avec un réajustement de 4% pour 1993.

Le temps de travail sur 12 mois a été ramené à 21 jours ouvrables/mois x 10. En regard du temps passé, le coût pour une référence traitée a été de 4,467 F.

De plus, le CIRAD étant un EPIC, à ce titre, la totalité de la masse salariale n'est pas couverte par le budget assuré par l'Etat (titre III du Budget Civil de la Recherche: BCRD). Cette couverture des coûts salariaux était de 85%. 15% des salaires des actuels agent du SCIST restent donc à financer: cela induit donc une surcharge salariale, soit 4,467 F x 15% = 0,67 F.

Le coût total est de 4,467 + 0,67 = 4,534 F.

Matériel mis à disposition

Le fonctionnement a déjà été évoqué au point 3.2. Ne sont donc pris en compte que les amortissements et les consommables:

- amortissement du terminal, de l'imprimante;
- fonctionement de l'imprimante (encre et papier).

Ce coût est évalué à 0,238 par référence.

Frais généraux

Ils portent sur l'affranchissement postal. Le tarif moyen de l'envoi postal est de 30 F. Ramené à l'envoi postal d'une référence, cela fait: 0,605 F.

Frais indirects

Ces frais indirects portent sur l'entretien courant, les frais de téléphone, et l'amortissement de la construction sur la base d'un bureau de 20 m^2 par documentaliste. Rapporté à la référence, ce coût est 0,308 F. Le quart restant (28%) est lié à des frais structurels (tableau récapitulatif de l'analyse des coûts de production des DSI).

Discussion

Estimation de coût/chercheur

Le coût d'une référence envoyée à un chercheur dans le cadre d'une DSI peut être estimé à 13,64 F.

Les envois correspondent en moyenne à 132,66 références par an (moyenne établie de novembre 91 à décembre 92).

L'appui documentaire référentiel est donc d'environ 2000 F par an et par chercheur. Il conviendrait, pour être complet, d'y ajouter la fourniture des documents primaires: photocopies, ouvrages, éventuellement périodiques spécifiques.

L'évaluation du coût de cette fourniture de documents ne fait pas l'objet de la présente communication. Cependant, sur la base d'une moyenne établie sur deux ans en prenant l'ensemble des chercheurs du CIRAD expatriés et récipiendaires d'une DSI, nous avons un coût individuel de fourniture de documents de 1350 F. L'appui documentaire intégré, information référentielle et documents primaires, est donc de moins de 3500 F/an. Si l'on rapporte ce coût au salaire chargé d'un chercheur senior expatrié (base de 550 000 F), l'on obtient un ratio de 0,6 %.

Impact des charges affectées

La prise en compte des salaires, des charges directes et indirects, fait passer le coût d'une référence de 6,44 F à 13,640 F. Il ya donc plus qu'un

***Tableau 1**: Recapitulaf de l'analyse des coûts de production des DSI*

LIBELLES	COUT D'UNE REFERENCE
I REFERENCES	
a. Réglé au serveur (DIALOG)	
La référence coûte 1.17 $ (cours à 5.50 Frs le $)	
soit: 1.17 x 5.50 = 6.44 Frs	6.44
b. Télécommunications (TRANSPAC)	
–Connection: 33h 34mn en 03/93 pour 7433 ref à 0.09 F/mn	
soit 2.014 mn x 0.09 Frs = 181.26F / 7433	0.02
–volume d'informations transmis en segments	
(1 segment = 1k octet): 7793 seg x 0.08 / 7433	0.08
II TEMPS MACHINE	
Le coût est déterminé par des relevés mensuels de CPU	
En 1992, ce coût était de 5.433 F. Actualisation du coût:	
selon prévisions d'A. BASSO (SCI), augmentation de 10%	
Soit: 5433 + 10% = 5976.30 / 7433	0.80
III TEMPS DOCUMENTALISTE	
Le coût moyen salaires dadres calculé sur la masse	
salariale de 1992 + réajustement par rapport au	
coefficient de progression de 4% = 1581F/j x 21 jours	
ouvrables = 33201F / 7433	4.47
IV MATERIELS MIS A DISPOSITION	
a. Data Géneral	
La valeur d'achat du terminal sur Data Géneral = 5000F	
On tient compte d'un amortissement de 5 ans	
amortissement mensuel: 5000/5 ans / 10.5 mois / 7433	0.01
b. Imprimante	
–Papier: 0.20 feuille pour 1 ref x 0.50F /feuille	0.10
–Encre: 1 cartouche / mois à 700F / 7433	0.10
–Amortissement de l'imprimante: coût d'achat 12000F	
Amortissement 5 ans = 12000 / 5 / 10.5 / 7433	0.03
V FRAIS GENERAUX: Affranchissement	
On effectue en moyenne 150 envois par mois	
de 12 à 30 pages. Le tarif d'affranchissement appliqué	
est de 30F: 150 x 30 / 7433	0.61
VI FRAIS INDIRECTS	
a. Salaires indirects: titre III / Masse salariale = 85%	
Reste à financer sur salaires sur RP 15% soit: 4.47 x 15%	0.67
b. L'évaluation des charges de ménage, de l'entretien courant	
y compris les frais de téléphone et l'amortissement de la	
construction est de 1200f/m^2/an. Soit un bureau de 20 m^2	
20 x 1200 / 10.5 mois / 7433	0.31
TOTAL	**13.64**

doublement entre les royalties payées au serveur pour l'achat d'une référence à la fourniture de la référence dans l'assiette du chercheur.

Ce ratio est dû en large partie (72%) à la prise en compte du salaire du documentaliste.

Les limites du système

L'itinéraire technique de production par télédéchargement fait que les coûts de fourniture des DSI sont proportionnels au volume de chaque DSI et au nombre de ces dernières. Le coût du programme connaît donc une croissance linéaire proportionnelle au volume des activités.

Les gains de productivité possibles sont limités et ne portent que sur 15% environ des coûts (28% / 2).

Dans ce contexte, une réflexion a été entreprise pour rechercher un autre système de production des DSI au CIRAD.

Des négociations sont en cours avec différents producteurs de bases de données pour l'achat de bandes magnétiques pour un traitement en interne et une production de DSI dont les coûts seraient ainsi optimisés.

Summary

An Analytical Approach to the Costing of Documentary Support in a Research Establishment

CIRAD (Centre for International Cooperation in Agronomic Research and Development) is a scientific organization specializing in the agriculture of tropical and subtropical regions, with a staff of approximately 1,000 scientists. More than half of its budget comes from public funds. CIRAD has seven research departments. Research is carried out at CIRAD itself, as well as in those countries which are part of its sphere of operation, and additionally as a support service to development projects. Documentary support in these external locations is relatively poor. As a result, the Service Central d'Information Scientifique et Technique (SCIST—Central Scientific and Technical Information Service) at CIRAD set up in 1988 a special documentary support system integrated with an SDI service. An economic evaluation of this service is provided.

The documentary support system set up in 1988 supplies relevant bibliographic references to scientific research teams. To implement the system, CIRAD was connected online to the principal international hosts for bibliographic databases in the field of agronomy, and references were downloaded The end-user has a choice of formats and services: paper product, ASCII file, disk, electronic mail, and more recently, mailbox system. At present, the service is provided to 617 users and covers 468 research topics in 52 countries.

A cost-benefit analysis is drawn up in six sections: cost of bibliographical references; cost of machine time (at CIRAD, the accreditation of users is controlled by the accounts department); staff time (information specialists); hardware (depreciation of equipment and consumables); general expenditure (postal charges); and indirect expenses (maintenance, telephone charges etc.).

The cost of documentary support for the provision of references is approximately 2,000 F per year for each researcher. Salaries, direct and indirect costs must also be taken into account, which represents a virtual doubling of the costs after fees charged by the hosts for the supply of references have been paid. The route used for downloading the references adds to the cost of the programme in direct proportion to the volume of activity. It is very difficult to make further savings using this methodology, and it is envisaged that it will be necessary to investigate other systems to deliver SDI material. Negotiations are already under way with database producers for the purchase of tapes which will make it possible to carry out data processing internally.

Information Spécialisée et Formation de l'Avantage Compétitif

Specialist Information and the Competitive Advantage

Jean-Louis Coujard et Yvette Salaün
CERISE, ENSAIA-INPL, Nancy, France

Information et compétitivité sont deux termes dont l'association est récente mais semble destinée à un avenir prometteur.[1] En effet de nombreuses raisons plaident en faveur d'une meilleure prise en considération du rôle de l'information dans l'acquisition et la préservation de la compétitivité non seulement des entreprises mais du système économique dans son ensemble. Parmi les raisons empiriques qui ont conduit à considérer l'influence de l'information sur la compétitivité, trois paraissent déterminantes:

- l'ampleur et la rapidité du développement des technologies de l'information, qui ont non seulement conduit à la formation de nouveaux secteurs d'activité économique (apparition de constructeurs informatiques de dimension mondiale, multiplication de sociétés de services informatiques...), mais ont pénétré tous les autres secteurs d'activité, provoquant souvent leur réorganisation non seulement en termes de structures productives mais au sein même du procès productif.

1. C'est en effet le titre du rapport de la Commission Mayer, réalisée à la demande du Commissariat Générale au Plan (La Documentation Française 1990), et c'est l'une des idées directrices des numéros spéciaux de la prestigieuse série Réalités Industrielles publié par les Anales des Mines, et qui s'adresse aux décideurs des services de l'Etat et des gandes entreprises.

- le développement de la réflexion stratégique, qui, à la suite notamment des travaux de M. Porter puis de leur vulgarisation, a nourri une conception de l'entrepreneur stratège dont l'habileté décisionnelle ne pourrait résulter que d'un trop rare génie, si elle ne se fondait sur une mobilisation méthodique de l'information. De nombreux écrits filent ainsi la métaphore militaire sur le 'renseignement' et l''intelligence' (au sens britannique du terme), fondements de toute démarche stratégique.

- l'observation des modes d'organisation mis en place à l'étranger, que ce soit pour constituer de puissantes bases d'informations spécialisées ou pour assurer la circulation et la mise en valeur d'informations économiques et technologiques; les États-Unis et le Japon constituent des cas polaires, dont les succès économiques et la puissance technologique invitent à examiner sinon à imiter les réalisations.[2]

L'importance du rôle de l'information n'est pourtant pas chose véritablement nouvelle et si aujourd'hui on voit se manifester une attention particulière à son égard, de même que le soucis d'en acquérir la maîtrise dans la recherche et l'obtention d'un avantage compétitif, cela ressemble davantage à une pétition de principe qu'au résultat d'une démarche analytique qu'il semble donc opportun d'engager.

Cette communication se propose, dans un premier temps de préciser les voies et moyens de la formation d'un avantage compétitif dans un contexte concurrentiel. On examinera ensuite les rôles qu'est appelée à jouer l'information dans la genèse de l'innovation dont la place est désormais déterminante dans la recherche d'un avantage compétitif. On tentera enfin de montrer par quels mécanismes l'information spécialisée contribue à la réussite des processus de spécification des ressources, d'apprentissage et d'amélioration de l'efficacité organisationnelle au travers desquels se constituent les formes actuelles de l'avantage compétitif.

2. La création au sein de l'Institut National de l'Information Scientifique et Technique de CNRS, d'une cellule Japon en 1985 est symptômatique de cette recherche de 'modèles'.

De la concurrence à la recherche d'avantages compétitifs

Le mécanisme concurrentiel

Le modèle canonique de la concurrence pure et parfaite ne traite pas en fait de la concurrence dont il présuppose le jeu, mais de ses conséquences et de leur optimalité. L'agent économique rationnel, doté d'une connaissance préalable de la structure de ses coûts de production d'un bien ou d'un service, ainsi que de la productivité des moyens de production qu'il peut acquérir sur leurs marchés respectifs, ne connaît du marché sur lequel il présente sa production que le prix d'équilibre,[3] celui qui, à la criée, assure l'égalité des quantités offertes et demandées. C'est une telle situation qui conduit à parler à son propos d'un 'price taker', que la rationalité qui lui est attribuée et les hypothèses du modèle conduisent à considérer comme ne décidant véritablement que des quantités à offrir et donc à produire.

Ce modèle 'hyperfluide' ne nous apprend rien sur la concurrence, et ce n'est que lorsqu'on envisage des écarts aux hypothèses constitutives du modèle que l'on entrevoit en quoi peuvent consister les *pratiques* de la concurrence. Ces pratiques, que les agents qui les mettent en oeuvre en aient ou non conscience, consistent en effet à tenter d'accentuer ou à tout le moins de pérenniser l'écart entre la situation réellement observable et les conditions de l'équilibre décrites par le modèle.

Par analogie avec l'avantage comparatif dont Ricardo a posé les fondements et les conséquences, on peut évoquer un avantage compétitif, qui consiste aussi en la mise en valeur d'une spécificité, mais en s'efforçant de n'en pas partager les profits. Il s'agit donc bien d'une rente ou d'un profit de monopole, mais à la différence des monopoles naturels qui sont durables, cet avantage compétitif tend à être fugace car son succès même induit l'imitation et provoque sa résorption.

Ce que ne montre pas ce modèle canonique, et qui pourtant est essentiel à la compréhension de la concurrences, qui en constitue l'essence même, c'est *que ce sont les efforts que mettent en oeuvre les agents pour lui échapper qui la réalisent.* Chacun en s'essayant à échapper à la

---

3. un équilibre déjà réalisée et sur lequel il ne dispose d'aucun moyen d'influence.

situation moyenne par un écart qui lui soit profitable, contribue, du fait des comportements d'imitation et des phénomènes de diffusion, au relèvement de cette norme moyenne et voit ce relèvement s'imposer à lui, réduisant ses efforts initiaux à néant. Cette conception dynamique de la concurrence laisse ouverte la possibilité de rentes ou quasi-rentes provisoires et c'est elle qui fonde le rôle essentiel de l'innovation au coeur même du mécanisme concurrentiel. L'innovation, si on en admet une définition la plus générale, 'à la Schumpeter', est recherche de rente.

Différents types d'avantage compétitif

Lorsqu'on cherche à identifier les différents types de pratiques concurrentielles on est conduit à s'écarter des hypothèses du modèle le plus abstrait qui suppose une concurrence 'pure et parfaite'. On se limitera ici à une rapide revue avant de reconsidérer ceux d'entr'eux qui ouvrent particulièrement la voie à un recours à des informations spécifiques.

Les *économies d'échelle*: elles autorisent un abaissement des coûts unitaires et constituent un avantage lorsqu'elles ne sont pas communes, c'est-à-dire lorsque des différences de dimensions significatives sont observables entre firmes opérant sur un même marché. Leur existence pose cependant le problème théorique des conséquences des rendements croissants qui conduisent à une augmentation de production que seule l'apparition d'une zone de rendements décroissants peut limiter.

Les *économies de capacité* s'apparentent aux économies d'échelle mais renvoient à une approche plus concrète: elles différencient les coûts en référence aux capacités de production installées et à leur taux d'utilisation, ce qui résulte de décisions d'investissement antérieures et de leur non réversibilité. Ces économies de capacités peuvent différencier des entreprises qui n'ont pas la même chronique d'investissements.

Les *économies de variété*, de champ ou de gamme (scope): elles considèrent des interdépendances entre produits, générant des effets positifs sur les coûts, et peuvent différencier par là les positions concurrentielles d'entreprises qui présentent un produit comparable sur un marché déterminé.

Les *effets d'apprentissage* font apparaître ce qui est parfois présenté comme une 'courbe d'expérience', c'est-à-dire un abaissement progressif des coûts au cours du temps, résultat d'un rodage des méthodes et procédés, d'un véritable apprentissage de l'entreprise et, éventuellement, de ses fournisseurs. Pour être durable un tel effet doit impliquer une 'proprietary knowledge', une connaissance interne, non immédiatement diffusable auprès des concurrents.

D'une façon générale, la formation d'un avantage compétitif pourra résulter en outre de toutes les entraves qui peuvent être mises à la vérification des hypothèses de la CPP:

- l'acquisition d'un pouvoir de marché significatif est lié à la conquête de parts de marché assez importantes pour que l'atomicité de l'offre ne soit plus réalisée: constitution d'une position dominante, formation d'oligopole et/ou de cartel, segmentation du marché jusqu'à constitution de 'niches' abritées...
- l'existence de barrières à l'entrée de nouveaux concurrents, quelle qu'en soit la nature, favorise la constitution du pouvoir de marché qui n'est donc concevable que comme écart à la concurrence idéale.

Par delà la variété des sources de capacité compétitive, qui peuvent faire l'objet de désignations diverses selon l'optique adoptée, il est possible de ne retenir qu'un petit nombre de phénomènes, que la littérature 'managériale' regroupe en quelques principes stratégiques: recherche d'une *domination* des concurrents généralement obtenue par des coûts plus faibles permettant une baisse des prix, recherche d'une *différenciation* du produit permettant de s'extraire du risque de substitution qui est une condition de la concurrence, ou recherche d'une *segmentation* de la demande qui vise à capter une partie du surplus du consommateur.

Information, décision, coordination.

Le modèle néoclassique est comme le souligne O. Favereau (1989a) fondé sur deux concepts de nature considérablement différente: l'agent économique individuel et le marché. L'agent est caractérisé par une rationalité qui se résume à une capacité d'optimisation, tandis que le marché est une construction plus abstraite, résultat de l''équilibration' des agrégats de décisions individuelles en présence lors des transactions.

Dans cette approche, l'entreprise est un agent ce qui explique que l'on se soit longtemps intéressé à sa seule prise de décision, sans faire porter l'interrogation sur sa nature, ses contours, son organisation. Dans cette tradition, la recherche de l'avantage compétitif repose fondamentalement sur l'optimalité des décisions prises à tout moment. Si l'on admet une approche paradoxale et circulaire de la concurrence *comme résultant de l'ensemble des tentatives faites pour échapper à ses effets*, alors l'habileté concurrentielle du décideur consistera à optimiser à tout moment son écart favorable à la norme que décrit le modèle. Cette conception conduit à mettre l'accent sur les conditions de l'optimalité décisionnelle: information parfaite et instantanée, univers certain. En pratique toutefois, les asymétries informationnelles sont nombreuses, l'univers est incertain et la décision est souvent conduite à s'inscrire dans une rationalité limitée (cf. Simon, 1947), en ce sens que l'optimisation qui est toujours pratiquée parmi les seules possibilités qu'une information incomplète a permis d'envisager, peut n'être qu'un sous-optimum.

La recherche de l'avantage compétitif doit alors tenter de s'accommoder de problèmes d'irréversibilité qui peuvent résulter des décisions déjà prises. On aborde là la notion de flexibilité qui peut être définie comme la possibilité, au vu d'informations nouvelles sur une nouvel état de l'environnement concurrentiel, de prendre des décisions 'néo-optimales' sans être limité par les effets des décisions antérieures: on a alors affaire à une *flexibilité décisionnelle* (cf. Cohendet et Llerena, 1989). C'est dans cette direction que s'est développée une réflexion économique sur le prix qui peut être attaché par un agent à la possibilité de réviser ses décisions ou, ce qui revient au même, de prendre un nouvelle décision non contrainte: c'est la notion de valeur d'option[4] qui peut être réinterprétée comme mesurant l'attrait d'une possible utilisation d'informations futures susceptibles d'inciter à une révision de décisions passées. On reste dans le cadre du raisonnement optimisateur, mais examiné dorénavant comme inscrit dans des processus séquentiels d'information partielle et discontinue (cf. Willinger, 1989; Favereau, 1989b).

Dans une approche plus hétérodoxe, l'avantage compétitif ne sera plus recherché dans ce qui s'apparente à une optimisation au second degré (optimisation par révision, de l'optimalité des décisions passées) mais par une action menée sur l'organisation de la production, qu'il s'agisse d'en contenir ou d'en réduire les coûts, d'en améliorer la variété et la qualité, ou plus généralement de donner à l'avantage compétitif un contenu vérita blement productif... A la différence du point de vue néoclassique qui ne permet d'interroger la recherche de l'efficacité compétitive que dans l'exploitation des imperfections du marché, on considère ici que l'entreprise n'est pas un simple centre décisionnel, mais

4. introduite d'abord par B.A. Weisbrod (1964), puis repris par C. Henry (1974).

une structure organisée et productive dotée d'inertie, c'est-à-dire qui n'est pas instantanément ajustée à son contexte concurrentiel. Dans une telle conception, on s'intéressera à l'action que peut conduire l'entreprise *sur elle-même* et dans la durée, pour conquérir une position favorable dans le jeu concurrentiel: 'le problème posé à la firme (...) est moins d'exécuter un choix optimum parmi un ensemble donné de possibilités offertes de l'extérieur, que de *mettre en place*[5] et d'appliquer des règles ou procédures dont la principale vertu est une vertu créatrice, une vertu d'exploration d'un ensemble d'alternatives qui, autrement ne pourraient pas être connues' (Gaffard, 1990) .

On est à nouveau conduit à s'intéresser à des formes de flexibilité de l'entreprise, mais celle-ci est pour l'essentiel interne c'est-à-dire technologique et organisationnelle, et consiste moins à procéder à des ajustement quantitatifs qu'à recombiner son potentiel en vue d'en obtenir de meilleures performances compétitives par la recherche de meilleures solutions aux problèmes productifs rencontrés (cf. Amendola, 1983). C'est dire que l'information qui est alors nécessaire et dont il est maintenant question n'est plus de même nature que celle évoquée jusqu'à présent: il ne s'agit plus d'*une information générique*, support d'une meilleure perception de l'environnement concurrentiel et donc de meilleures décisions (on peut alors parler d'information décisionnelle ou stratégique quoique ce terme désormais galvaudé devienne d'emploi délicat) mais d'*informations spécifiques* destinées à nourrir les aménagement de l'organisation productive: il y aurait lieu de parler d'*information de coordination.*

Information de coordination et innovation

S'intéresser à l'information de coordination, c'est, ainsi qu'on l'a déjà suggéré, refuser de privilégier *une* information singulière (et qui par là même peut difficilement constituer un objet de recherche), et qui ne pourrait s'avérer stratégique (ou non) qu'*ex post*, pour viser des flux plus ou moins réguliers d'informations spécifiques. Celles-ci pourront alors être utiles aux exigences de la coordination plus par leur assortiment, leur assemblage pertinent et *l'aptitude de l'entreprise à les matérialiser*

---

5. souligné par nous

que par on ne sait quelle valeur intrinsèque préexistante. Ce qui importe dans cette perspective, c'est le processus ordinaire au travers duquel l'information spécialisée s'incorpore à la production non pas tant des biens ou des services que de l'entreprise par elle-même, grâce à l'innovation dans les deux grandes formes que constituent l'élaboration de technologie et la création d'organisation.

L'innovation technologique

Les conceptions de la technologie

L'approche néoclassique de la technologie tend à rejeter celleci en dehors du champ de l'analyse économique: selon Arrow (1962) l'activité de recherche des scientifiques produit des connaissances constituant un bien public non rival, accessible aux entrepreneurs. 'La non-rivalité implique que l'élément de connaissance ne se détruit pas dans l'usage et peut don être exploité un nombre infini de fois. On retrouve don ici la principale caractéristique d'un bien public pur (...). Un élément de connaissance défini de cette façon n'est donc pas appropriable et se propagera au seul coût de sa duplication' (Foray, 1991). Dans cette perspective, l'innovation consiste, pour l'entrepreneur, à adopter une combinaison productive déjà définie et caractérisée par les travaux antérieurs des chercheurs et qui pour n'avoir pas encore été pratiquée n'en est pas moins déjà connue et immédiatement applicable. Cette conception renvoie au point de vue que nous avons écarté en ce qu'il suppose une simple décision pertinente de la part de l'entrepreneur innovateur, sans qu'il soit possible de soumettre à l'analyse un processus innovant qui est ici réduit à sa plus simple expression: l'éclair d'une 'bonne' décision.

En rupture avec cette conception, dont nous examinerons ci-dessous les implications sur le rôle de l'information, se sont affirmées des approches visant à souligner le caractère 'construit' de la technologie, l'existence de ruptures fortes liées à l'émergence de nouveaux 'paradigmes technologiques' (Dosi, 1980) et l'inscription de l'innovation technologique dans des trajectoires d'entreprises lourdes d'irréversibilités (cf. Amendola et Gafard, 1988). Dans ces approches qui se rattachent plus volontiers à l'économie industrielle, le changement technique devient en lui même objet d'analyse, processus à décrire et appréhender, et qui autorise un dédoublement de la fonction de production de l'entreprise: celle-ci ne se définit plus simplement par une activité de production de biens et/ou de services mais simultanément par une production de technologie résultant notamment d'un processus à caractère permanent de spécification de ses ressources de toutes natures. Ce processus de spécification qui peut être décrit en termes de trajectoire d'entreprise a pour corollaire un déplacement du 'point de vue': on tend ainsi à substituer au concept générique de ressources (malléables, indifférenciées ou d'une absolue polyvalence) celui de ressources spécifiques, mutuellement adaptées, peu reconvertibles et pour lesquelles se poseront les questions de la flexibilité interne de l'organisation productive.

Les ressources spécifiques 'n'existent que par leur participation à des processus de production particuliers dont elles sont la manière d'être, et qui sont de ce fait in transférables d'un processus à l'autre. (...) Des ressources matérielles sont des ressources spécifiques,(...) la spécificité est ici le résultat de la division du travail et de la spécialisation des tâches.(...) Cependant les ressources humaines peuvent aussi être des ressources spécifiques' (Gaffard, 1990).

Technologie, connaissances et information spécialisée

Les deux types de conceptions de la technologie dont on vient de brièvement rappeler les principales caractéristiques entretiennent avec l'information des relations très contrastées.

Pour les néoclassiques, la technologie est assimilable à un savoir déjà constitué, dans lequel il est possible de puiser à tout moment de façon gratuite ou quasi-gratuite. En effet la communication de ce savoir passe par une information indéfiniment duplicable et donc non monopolisable. Arrow y voit la raison principale d'une déficience du marché à l'égard de la production scientifique: une entreprise courant le risque de voir ses concurrents accéder librement et à un coût négligeable aux connaissances qu'elle a produites en supportant des coûts de recherche qui peuvent être élevés, il existe un défaut d'incitation à la recherche, ce qui justifie le rôle d'une recherche publique, générateur du bien public que constitue la connaissance technologique. On se trouve ici face à un enchaînement par lequel la recherche produit des connaissances intégralement consignables sous forme d'informations, donc non monopolisables, qu'un entrepreneur peut instantanément mettre en oeuvre pour peu qu'il acquière ou dispose déjà des ressources nécessaires.

Un tel enchaînement qui conduit finalement à une totale assimilation entre technologie et information invite à considérer que tout entrepreneur peut accéder à un catalogue exhaustif des technologies déjà conçues par les chercheurs, et que ce catalogue est réductible à de l'information.

A partir d'une telle vision il est impossible de comprendre comment peut se former un avantage compétitif fondé sur la technologie: en toute hypothèse il ne peut résulter que d'une pertinence supérieure de la décision d'un entrepreneur, c'est-à-dire de l'incapacité de ses concurrents à optimiser leur choix d'une technologie économiquement pertinente, ce qui contredit soit la rationalité commune, soit le libre accès à l'information traduisant les connaissances produites par la recherche.

C'est le caractère peu satisfaisant de cette conception, sa faible adéquation à la réalité observable de la vie des entreprises qui a conduit dans ce domaine au développement d'une pensée hétérodoxe considérant l'élaboration de technologie comme un procès interne à l'entreprise, générateur tout à la fois d'irréversibilités et de mécanismes cumulatifs.

Technologie, information, connaissances tacites et apprentissage
Dans cette conception il n'est plus question de considérer une technologie comme déjà constituée et consignée, mais plutôt comme résultant d'un processus d'élaboration se perpétuant au travers des perfectionnements apportés en continu au procès productif (innovations incrémentales). Cette vision de l'entreprise comme lieu de l'élaboration technologique n'a bien sûr pas pour conséquence de réfuter le rôle de la recherche ni celui des connaissances préexistantes à l'extérieur de l'entreprise et accessibles par le moyen de flux d'informations spécialisées, mais elle implique le déroulement d'un processus intégrateur au sein duquel *des informations s'incorporent dans des ressources qu'elles contribuent ainsi à spécifier.* Ceci vaut pour les moyens de travail dont les réglages, les reconfigurations, les modifications fréquentes résultent de ce procès de matérialisation de l'information qui est au coeur de l'innovation technologique et cependant ne suffit pas à la résumer.

Mais cela vaut aussi pour les agents de la production, travailleurs et encadrement, dont la 'spécification' c'est-à-dire l'acquisition et la mise à jour de compétences se nourrit notamment d'informations spécialisées.

En effet l'observation suggère que la tentative de construire un avantage compétitif à partir de l'innovation technologique ne conduit pas à un processus continu. Des ruptures se produisent constituant véritablement les innovations, mais entre leur conception c'est-à-dire leur première mise en oeuvre[6] et leur véritable maîtrise productive, se déroule

6. Rappelons que, au sens strict, l'innovation n'existe que déjà mise en oeuvre dans les conditions de la production.

tout un *processus d'apprentissage* au sein duquel, au côté de la matérialisation d'informations spécifiques, s'opère aussi une *production de connaissances pratiques* non consignées. 'La connaissance codifiée et, d'une certaine manière, publique est complémentaire des formes plus spécifiques de connaissance, engendrées par les unités innovatrices elles-mêmes' (Cohendet et Gaffard, 1991).

Dans ces conditions, il n'est plus possible d'accepter l'assimilation qui est généralement et implicitement admise entre connaissance et information; l'un des problèmes que pose la gestion des 'ressources humaines' est d'ailleurs celui de la prise en compte non pas des qualifications, telles que les définissent de façon générale des grilles de classification, mais bien les *compétences réelles*, largement acquises 'sur le tas', c'est-à-dire résultant d'une spécification, au sein de l'entreprise d'une qualification initiale. La transmission des compétences au sein de l'organisation productive implique en particulier l'acquisition de telles connaissances tacites dont la formation par l'apprentissage ou les stages constitue la plus fréquente modalité (Dosi, 1988).

On voit d'ailleurs apparaître, à la suite du développement des travaux relatifs aux systèmes experts, des tentatives de consignation méthodiques et donc d'explicitation des savoirs pratiques détenus par des salariés expérimentés proches de la retraite et dont on prend conscience qu'il convient de les transmettre ou de les conserver.[7]

Il apparaît ainsi que la maîtrise de l'innovation technologique, considérée dans sa double dimension d'un potentiel matériel toujours plus spécifié et d'un potentiel de compétences en perpétuelle construction et reconfiguration, appelle de façon nécessaire des innovation d'organisation destinées à en assurer la cohérence.

7. On sait que les exemples abondent, à tout niveau de qualification, de ces mises en préretraite ou retraite qui, conduisant l'entreprise à prendre soudain la mesure du coût d'absence de ces savoirs pratiques, l'incitent à faire à nouveau appel, en qualité de consultant et à un coût très supérieur à ce qu'était la charges salariale, à l'expert dont la compétence a été sous-estimée, et qui revient au sein de l'entreprise former le successeur qui, bien que souvent plus 'qualifié' n'est pas doté de la compétence spécifique indispensable.

L'innovation d'organisation.

L'apprentissage organisationnel
Les travaux développés à la suite de Coase sur l'organisation et sa raison d'être, ont conduit à la constitution d'un certain nombre d'acquis:

- l'organisation n'existe que dans la mesure où elle se justifie par l'efficacité de la coordination qu'elle s'avère capable d'opérer entre des activités réunies en son sein: elle est toujours susceptible de 'restructurations' ou d'externalisations dès lors que le marché, longtemps considéré comme la forme normale sinon exclusive de 'mise en ordre', se montre plus avantageux.
- l'organisation est une conséquence de l'existence de coûts de transactions, elle s'inscrit comme cadre de la pratique des routines qui du fait d'une rationalité limitée, sont suffisamment efficaces pour remplacer avantageusement un flux perpétuel et de très grande ampleur de décisions optimisatrices.

Pourtant, ces indications, si elles permettent de comprendre l'existence des organisations productives que sont les entreprises, ne suffisent pas à préciser comment s'organise en leur sein la coordination des activités. Il est en particulier tentant de transposer au sein même de l'organisation le raisonnement optimisateur si familier aux économistes, et de supposer que l'entrepreneur a fait choix de la meilleure forme de coordination possible.

On pourrait, en poussant la comparaison avec ce qui a été indiqué ci-dessus, considérer que de même que l'entrepreneur néoclassique choisit sa technologie au sein d'un catalogue déjà constitué, il adopte un mode de coordination 'clés en main', à choisir dans la panoplie que peuvent proposer les sciences de l'organisation.

L'approche en termes de processus continu de spécification des ressources est évidemment incompatible avec une telle conception et conduit à considérer l'organisation comme largement autoproduite. L'organisation ne vise pas seulement en effet à assurer la coordination mais à l'améliorer ce qui revient à dire que l'*organisation a notamment pour mission de produire des innovations d'organisation* ce qui va encore nécessiter un apprentissage organisationnel[8] au sein duquel l'in-

8. O. Favereau (1989a) souligne que l'efficience de ce qu'il appelle le marché interne du travail, et qui est constitué par l'aptitude de l'organisation à gérer et constituer en son

formation spécifique est appelée à tenir un rôle important quoique non exclusif.

Tout ce qui a trait à la production et à l'élaboration de règles, considérées comme expression d'un savoir collectif, tant formalisé qu'empirique, peut s'interpréter comme innovation d'organisation et apprentissage organisationnel, traduisant, synthétisant et accumulant, même sous une forme qui peut rester elliptique et partiellement tacite, les acquisitions d'une recherche pratique ayant pour but l'amélioration de la coordination. La codification de ces règles qui seule permet la transmission du savoir ainsi constitué conduit à produire des informations spécifiques dont l'utilisation interne dans le processus de consolidation de l'innovation d'organisation est essentiel.

Information et organisation.
Si l'acquisition d'un avantage compétitif passe en particulier par l'innovation technologique, on a vu que celle-ci résulte largement, dans le cas d'une entreprise industrielle, d'un processus de spécification des ressources qui tend à accroître les irréversibilités et donc à accroître les rigidités du système productif. Le défi auquel se trouve confrontée l'organisation industrielle est de parvenir à surmonter ces rigidités en instaurant la flexibilité interne déjà évoquée. L'innovation d'organisation va alors principalement consister à mettre en place des formes de coordination souples et réversibles compensant les rigidités incorporées dans les ressources et permettant de restaurer les polyvalences qu'autorisaient des moyens de productions moins étroitement dédiés.

'Dans un régime de production riche en information où la valeur ajoutée provient essentiellement de combinaisons particulières de propriétés la capacité à intégrer des innovations devient déterminante pour la compétitivité quotidienne de la firme' (Foray et Zuscovitch).

L'une des formes les plus citées de cette flexibilité interne est celle qui se manifeste dans les 'ateliers flexibles' qu'a permis de créer le développement des machines à commandes numériques. Ces ateliers illustrent de façon très convaincante le rôle central des informations spécifiques dans la reconfiguration non seulement des opérations mais

---

sein les compétences qui lui sont indispensable, est dynamique et 'se mesure en termes d'Apprentissage Organisationnel rendu possible par le transfert du jeu de la concurrence, du marché du travail vers le marché des biens' (p.312).

des machines et de leurs ordonnancement. On a des exemples éclairants de la 'matérialisation' des informations spécifiques au travers d'une chaîne qui va des cotes caractéristiques de la pièce à usiner, généralement fournies par le donneur d'ordre, à l'opérateur qui traite et traduit ces informations en réglages des machines et programmation de l'atelier, pour aboutir à un produit 'informé'. Le produit peut alors être défini comme 'une collection de caractéristiques dont une est le prix' (Lancaster, 1979).

Une telle forme d'organisation et de coordination, même si elle se développe dans les systèmes industriels, n'est toutefois qu'un archétype et ne doit pas masquer les fonctions moins visibles de l'information dans la constitution de la flexibilité. Les informations spécifiques mobilisées ne concernent pas seulement les caractéristiques intrinsèques des produits, elles touchent aussi à ce que l'on appelle parfois paradoxalement l''environnement interne' de l'entreprise (charge des différents services, disponibilités et goulots d'étranglement...), à la prise en considération des caractéristiques de la 'demande' du marché, (variabilité des options concernant l'emballage et le conditionnement, adaptation aux divers canaux de distribution...), à la prise en compte concurrentielle des données recueillies sur les caractéristiques techniques et commerciales des produits concurrents.

Au delà de cette information de coordination ordinaire, *l'organisation a besoin d'information sur elle-même pour évoluer*: le retour d'expérience, l'analyse des dysfonctionnements, éléments constitutifs de l'apprentissage organisationnel, nécessitent la consignation d'information spécifiques destinées à être réinjectées dans le processus de reconfiguration de l'organisation par lequel s'acquiert la flexibilité interne.

L'organisation nécessite ainsi des flux continus d'information sans lesquels la coordination ne pourrait être que statique c'est-à-dire réfractaire à l'innovation ; réciproquement pour n'être pas débordante, inexploitable par surabondance, l'information doit être organisée.

Organisation de l'information.
Si l'organisation a besoin d'informations pour assurer les coordinations nécessaires et pouvoir se réformer, elle se trouve confrontée à la nécessité d'organiser ces informations, ce qui implique de définir les conditions de leur production et de leur acquisition, de leur caractérisation et de leur stockage, de la constitution de leurs réseaux de circulation interne.

Dans ce domaine aussi il y a lieu de produire des règles de collecte, de définir des procédures de mise en circulation, qui conditionneront la flexibilité et la vitesse de réaction de l'organisation.

Les techniques actuelles d'enregistrement permettent de produire et stocker une quantité considérables d'informations dont la surabondance même interdirait une utilisation pertinente. Une première mesure d'organisation consiste à définir les champs spécifiques à l'égard desquels des informations sont potentiellement utiles. L'appréciation de leur durée de validité est essentielle pour opérer une distinction entre des informations dont l'utilisation est possible ou probable, et celles dont la prudence conduit à réaliser un archivage qui est d'abord un allégement organisationnel avant d'être une conservation.[9]

Mais organiser l'information spécifique, c'est avant tout créer les conditions de sa *mobilisation en temps et lieu opportuns*. Cela suppose d'opérer une conversion de flux à caractère permanent, en stocks renouvelés et structurés, propres à des extractions rapides et sélectives. C'est aussi définir les contours de ce qu'il apparaît nécessaire de détenir *dans* l'entreprise et identifier des informateurs externes permettant de satisfaire des demandes toujours urgentes. Ce qui au fond constitue le critère à privilégier dans l'organisation d'un système d'informations de coordination c'est sa capacité à assurer la *mobilisation juste à temps des informations utiles*, et ce avec le moindre encombrement pour l'organisation générale de l'entreprise. C'est dire que ce système est inconcevable sans une redéfinition des fonctions, des connexions, et même de la distribution de l'autorité qui constitue l'un des principes de la coordination: toute les entreprises qui se sont engagées dans une informatisation de grande ampleur se sont trouvées confrontées, le plus souvent sans les avoir vus venir, à un développement des délégations et des autonomies sans lesquelles la flexibilité est illusoire, à un foisonnement de 'courts-circuits' permettant en fait des circulations d'informations non prévues par les organigrammes, bref à une recomposition des relations hiérarchiques. Organiser ou réorganiser l'information conduit selon les cas à réformer ou révolutionner l'organisation toute entière.

C'est l'observation comparative des performances compétitives des entreprises américaines et japonaises qui a conduit à distinguer les

9. En explorant le contenu de son disque dur, tout utilisateur de micro-ordinateur peut constater non seulement la difficulté de ranger les information d'une façon permettant un rappel efficace, mais surtout la difficulté d'échapper à un gonflement largement inutile de stocks bons pour l'archivage.

organisations 'A', hiérachiques, verticales, peu propices au mélange sans lequel il n'y a pas d'intégration possible, et les firmes 'J', organisées horizontalement, réduisant les lignes hiérarchiques et privilégiant des liaisons fonctionnelles de coordination (Aoki, 1986).

En situation d'environnement changeant, la variabilité des informations collectables qui conduit certains auteurs à évoquer un 'régime d'information perurbée (*dans lequel...*) c'est la mise en oeuvre de processus locaux d'apprentissage qui constitue la réponse organisationnelle la plus appropriée' (Cohendet et Llerena, 1990). Cet apprentissage local mobilise et produit de l'information spécialisée en mettant au point des coordinations nouvelles qui n'ont pas été préconisées par la hiérarchie.

Conclusion

En renonçant à mettre l'accent sur ce que l'information peut avoir de spectaculaire dans certaines singularités et en ne la considérant pas comme le simple préalable de la prise de décision, on se met en situation d'en prendre en compte le caractère ordinaire, répétitif et routinier qui implique son inscription au coeur des processus industriels de production et d'innovation.

Cette approche conduit au constat d'une liaison étroite entre innovation technologique et innovation d'organisation et invite par conséquent à ne pas privilégier abusivement une information scientifique et technique qui ne constitue qu'une part de l'information de coordination.

Enfin si l'information est indispensable à l'organisation innovante, l'organisation de l'information est réciproquement une condition de sa matérialisation efficace.

On a renoncé ici à évoquer la notion empirique de veille, car elle n'est pas dépourvue d'ambiguïtés: s'il s'agit de 'pêche au gros', d'être à l'affût du 'scoop' décisif, la veille renvoie en effet à la conception de l'information que nous avons écartée, et elle ne peut être que génératrice de déceptions pour les entreprises qui s'y livrent dans une telle optique ; si au contraire la veille consiste à 'chaluter' voire à 'filtrer le plancton' en vue d'assurer l'alimentation des processus d'innovation dans les systèmes industriels, alors elle s'inscrit bien dans le fil des réflexions qui précèdent et qui ont voulu commencer l'exploration des processus par lesquels l'information spécialisée participe à la construction quotidienne de l'avantage compétitif.

Summary

Specialist Information and the Competitive Advantage

This paper sets out to specify a methodology for the application of specialist information in developing a competitive advantage in the marketplace. The role of information in innovation is considered, as well as the results of specialist information distribution on the effectiveness of organizations. Innovation is a mechanism which operates at the centre of a competitive strategy.

New developments in information technology have led to the growth of new sectors of economic activity (such as information processing services), and at the same time, have penetrated most other areas of activity, which often require reorganization as a result. This has necessitated the development of a strategy for the mobilization of information. Overseas institutions are studied, with a view to understanding the process of integration of economic and technological information in countries as different as the United States and Japan.

Different forms of competitive advantage are detailed: economies of scale; reduction of capacity; definition of scope; effects of the 'learning curve' in the acquisition of new technology, which highlights the importance of proprietary knowledge accumulated within the firm.

The concept of competition is presented as the end-product of a series of initiatives, resulting from decisions based on the provision of specialist information. Management literature considers three principal strategies: domination of the market; product differentiation; and segmentation of demand. The competitive advantage is generated by flexibility of decision-taking in the organization of the production process. The degree of flexibility depends on the coordination of specialist information.

The development of a competitive advantage is linked with the capacity of the organization to implement the specialist information acquired. Innovation consists of recombining the elements of production in the light of new technological developments, and is at the heart of the continuing process of specification within the organization.

The object of research, which utilizes the specialist information coordinated internally by the organization, is to facilitate innovation. The importance of factors in the 'internal environment' of the organization is noted, and a comparison is drawn up between the competitive performances of American and Japanese firms.

A direct link is shown between technological innovation and innovation within the organization itself. Organizational innovation in turn relies on the internal organization of information. The anticipation of market trends is not as important as encouraging the innovation process in industrial organizations.

Références

Amendola, M. (1983). **A change of perspective in the analysis of the process of innovation**. Metroeconomica.

Amendola, M. et Gafard, J.L. (1988). **La dynamique économique de l'innovation**. Economica.

Aoki, M. (1986). Horizontal versus vertical information structure of the firm, **American Economic Review**, 76(5), 971-983.

Arrow, K. (1962). Economic welfare and the allocation of resources for invention. In **The rate and direction of inventive activity: economic and social factors**, edité par R. Nelson.

Cohendet, P. et Gaffard, J.L. (1991). Innovation et entreprise. In **Encyclopédie économique**. Economica.

Cohendet, P. et Llerena, P. (1989). Flexibilité, risques et incertitude dans la théorie de la firme: un survey. In **Flexibilité information et décision**, edité par P. Cohendet et P. Llerena. Economica.

Cohendet, P. et Llerena, P. (1990). Nature de l'information, évaluation et organisation de l'entreprise, **Revue d'Economie Industrielle**, 51, 162.

Dosi, G. (1980). Technological paradigms and technological trajectories: a suggested interpretation of the determinants and directions of technical change, **Research Policy**, 11, 147-162.

Dosi, G. (1988). The nature of the innovative process. In **Technical Change and Economic theory**, edité par G. Dosi. London: Pinter Publisher Ltd.

Favereau, O. (1989a). Marchés internes, marchés externes, **Revue Economique**, 2, 273-328.

Favereau, O. (1989b). Valeur d'option et flexibilité: de la rationalité substantielle à la rationalité procédurale. In **Flexibilité information et décision**, edité par P. Cohendet et P. Llerena. Economica.

Foray, D. (1991). Economie et politique de la science: les développements théoriques récents, **Revue Française d'Economie**, VI(4).

Foray, D. et Zuscovitch, E. (undated). L'innovation entre la production et le système technique, **Traité de'Economie Industrielle**.

Gaffard, J.L. (1990). **Economie industrielle et de l'innovation.** Dalloz.

Henry, C. (1974). Investment decision under uncertainty: the irreversibility effect, **American Economic Review**, 14, 1006-1012.

Lancaster, K. (1979). **Variety, equity and efficiency: product variety in an industrial society**. Oxford: Basil Blackwell. (Cité par Favereau 1989.)

Simon, H.A. (1947). **Administrative Behaviour, a Story of Decision Processes in business Organization**. Macmillan.

Weisbrod, B.A. (1964). Collective-Consumption Services of Individual Consumption Goods, **Quarterly Journal of Economics**, août, 471-477.

Willinger, M. (1989). Flexibilité et valeur de l'information. In **Flexibilité information et décision**, edité par P. Cohendet et P. Llerena. Economica.

CHANGES IN THE POLITICAL AND LEGAL CONTEXT

Développements dans la Domaine Politique et Légale

How Can Digital Information be Protected?

La Protection de l'Information Digitale

Michael Lesk
Bellcore, Morristown, New Jersey, USA

Electronic information delivery poses great risks to publishers; how can these be overcome? The technology of software publishing may well offer some answers, and digital cryptography may offer others. Failure to solve these problems will continue to drive us towards CD-ROM type solutions, rather than networked solutions.

Introduction

The development of electronic information systems has been greatly delayed by our inability to devise suitable delivery and accounting schemes for scholarly information. Libraries hope that many paper copies will be replaced with one electronic copy, and publishers fear that many paper copies will be replaced with one electronic copy. These economic problems arise from simple technological facts:

1. Printing, binding, and mailing are only a small part of the costs of scholarly publishing, perhaps only 25 per cent; so that eliminating these does not greatly reduce the cost of the journal.

2. Electronic information can be copied and transmitted easily, raising the expectation on the part of users that it will be easy to make multiple uses of the same information for low cost, and raising the fear on the part of publishers that copying will be rampant.

Many scholarly journals today are published as a small press run of high-priced copies sold primarily to libraries. Economically, this is a strange use of print technology, which is well adapted to mass production. As universities and their staff members cut back on subscriptions to save money, the publishers must raise prices to keep the journal solvent. Thus we wind up using a mass-production technology in an inefficient way and providing very few people with the paper journal even though it would cost relatively little more to provide the extra copies. People start relying on photocopies of articles (whether 'fair use' or illegal) to avoid paying the subscription price, even though it is clear that the cost to the economy as a whole of making copies one page at a time must be higher than the cost of printing the journal in bulk. These and related problems have been described many times before (see for example Curtis, 1985 and 1986).

Everyone wishes that there were a simple answer to the problems of research distribution, and many have hoped that in the electronic world things would be easier. Unfortunately, electronic copying is even easier than paper copying. Thus, the same incentives that cause people to copy rather than purchase in the paper world exist electronically, and are much more serious in that world because of the ease, rapidity, and quick redistribution of the copies.

All of these problems are difficulties with economy of scale; because the incremental cost of producing another copy of an electronic file is so low, much less than average cost, it is not possible to price at incremental cost and have a successful business. There are various straightforward economic solutions, but none seems to work out.

A simplistic solution is for the government to pay the start up costs, leaving the users only the incremental costs. This is the way we fund road transportation for example. But expecting direct government funding of initial publication costs is clearly unrealistic in the United States or any other major country, as suggested by Olaisen (1989).

Publishers have looked, not surprisingly, for techniques to make copying more difficult. CD-ROMs are relatively difficult to duplicate, for example, so that this form of information distribution is attractive to publishers. Unfortunately, it also interferes with rapid updating, and interferes with the simultaneous use of different information sources by users. It would be unfortunate if the advantages of networked data could not be exploited because of the fear of copying. CD-ROMs are also becoming easier and easier to copy—the price of a drive to write one's own CD-ROMs is now below $10,000 and dropping steadily.

Worse yet, the CD technology is even more directly adapted to mass production than the conventional printing process. It was designed (and is used) for producing millions of copies of audio recordings. Although many CD-ROMs are priced in the neighborhood of $1,000, the actual incremental cost of making another one is only a few dollars. Once again, a small number of copies are being sold at a price far above incremental cost, making it economically advantageous to copy rather than to buy information, and encouraging complex networking arrangements for CD-ROMs rather than just getting more copies.

It is possible that substantially lower prices for information would be more effective. At the moment, a great many users of scientific information do not actually subscribe to any journals themselves; they read everything in the nearest library. There is thus an untapped market of individual scientists and engineers who might, if they could buy one article easily and cheaply, pay for it. Against that, of course, is the fear that if one article could be bought easily, people would stop buying whole journals. And it is not clear whether people who had paid relatively little for an article would be more likely to think that because it was cheap it didn't matter if it were copied illegally, or that because it was cheap there was no point in trying to get an illegal copy instead of a legitimate one. Nothing short of some real experience will help here.

Given that we do not have a known economic solution right now, we must ask what else could be done. Can alternative arrangements be found that would provide a suitable economic basis for disseminating scholarly results and not encourage theft?

Page charges

One economically suitable way to support the journal publication system would be to rely on page charges instead of reproduction charges. In actual fact academic journals are largely driven and supported by the need of authors to publish papers for academic credentials. Such organizations as the National Science Foundation and Harvard Medical School now request authors to list only a few publications, hoping to discourage researchers from dividing their accomplishments into as many papers as possible, producing a superfluidity of publications many of which are rarely read. If this system is recognized as author-driven rather than reader-driven, and the costs were divided among both the authors and the readers, with readers paying only for duplication costs, a sensible financial platform could be developed. In such a world the cost of a journal would be divided among some hundred publishing institutions. Faculty and students at an institution which did not 'super-scribe' to the journal would not be able to publish in it. Subscription costs would cover only the costs of producing the copies; thus, electronic subscriptions would be free. In this world, there would be no difficulty about copyright violation.

Page charges have been around for years, but have been losing ground. Authors have been able to publish in journals that did not require page charges and the competition for high quality articles has inhibited publishers from raising page charges to the level that would be required to balance front-end costs.

Software publishing and site licenses

The software publishing industry has had many of the same problems. Copying of videogame software, and international problems with countries where copying is widespread, have both cut into the sales of standard software packages. Ten years ago, 'copy-protection' was tried, but has been virtually abandoned. Site license agreements exist but have the problem of complexity (since companies of different sizes must negotiate different kinds of licenses).

In sales to large corporations, the 'simultaneous use license' is now common. In this form, the user buys the right for one person at a time to use a program. So, a company might buy three licenses if they expected either three people to use the program most of the time, or thirty people to each use the program one-tenth of the time. This form of pricing is easily understood, adapts to companies of different sizes, and avoids case-by-case negotiation. It does, however, require some controlled systems administration, with a program called the 'license server' handling the distribution of authority to run the software. In many cases, given the highly heterogeneous systems running in many universities, it is effectively impossible to impose any kind of standard administration on the computers.

Unfortunately, in some respects the site license procedure is counterproductive. Since no individual user has paid anything for the access to the information, they are likely to think of it as free. Thus, although the problem of copying between students at the same university disappears, for example, the problem of a student at a university which does subscribe to some service helping a friend at a different university may be aggravated. More seriously, this procedure is too hard to set up for a small price; it is not likely to be an effective way of sending one person one article unless we get some kind of standardization of terms so that enrollment in such systems becomes relatively straightforward.

Networking

Networked distribution of data also alleviates some of the economic problems. Systems such as Dialog and Lexis exist successfully on central networks. If users receive only a small part of the total information at a time, it is difficult for them to steal large parts of a file (and an attempt is more likely to be noticed). As networks get cheaper, it becomes more practical for publishers to move to centralized data stores and deliver data on demand.

To the extent that different users in an area want the same information, however, they are likely to find it economically attractive to share it rather than buy it again. In fact, in a complex network environment it may not be clear whether a 'copy' in the traditional sense is even made when one person fetches an article from an electronic system and ten people read that particular file; but nevertheless publishers may feel they are losing an opportunity to gain revenue in such a situation.

Note that the more information supplied, the harder it is to copy. Thus, another way to interfere with the ease of copying is to distribute bitmaps rather than ASCII streams to the user workstations. At present it is conventional to display on a user workstation by sending the bytes of text to the user. Instead of that, we can imagine an architecture in which we format the text into the window display bitmap, and transmit the bitmap to the end user terminal. This increases the network bandwidth required, but networks are growing very quickly in speed. Although in theory the increase in bandwidth is a factor of 10 or so, compression can reduce this to perhaps a factor of 3. A user who attempts to copy what is on the screen would find himself forced to copy the bitmap, having received nothing else, and to actually get ASCII would require running an OCR program on the bitmap, which is at least tedious and in reality likely to be error-prone.

Complex graphical user interfaces may serve somewhat the same function. Although the stream going to an X windows server contains ASCII characters for the text on the screen, if the interface designer does not provide a button or command for saving that text, the user will need some rudimentary knowledge to be able to capture it. It is fairly easy to do, but if the only goal is to make copying as difficult as making Xerox copies, this probably meets the test. This paragraph should not be read as an argument for making computer interfaces as difficult as possible to program.

Instead, the most important function of a good networked interface should be to encourage users to get only small fractions of the material available. To the extent that what users do is skim the article remotely, looking at only a few paragraphs or illustrations, they do not get enough of the data transmitted to their screens to be able to retain a copy that is likely to be useful to somebody else. Also, to the extent that the network interface and database itself provides a great deal of skimming or searching functionality, people will wish to use it rather than work with a copy that someone else has retained illegally.

As examples of these techniques, Figures 1 to 3 show example screens from the CORE project (an information delivery system for chemical journal articles done by a collaboration of the American Chemical Society, Bellcore, Chemical Abstracts, Cornell University, and OCLC (Lesk, 1991)). Experimental studies done with this system have been reported earlier (Egan et al, 1991). Figure 1 shows some display windows for an image-oriented system. The various windows include a welcoming window, a search window, a list of titles matching the search, a table of contents for one issue, and two page excerpts at two different sizes. In this system all full article displays are images, and the 'print' button prints from page images, giving something akin to a xerox copy. If the user retains anything, all that is retained is a bitmap, and there is no simple way for the user to retain any access to the search system. Except for the print command, in fact, the user can't even get a full bitmap because the high-resolution bitmap does not fit on the screen and will always be truncated before being shown. Figures 2 and 3 show a variant of the SuperBook system (Egan et al, 1990) whose display is based on ASCII. In this system, as shown in Figure 2, the user gets a structured table of contents and a page of text, with icons indicating graphic figures. Figure 3 shows the result of clicking on the graphic icon to pop up the full figure. Again, the screen displays are only portions of an article, a large full-resolution graphic display does not fit on the screen, and it is difficult for a user to capture any useful bit of information.

These partial displays make sense even in fast networks. The network may be fast, but the user's display is still limited in resolution and may be short of cache memory for the display. Thus, it makes sense to use the full search power of the system to select portions of material which can be sent to the user's screen. The network will be more efficiently employed, the display more focused, and the user's time better spent. If, as a side benefit, it becomes harder to steal portions of material, that is all to the good. Although some people possess enough expertise, computer power, and interest to wish to write their own display software, it is likely they are few enough in number that negotiating specific deals with them is not hard.

Cryptography

Another way of easing the risk to publishers would be the use of cryptographic technology to protect data. It is straightforward to use cryptography to prevent people snooping on networks from taking copies of information they are not entitled to. This can be done using fairly routine technology since this application is not dealing with military or commercial secrets; it is only necessary to make the cost of code-breaking higher than the cost of buying the service. Cryptography of this sort also has the minor advantage of improving the integrity of published documents—it becomes harder for someone to write something and present it as if it had been issued by a real publisher, or to take an existing document, make a few changes, and re-issue it.

What is more important in this context is whether it is possible to dissuade people from copying information they are entitled to read themselves (but not redistribute). It is possible, cryptographically, to add a coded signal to a bit string which is unforgeable and, in the case of a bitmap, unobtrusive. This could uniquely identify the license copy of any piece of information which someone had, and thus permit tracking of the source of a stolen piece of digital information. This technique has been patented under the name 'digital watermark' (see Komatsu and Tominaga, 1990). Unfortunately, it is much easier to hide the signal in an image than in a text file, because of the greater redundancy of the image. It is also much more likely that an image system can make it difficult for the user to remove the signals (although a simple low-pass filtering would seem to suffice). Komatsu explains the tradeoffs between image degradation, amount of hidden information, and resistance to modification.

Although this technique is particularly suited to image distribution of material, that may not be a problem. Image distribution appears to be gaining favor. Although character-style (i.e. ASCII) text is shorter, searchable, and easier to manipulate, there are no generally used standards for complex text formats, there is no general agreement about how to include graphics, and the systems to distribute ASCII are more complex, harder to build, and more specific to subject areas. At the same

***Figure 1**: CORE image display screen*

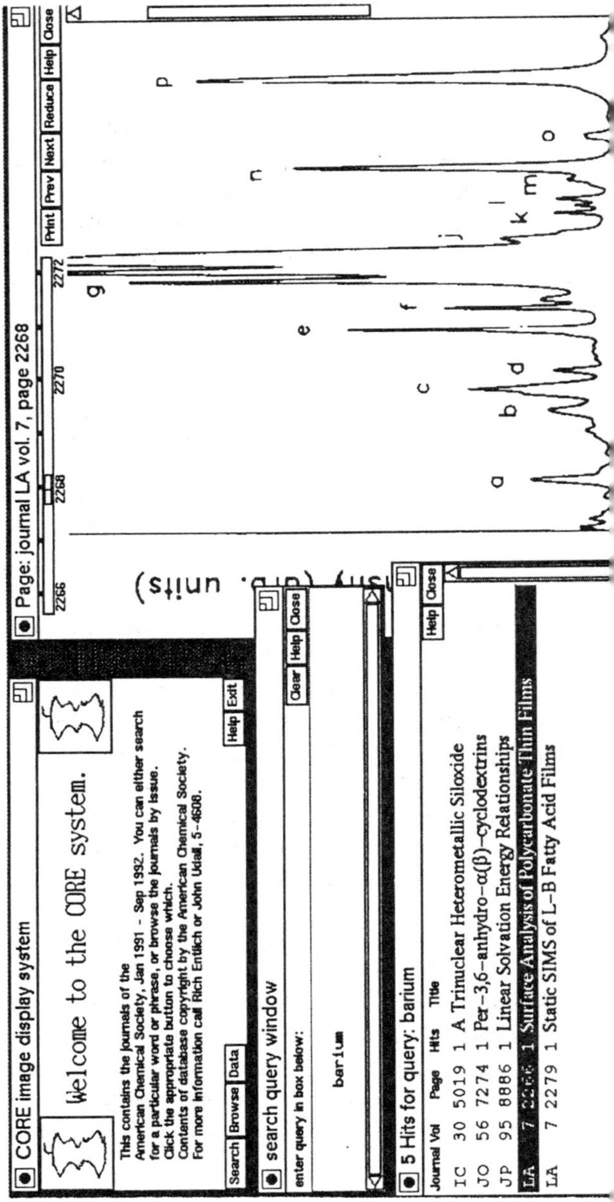

convient mal aux fonctionnalités de produits ou d'outils de traitement et de recherche de l'information.

Les juges qualifient d''œuvres de l'esprit originales' des objets qui ne révèlent aucune subjectivité mais résultent d'opérations ou de mécanismes plus ou moins complexes. Le concept d'originalité—critère de la réservation au titre de la propriété littéraire et artistique—a donc été 'forcé'. Il a été reformulé en matière de logiciels. Il trouve ses limites à propos d'autres produits recueillant ou présentant des informations et il paraît inapplicable aux documents issus de systèmes de traitement de texte de même qu'aux synthèses de langage, sons ou images générées automatiquement. L'inadaptation du droit d'auteur aux nouvelles technologies de l'information est avérée. Face à ce constat, on peut bien entendu regretter la diversification du régime juridique des biens—sans qu'il y ait à déplorer un bouleversement de leurs classifications—il est heureux que des solutions plus appropriées à la gestion documentaire et d'informations se dessinent en droit positif. Il n'est cependant pas certain qu'elles permettent aux producteurs de bases de données de s'affranchir complètement de l'épineuse condition d'originalité.

L'évolution du critère d'originalité aux confins du droit d'auteur

En tant que révélateur de la personnalité d'individus créateurs, l'originalité paraît devoir évincer de la protection tout ce qui est brut, factuel, donné ou résultat d'une nécessité objective, qu'il s'agisse de mettre en œuvre un mécanisme ou de recourir à un ordonnancement banal ou commun tel que l'ordre alphabétique. Pourtant, la condition de la protection par le droit d'auteur s'applique aux programmes d'ordinateur et à des systèmes logiques et/ou automatiques d'information.

C'est au profit des logiciels que le concept d'originalité a d'abord subi des distorsions. En ce qui concerne des programmes informatiques accomplissant des fonctions, ce n'est pas l'empreinte de la personnalité de l'auteur qui est recherchée. Ce qui est pris en compte, c'est 'l'apport intellectuel' du concepteur dont la marque est à rechercher dans 'l'effort personnalisé allant au-delà de la simple mise en œuvre d'une logique automatique et contraignante' et matérialisé dans une structure individualisée. L'arrêt rendu par la Cour de cassation siégeant en Assemblée plénière le 7 mars 1986 dans l'affaire Pachot indique en ces termes que la condition d'originalité est remplie dès lors que peut être apportée la preuve de l'existence d'un effort intellectuel particulier révélateur de la personnalité de son auteur.[4]

Il est couramment fait référence à la formule de l'Assemblée plénière et une application récente de cette jurisprudence concerne des modules mémoires d'un logiciel de traçage[5] dont il est jugé que les indications qu'ils contiennent 'résultent de choix créatifs caractéristiques de véritables programmes, protégeables du fait de leur originalité au regard de l'apport personnel de leur auteur'.[6]

En ce qui concerne les banques de données, leur protection par le droit d'auteur a été indirectement reconnue dans les arrêts rendus dans l'affaire fameuse Microfor/Le Monde.[7] La Cour de cassation était appelée à statuer sur l'étendue des droits de citation et d'analyse, autrement dit sur la portée d'exceptions légales[8] au monopole d'exploitation de l'auteur qui sont essentielles pour le libre exercice d'activités documentaires. A cette occasion, elle a qualifié 'd'œuvres d'information' les banques de données 'constituées sans commentaire ni développement personnel de leur auteur, par la réunion et le classement de courtes citations empruntées à des œuvres préexistantes'. Le principe de la protégeabilité des bases et banques de données étant ainsi posé et admis,[9] l'originalité d'ensembles tels que bibliographies, annuaires et tous types de recueils d'informations brutes non protégées en tant que telles est à rechercher dans 'le choix et la disposition des matières, la structure et la présentation des données'.

Pour d'autres corpus d'informations exprimés en langage naturel, on note une évolution analogue de la notion d'originalité, illustrée par diverses décisions rendues récemment à propos de dictionnaires, répertoires et catalogues.

Dans une affaire opposant une société française éditrice d'un dictionnaire bilingue d'informatique et une société d'édition anglaise diffusant des ouvrages du même type en France, cette dernière, poursuivie en contrefaçon d'œuvre littéraire, faisait notamment valoir qu'un tel dictionnaire ne peut bénéficer de la protection instituée par la loi du 11 mars 1957 faute d'originalité, compte tenu du caractère de bien commun propre à tous les mots de la langue, le langage informatique étant par nature insusceptible d'appropriation au titre des droits d'auteur. Rejetant l'argumentation, la Cour d'appel de Paris relevait les éléments d'un 'travail positif suffisant à démontrer une activité impliquant des choix, c'est-à-dire des opérations intellectuelles qui contribuent à donner à l'ouvrage, si technique soit-il, une originalité certaine'. Plus particulièrement, 'l'opération (de tri, parmi les termes courants,) qui requiert culture et attention, orientée par la vision de l'œuvre à réaliser, doit être qualifiée d'œuvre de l'esprit'.[10]

La qualification de diverses 'sommes' d'informations est de la même veine. Ainsi, constituent des créations originales une enquête sur les prix, 'par son ampleur et la présentation des données concrètes recueillies';[11] un répertoire professionnel constitué par la liste d'agences de promotion suivie de divers renseignements, 'l'ensemble étant le résultat d'un travail intellectuel d'élaboration et de présentation';[12] un guide local de renseignements administratifs dont l'originalité réside dans sa seule structure.[13]

En 1992, la Cour d'appel de Paris a jugé qu'un catalogue recensant des logiciels d'EAO et des systèmes-experts en matière médicale en présentant par ordre alphabétique des fiches remplies par les concepteurs de ces logiciels est 'le résultat d'un travail intellectuel d'élaboration et de présentation qui le rend protégeable au titre du droit d'auteur'.[14] Et quelques mois plus tard, elle a décidé que bénéficiait de la protection une compilation d'histoires drôles dont 'la sélection et le classement dans un ordre ne découlant d'aucune nécessité contraignante caractérisaient une œuvre créatrice'.[15]

Mais peu de temps auparavant, en affirmant que la simple compilation n'est pas protégeable par le droit d'auteur, la Cour de cassation rappelait que l'information n'est pas en soi susceptible d'appropriation.[16] (Il s'agissait d'un 'organigramme' des principales entreprises mondiales de construction automobile que la société Coprosa, éditrice du journal l'Automobile, avait publié sous la forme de liste de leurs administrateurs et directeurs). Un mois plus tard, la même solution était adoptée à propos d'informations boursières dont une sélection de la cote Desfossés avait été proposée au public sur un service du Minitel.[17] Ainsi que l'observe Madame C.Ginsburg, 'on aurait beau revêtir les données d'une structure, si un autre se passait de la structure et ne volait que l'information, il n'y aurait pas de contrefaçon'.[18] Autrement dit, 'la protection attachée au recueil original ne s'étend pas à des éléments d'information qui, une fois publiés, échappent à toute appropriation, leur synthèse et leur présentation étant faites dans des formes différentes'.[19]

Aux Etats-Unis, les compilations sont expressément visées dans les lois sur le droit d'auteur. Les banques de données sont considérées comme telles et définies comme des 'œuvres formées par la réunion et l'assemblage des éléments préexistants ou des données qui sont sélectionnés, coordonnés ou agencés de telle manière que l'œuvre qui en résulte constitue dans son ensemble une œuvre de l'esprit originale'.[20] C'est donc 'la manière' qu'il faut considérer et l'originalité est repérée dans la sélection de données, révélatrice d'un parti pris qui s'exprime dans leur représentation. A cet égard, l'affaire Feist[21] a bien montré que le droit d'auteur sur une compilation d'informations brutes—en l'espèce, un annuaire des abonnés au téléphone—est faible. Faute d'un minimum de créativité—l'équivalent de l'apport intellectuel dans la jurisprudence française—il est inexistant. De sorte que paradoxalement, l'exhaustivité d'une banque de données en exclut toute manifestation de subjectivité et la fait sortir du champ de la protection légale.

Quelles que soient les divergences des solutions rendues, dans les deux systèmes français et américain de droit d'auteur ce sont donc le travail de tri, la sélection et le choix, synonymes de parti pris, qui caractérisent l'originalité des productions qui en résultent, le plus souvent par opposition à ce qui ne serait que 'simple présentation' ou 'simple compilation' (Paris, 29 juin 1992). Mais, au nom de la 'complexité' des opérations intellectuelles, n'est-ce pas en réalité l'importance des investissements qui est indirectement prise en compte?

Cette évolution rend compte d'une extension économiquement utile mais juridiquement extrême du champ du droit d'auteur. Il n'en reste pas moins qu'en deça d'une objectivation certaine de la notion d'originalité, c'est toujours une intervention humaine qui est recherchée. Et même s'il s'agit en réalité de réserver les résultats d'un travail complexe, la marque intellectuelle d'une personnalité[22] reste caractéristique de l'œuvre de l'esprit qui ne se confond pas avec l'information qu'elle élabore ou véhicule.[23] Tant bien que mal, la conception traditionnelle et subjectiviste du droit d'auteur est sauvegardée. Mais on ne voit pas comment elle pourrait l'être s'agissant 'd'œuvres' qui n'ont de 'l'esprit' que l'apparence des langages—naturels ou artificiels—dans lesquels elles s'expriment.

Vers la reconnaissance d'un mode de réservation spécifique en marge du droit d'auteur

Tributaire de la condition d'originalité, la protection des corpus informationnels en tant qu'œuvres de l'esprit est aujourd'hui soumise aux aléas d'une jurisprudence qui tente de borner le champ démesuré des œuvres d'information qu'elle a ouvert. Limité au 'contenant'—seuls l'agencement de données brutes et la disposition des matières y donnant prise—le droit d'auteur reste une cote mal taillée pour des collections, anthologies, compilations ou sommes exhaustives dont les éléments considérés isolément, bien qu'utilisables et exploitables séparément, ne sont pas couverts.

De plus, à l'heure actuelle, de nombreux textes sont générés par des ordinateurs à partir de corpus de références, c'est-à-dire de documents en langage naturel saisis et traités à cette seule fin. Par exemple, des logiciels de constitution ou d'interrogation de bases de données, fonctionnant dans des systèmes de recherche précisément performants en matière documentaire, produisent—à partir de textes mémorisés ou dictionnaires électroniques—d'autres textes qu'il est difficile pour ne pas dire impossible de considérer en tant que tels comme des créations originales, témoins d'un quelconque apport intellectuel individualisé. Les produits des 'industries de la langue'—ainsi qu'il est convenu de désigner l'ensemble des applications réalisées[24] en traitement automatique des langues naturelles—posent notamment les deux questions particulières et délicates du choix de leur régime juridique—différent selon qu'on les qualifie de logiciels ou d'œuvres de langage[25]—et de la détermination de leur auteur.[26]

Ainsi, partout où les techniques de numérisation permettent la réalisation de produits de langage ou d'images de synthèse[27] sans intervention humaine—sinon tout à fait en amont ou en marge, aux niveaux de la conception et de la maintenance des systèmes—l'entreprise d'information se trouve particulièrement démunie de moyens propres à protéger et activer les valeurs en jeu. Le statut juridique du texte informatisé reste en effet à élaborer.

Sans doute ce contexte permet-il d'expliquer la tentative récente d'instaurer 'une protection temporaire et sans droit moral pour des créations non originales ou non inventives', ainsi qu'il est dit dans l'exposé des motifs d'une proposition de loi relative à la protection des créations réservées présentée le 30 juin 1992 par Mr. J.Godfrain.[28] L'article 1er dispose que 'toute création exploitable à des fins lucratives, qui résulte d'un travail intellectuel accompli avec ou sans l'aide d'un logiciel est constitutive d'un intérêt patrimonial susceptible de protection juridique'. Et l'article 3, sans faire aucun cas des protections existantes,[29] énumère pêle-mêle 'les banques de données, circuits électroniques, photographies, numérisations d'images ou de sons, résultats de calculs, savoir-faire, compilations, solutions commerciales, méthodes administratives, formes utiles, formules promotionnelles'.[30]

Les propriétés intellectuelles ont un champ limité aux droits privatifs expressément institués par la loi et érigés en monopoles temporaires à des conditions particulières. Si contre toute vraisemblance le texte proposé venait à être voté, ces dispositions créeraient une catégorie de biens nouvelle et indéfinie, susceptible d'accueillir toutes les matérialisations concevables de 'matière grise' et toutes les formules utiles d'abstractions—méthodes, résultats et fonctionnalités—dont le dénominateur commun est précisément l'information. En droit positif, de tels éléments de connaissance et de compétence ne sont pas réservables. Ils ne sont protégés que par le droit de la responsabilité civile, délictuelle ou contractuelle. L'utilisation sans droit du travail intellectuel d'autrui peut notamment être sanctionnée dans le cadre de l'action en réparation du dommage fondée sur la faute,[31] la déloyauté du concurrent ou le parasitisme d'un quidam qu'il faut prouver.

A l'inverse, dans le régime envisagé d'un 'droit exclusif temporaire (de dix ans) opposable à tous'[32] assorti de sanctions civiles et pénales, des prérogatives exorbitantes et analogues à celles du monopole de l'auteur seraient octroyées au concepteur ou au producteur[33] desdites créations. L'exposé des motifs indique que 'par création, il faut entendre toute œuvre de l'imagination ou de l'industrie humaine qui est susceptible d'exploitation à des fins lucratives, l'objectif étant de proposer une solution simple et pratique qui encourage l'investissement en matière de création'. Le seul critère proposé réside ainsi dans la potentialité à être exploité de sorte que pourrait être monopolisée n'importe quelle somme de données concrètes ou manifestation de connaissance objective dont la rentabilité ne reposerait en définitive que sur l'arbitraire d'investisseurs décidant d'en réserver l'exploitation à leur profit exclusif. Sur ce point d'ailleurs, aucun acte précis d'exploitation—reproduction, représentation, édition, diffusion—n'est déterminé. Même dans un contexte 'protectionniste', il paraît donc inconcevable que le législateur entérine ce dispositif qu'un commentateur qualifie à juste titre de 'brutal'.[34] Il n'aurait d'autre effet que d'obérer gravement l'accès à la connaissance, d'entraver le libre exercice d'une multitude d'activités—études, recherche, promotion ou communication—et de freiner le progrès des technologies de l'information.

Les visées de la directive communautaire concernant la protection juridique des banques de données[35] sont plus ciblées et réalistes. La finalité du texte en préparation est de réserver les droits des producteurs et d'assurer la libre circulation des banques de données.[36] Il s'agit tout à la fois d'encourager leur développement qui 'exige la mise en œuvre de ressources humaines, techniques et financières considérables (...)[37] et de satisfaire les besoins en information'.

Son domaine d'application est limité aux collections faites par des moyens électroniques.[38] La base de données y est définie comme 'une collection d'œuvres ou de matières disposées, stockées et accessibles par des moyens électroniques, y compris les éléments électroniques nécessaires au fonctionnement de la base de données, tels que le thesaurus et le système d'indexation et de consultation de la base. Le terme ne s'applique pas aux logiciels à utiliser dans la création ou le fonctionnement de la base de données'.

Le projet de directive prévoit une protection des bases de données qui peut relever du droit d'auteur ou bien d'un régime spécifique tout à fait 'inédit'.

- Le principe de la protégeabilité au titre du droit d'auteur est posé dans ces termes: 'les bases de données en tant que collections au sens de l'article 2 §5 de la Convention de Berne, si elles sont originales, bénéficient d'une protection de même durée que celle prévue pour les œuvres littéraires'.[39] Et, selon le texte en projet, 'une base (...) est originale en ce sens qu'elle est une collection d'œuvres ou de matières qui, par le choix ou la disposition des matières, constitue la création intellectuelle propre à son auteur'.[40] Il est précisé que 'la protection par le droit d'auteur ne s'étend pas aux œuvres ou aux matières qui y sont contenues, qu'elles soient elles-mêmes protégées ou non par le droit d'auteur'.[41] Ces dispositions entèrinent l'ensemble des solutions admises dans la jurisprudence française. Elles les précisent en divers points[42] sans toutefois lever les incertitudes relatives à l'appréciation de l'originalité.
- La directive innove par ailleurs en obligeant les Etats de la Communauté à prévoir 'un droit pour le créateur d'une base de données d'interdire, pendant une durée de dix ans, l'extraction et la réutilisation non autorisées du contenu d'une base de données, en tout ou partie, à des fins commerciales'. L'article 2-5 du texte instaure en ces termes un droit sui generis, parfois qualifié de droit voisin. Ce droit spécifique distinct du droit d'auteur porte sur les informations indépendamment de la forme sous laquelle elles se présentent. Il paraît précisément adapté aux compilations d'informations, factuelles ou banales, ainsi des horaires, tarifs, listes de services, statistiques ou données météorologiques, peu important que leur ensemble obéisse ou non à la condition d'originalité.

Il est certain que la reconnaissance d'un droit pour les producteurs de s'opposer à l'extraction déloyale du contenu des bases de données serait de nature à encourager les investisseurs, sinon à offrir les conditions les meilleures pour que se développe dans ce secteur une industrie performante et compétitive. En accueillant favorablement l'initiative de la Commission, le Comité économique et social européen a tout de même émis un certain nombre de réserves sur la proposition et des recommandations dans un avis publié en janvier 1993.[43] Soulignant la difficulté qu'il y a à établir la limite entre une base de données constituant une création intellectuelle et une base résultant d'une simple compilation laborieuse, l'organe consultatif européen conteste l'opportunité de recourir à cette distinction 'ne servant qu'à offrir une protection limitée aux bases qui pourraient être le fruit d'un labeur et d'efforts financiers considérables sans toutefois satisfaire au critère d'originalité'.[44] Il estime que la Commission devrait ou bien inclure ce 'droit d'extraction'[45] dans le droit d'auteur général, c'est-à-dire le ranger au côté des autres prérogatives parmi les actes d'exclusivité visés à l'article 5 de la proposition,[46] ou bien étendre son domaine d'application au contenu de bases composé d'œuvres déjà protégées par un droit d'auteur ou par un droit voisin.

Dans la première hypothèse, la protection du contenu ne jouerait qu'au profit de bases susceptibles d'obéir à la condition d'originalité et d'être qualifiées d'œuvres d'information. A l'inverse, la seconde solution aurait l'avantage d'instituer la protection propre aux données et aux matières qui fait défaut, sans considération de la qualité d'œuvres ou non des divers éléments du contenu et sans préjudice de la protection de la collection qui les assemble, autrement dit du contenant. Il est d'ailleurs noté dans l'avis du Comité que la durée—de dix années—envisagée pour cette protection spécifique est trop courte.[47]

Comme les dispositions longtemps débattues et plusieurs fois remaniées de la directive concernant la protection des programmmes d'ordinateurs, le texte en projet fera certainement l'objet d'améliorations et de modifications et le Comité observe sans ambages que la date d'entrée en vigueur de la directive, prévue au 1er janvier 1993 est parfaitement irréaliste. Aujourd'hui, on doit donc se référer aux solutions de la jurisprudence avec ses aléas.

La protection de formes et la dématérialisation des supports et flux d'information

A l'heure actuelle en droit français, des données brutes telles que chiffres, dates, mesures ou formules ne sont pas appropriables. Pour être protégées, il faut qu'elles fassent l'objet d'un agencement relevant d'une opération intellectuelle créatrice. 'L'œuvre d'information' n'est donc jamais rien d'autre que l'enveloppe des données objectives et concrètes qu'elle élabore, organise et véhicule—ainsi des noms, adresses, horaires, résultats ou réponses à questionnaires. Or, seule la forme et l'expression que revêt la création donnent prise au droit d'auteur. Aussi, pour accéder au statut de propriété intellectuelle, l'œuvre d'information doit s'exprimer dans un langage et des signes.[48] Mais juridiquement il n'est pas indispensable qu'elle prenne corps dans un support qui la met à la disposition ou la transmet au public. En réalité, il en va autrement parce que sa présentation obéit à des considérations fonctionnelles. C'est pour pouvoir être sélectionnés et édités automatiquement ou transmis par voie électronique que des éléments, documents et données, subissent le traitement et la formalisation qui font d'eux l'œuvre ou la base protégeables. Le conditionnement formel de l'information d'une part, ses modes de diffusion d'autre part sont à cet égard essentiels. Mais la technologie a bouleversé les procédés d'édition et de diffusion, suscitant pour l'application du droit d'auteur aux intérêts patrimoniaux en jeu dans ce secteur des difficultés particulières tenant à la spécificité des supports et aux flux des données.

Le conditionnement de l'information

Le régime du support de l'œuvre, bien corporel, se distingue fondamentalement de celui de la création intellectuelle qui y prend forme en même temps qu'elle s'y incorpore et généralement s'y multiplie à des fins de diffusion et de commercialisation. Ainsi, l'acquisition en pleine propriété d'un exemplaire ou d'une copie, quelle que soit la technique d'édition, n'emporte pas transfert des droits de propriété intellectuelle attachés au contenu et à la valeur incorporelle que peut constituer la collection des informations recueillies et traitées. De même, le prêt pour consultation d'un ouvrage ne confère à l'emprunteur qu'un droit temporaire de détention éventuellement assorti d'autorisations particulières d'utilisation.

A priori, le régime du support intéresse davantage l'éditeur que l'auteur. En matière d'informations dont le marché s'effectue au moyen de banques et bases de données exploitées sur des supports magnétiques et souvent diffusées électroniquement, c'est-à-dire télétransmises sans transfert d'aucun support, il en va différemment à deux égards.

1. Traditionnellement, l'éditeur n'est pas propriétaire de la 'matière première' qu'il diffuse mais ayant-droit cessionnaire des droits des auteurs des œuvres éditées. Il est par ailleurs titulaire d'un droit dérivé sur un produit alliant à l'objet édité un apport créatif qui peut résider dans la collection, la composition, la typographie ou l'iconographie des ouvrages édités, entre autres éléments susceptibles de présenter une originalité. Autrement dit, d'un côté les prérogatives de l'éditeur dépendent du droit de reproduction qu'il s'est fait consentir par les titulaires du droit d'auteur (dans le cadre d'un contrat d'édition réglementé par la loi du 11mars 1957), de l'autre l'éditeur peut—par certains aspects de l'œuvre qu'il publie—être l'auteur d'une création qui a le statut d'œuvre dérivée. Mais enfin, lorsqu'il édite des recueils d'informations brutes ou des catalogues de données objectives ou des collections de documents libres de droit, il suffit qu'il fasse preuve d'originalité dans son élaboration, sa structuration et son agencement pour être un auteur à part entière et ériger ces éléments en une œuvre dite d'information.

Ainsi, les qualités d'auteur et d'éditeur d'ensembles dont la protection ne tient qu'à la formalisation se confondent naturellement. Ceci concerne au premier chef les producteurs de bases de données électroniques. Il y a une 'consanguinité'[49] entre éditeur et producteur de banques de données. L'administration notamment, lorsqu'elle produit de l'information, se comporte comme un éditeur. De fait, il est fréquent que des éditeurs d'ouvrages d'information tels qu'annuaires, catalogues, dictionnaires et encycopédies réalisent à la fois des éditions papier et des éditions informatisées. Ces dernières—l'annuaire électronique des abonnés au téléphone en offre la meilleure preuve—tendent d'ailleurs à supplanter les premières au fur et à mesure que se répand le média télématique. Et aux Etats-Unis, les sociétés d'informatique et d'électronique sont les premiers producteurs de banques de données. Si l'œuvre d'information n'existe pas sans mise en forme et que précisément la spécialité de l'éditeur consiste à formaliser des informations non protégées dans un support, alors œuvre et support se confondent pour faire de l'éditeur un auteur.

A propos de supports d'édition, il convient d'observer que les disques optiques numériques de type CD-ROM[50] sur lesquels sont édités de volumineux imprimés et commercialisées de nombreuses banques d'images ne doivent pas être qualifiés de vidéogrammes. Ces derniers sont soumis au régime particulier du droit voisin institué par l'article 26 de la loi du 3 juillet 1985. Leurs éditeurs sont seuls habilités à en autoriser la reproduction, mise à disposition ou communication au public. Selon ce texte, les vidéogrammes fixent des 'séquences d'images sonorisées ou non' auxquelles on ne saurait assimiler des collections d'images ou iconogrammes stockés sur disque optique. Peu importe en effet que l'utilisateur visualise occasionnellement des séquences de ces images sur l'écran de lecture car ces séquences sont le résultat des tris qu'il effectue lui-même lors d'interrogations.[51] Et, à supposer que des séquences d'images soient stockées dans une banque, le producteur de cette banque n'est pas 'celui qui a (eu) l'initiative et la responsabilité de leur première fixation', seul titulaire du droit voisin propre aux vidéogrammes.

2. Dans l'univers immatériel des bits et des octets, le régime du droit d'auteur se révèle particulièrement inadapté sinon absurde. Le droit d'auteur ne protège que des formes et c'est l'expression qui appartient à son auteur. Or la formalisation de nombreuses bases de données est commandée par leur fonction documentaire ou leur finalité informative. Ainsi, le classement alphabétique et l'ordonnancement chronologique, la collecte systématique et l'énumération exhaustive peuvent-ils offrir une plus-value à caractère technique ou documentaire.[52] Il est pourtant difficile d'y déceler l'apport intellectuel exigé pour la qualification d'œuvre appropriable, cet aspect de créativité pouvant au contraire apparaître dans l'analyse et l'organisation thématiques.

De plus, dans l'édition électronique et la génération automatique de corpus de données, l'exploitation se réalise essentiellement par des impulsions électriques. La mise à disposition du public a souvent lieu indépendamment de la diffusion de supports magnétiques tels que bandes et disquettes, à l'occasion d'interrogations en ligne dans le cadre de conventions d'abonnement. Mais en s'affranchissant pratiquement de toute matérialisation—autre que figuration ou formulation partielles à l'affichage sur l'écran de visualisation et à l'impression électronique sur listings—l'œuvre d'information sort de l'univers tangible du langage et des signes. Elle ne peut donc pas se reconnaître dans des éléments d'expression et de composition, pas plus que dans la structuration ou la typographie.

La doctrine juridique s'est surtout penchée sur les questions de formalisme et de preuve[53] tenant à la disparition du support écrit dans la transmission de documents et la réalisation d'opérations[54] ou EDI,[55] questions qui mettent en cause la validité et l'authenticité d'actes. Mais s'ils affectent la théorie des obligations, les échanges électroniques d'informations intéressent également le droit des biens. Il s'agit ici de déterminer le champ des propriétés immatérielles. Et pour ce qui est de la protection de l'information par le droit d'auteur, cet aspect de la dématérialisation—l'absence de support directement accessible et de forme tangible—a des conséquences qui touchent à la fois à la licéité, à l'existence et à la preuve d'actes d'exploitation relatifs à des valeurs dont la condition d'accès au monopole réside et s'apprécie précisément dans leur forme.

De fait, les techniques de numérisation des données permettent la réalisation de reproductions indécelables, du moins si on leur ajoute un traitement de nature à modifier l'agencement ou l'ordonnancement du contenu. Une tradition fictive et indépendante de tout support de tout ou partie d'un corpus peut s'effectuer lors d'une réception à distance par téléchargement[56] de fichiers informatiques sur disque dur ou disquette. Cette pratique consistant à reproduire par ordinateur des documents déjà informatisés permet la reconstitution—expressément convenue et prise en compte dans les coûts des services facturés ou au contraire illicite—de bases de données ou d'extraits de documents électroniques. En outre, les procédés de scannerisation permettent une reproduction de données brutes affranchie de leur formalisation. Sans copie servile de la mise en page, une telle réappropriation n'encourt pas le grief de contrefaçon.

La directive communautaire en préparation prend d'ailleurs en considération cette pratique. 'L'utilisateur légitime d'une base de données peut (en effet), sans autorisation du producteur, extraire et réutiliser des parties non substantielles d'œuvres ou de matières d'une base à des fins commerciales pour autant qu'il indique la source'.[57] Le téléchargement serait licite et la reproduction d'un ou plusieurs éléments contenus dans des bases de données électroniques—fiches, notices ou documents—libre d'autorisation sous réserve de ne pas 'toucher' à la substance de l'ensemble.

Le défaut de forme—sinon du tout—rend par ailleurs improbable la reproduction partielle de bases électroniques et les éditeurs de corpus de données souffrent économiquement de ne pouvoir établir la copie servile et contrefaisante de leurs produits, sauf à y réintroduire volontairement des éléments aberrants, autrement dit des erreurs illogiques et non aléatoires qui impriment leur marque et fonctionnent s'il y a lieu comme des indicateurs-témoins d'une appropriation illicite par téléchargement non autorisé. Il s'agit là d'une tactique probatoire et d'une pratique effective de la part d'éditeurs, valable pour tout ensemble de données où, comme en matière de dictionnaires, les tribunaux admettent que 'le plagiat est signé par la reproduction d'erreurs de classement orthographique qui ne sauraient être dues au hasard'.[58]

La transmission de l'information

Le plus souvent, la transmission de documents et notices d'informations a lieu directement sur le support labile que constitue l'écran de consultation du terminal d'ordinateur relié au réseau Transpac ou du Minitel raccordé au réseau téléphonique. Le système vidéotex notamment, qui permet l'échange d'informations textuelles, numériques ou graphiques sur des réseaux de télécommunications, est un instrument d'interactivité tel que la communication permet au receveur du message d'en compléter ou d'en modifier le contenu. De même, des systèmes d'information à disque optique autorisent non seulement la récupération de données mais aussi la modification de leur structure. Aussi, les fichiers des produits proposés dans ces conditions aux utilisateurs ou abonnés à des services de bases de données sont-ils en réédition constante.

Et parmi les questions juridiques diverses posées par l'expansion de la télématique, deux ont trait à la protection par le droit d'auteur.

- La première consiste à savoir si les clients de services télématiques et utilisateurs de systèmes d'information sont ou non des co-auteurs ou des co-éditeurs des bases qu'ils complètent à l'occasion de consultations. A priori évidente, la réponse négative lorsqu'il s'agit d'introduire des réponses à des questions, ainsi des éléments complémentaires d'identification ou d'actualisation, ne s'impose pas lorsqu'on est en présence d'un réseau d'opérateurs participant à l'élaboration en commun et permanente d'un produit composé de leurs contributions respectives. Resteraient néanmoins à déterminer la nature et à préciser l'importance de la part à prendre pour avoir la qualité d'auteur-collaborateur[59]...
- Liée à la précédente, la seconde question a trait à la détermination du point de départ de la durée de protection en cas de mise à jour de collections de données. L'article 9-4 de la directive précise à cet égard que 'des modifications non substantielles au choix ou à la disposition du contenu d'une

> base de données ne font pas courir un nouveau délai de protection de la base par le droit d'auteur' pas plus que de semblables 'modifications au contenu d'une base de données ne font courir un nouveau délai de protection de la base par le droit d'empêcher l'extraction déloyale du contenu'.

Dans son avis, le Comité économique et social estime à ce propos qu'un 'moyen plus pratique de déterminer le moment à partir duquel un nouveau délai de protection prend cours consisterait à munir, au moment de l'introduire, chaque unité de la base de données en question d'un timbre à date électronique ou autre. Chaque donnée serait protégée pendant un délai approprié qui prendrait cours à la date indiquée sur le timbre'.[60] Mais, théoriquement séduisante parce que prenant très précisément et indifféremment en compte toute information contenue dans une base de données, quelles qu'en soient l'importance et l'origine, une telle solution aurait pour effet d'instituer une protection distincte—du moins quant à son terme—propre à chaque élément nouveau ou composant séparable de la collection. Il importe de se demander si elle est raisonnablement praticable et économiquement utile.

Protection des banques de données par le droit d'auteur ou protection 'sui generis'? La question n'est pas neuve[61] et aucune des branches de l'alternative n'est dénuée d'inconvénients.

Dans le système de droit d'auteur, le statut des plus-values que génèrent les investissements consentis pour la recherche et la collecte, l'émission et la conservation, l'organisation et la distribution de données dépend de la formalisation et/ou du conditionnement des informations considérées. Or l'analyse de la forme s'avère particulièrement malaisée, voire artificielle compte tenu du caractère immatériel des procédés d'édition et de transmission d'une information qui est elle-même polymorphe et évolutive. Pourtant, la protection des logiciels s'inscrit déjà à l'intérieur de ce système,[62] dans un corps de règles dérogatoires dont l'élaboration a nécessité des adaptations répondant à des exigences semblables et au même type de considérations. A maints égards on peut le déplorer, mais le fait est que le droit de l'auteur a évolué vers un droit de l'investisseur.[63] Au nom d'intérêts considérables en jeu dans l'industrie de l'informatique, le législateur a institué une protection contre l'usage non autorisé des logiciels à raison de la valeur intellectuelle et économique ajoutée par leurs concepteurs et les S.S.I.I.[64] De même, la plus-value documentaire apportée à de l'information brute par les producteurs de bases offrant des données traitées, sélectionnées, enrichies et/ou actualisées devrait justifier que leur soit conférée une protection similaire.[65] Mais—et là réside sa limite infranchissable sauf à dénaturer davantage le concept—une telle protection ne peut et ne doit pas s'affranchir de la condition d'originalité caractéristique de la création ou de l'apport intellectuel personnalisés.

Et logiquement, lorsque les plus-values générées par les producteurs ou co-producteurs de collections d'informations sont purement techniques, qu'elles résultent exclusivement d'investissements consentis pour saisir, stocker, éditer et diffuser des données sans aucun apport intellectuel ni documentaire, seule une protection spécifique, distincte de celle de l'auteur créateur-concepteur et adaptée aux éléments composants—indépendamment du statut du produit de leur réunion—peut trouver à s'appliquer. La définition et les limites de cette protection sont en cours d'élaboration.

Summary

The Automation and Dematerialisation of Information—Originality and Form, Terms and Objectives for the Application of Copyright: The Legal Challenges

The question of the appropriation of 'information commodities' is considered in relation to the determination of the economic value of the information concerned, which should be specified by law. In this connection, a distinction is made between the information itself and information systems. Information may be said to constitute an 'immaterial good', and according to the Law of 3 July 1985, this category includes 'intellectual property' (patents are an example). However, the relevant European Community directive has not yet been permanently adopted, and as a result, the legal status of databases is thrown into confusion. In order to establish a case for the application of copyright for products incorporated in information systems, one is obliged to refer to the concept of 'spiritual endeavour'. The application and exploitation of copyright relies on a link being shown between the creation of a 'product' and the 'author', i.e a physical entity in the form of an individual or organisation.

Originality is the essential prerequisite for the definition of the products of information processing as diverse as indexes, directories, electronic dictionaries as 'works of spiritual endeavour'. The laws of copyright can be applied to the creation of works of this kind. Thus, the concept of originality has had to be redefined in order to incorporate the products and tools of information processing alongside works of a more subjective nature.

The criterion of originality is fulfilled as soon as the existence of a specific intellectual effort, which can be linked directly with an author, is established. For example, databases protected by copyright are described as 'works of information'. A mailing list distributed for advertising purposes could likewise be considered an 'original creation'. However, a simple listing would not be covered by copyright law, as it is in the United States.

The protection of data compilations as 'works of spiritual endeavour' is limited to 'content', that is to say, the organisation of raw data and the arrangement of material, but not the individual elements of a listing.

The legal status of information products produced by digital techniques without human intervention remains to be clarified. A recent initiative has been to introduce the concept of 'temporary protection without moral rights for non-original or non-inventive creations'.

Copyright does not apply to material in the category of 'grey literature'. Elements of knowledge such as formulae, working methods and modes of operation, are protected only by civil law. Exploitation refers solely to concrete data, whereas activities such as copying and distribution of data are not taken into account.

The Community directive concerning the legal protection of databases would restrict the application of copyright to compilations produced by electronic means. Furthermore, it reserves the right of the author to prevent the 'extraction and reutilisation of unauthorized data for commercial purposes' for a period of ten years.

Recognition of these rights for database producers would encourage investment and development in the relevant technologies, although serious reservations remain concerning the terms of application.

'Form' and 'expression' are essential concepts pertaining to the application of copyright to a particular work. The 'work of information' is the external form of the objective and concrete data which have been processed. The format of the information, as well as the distribution channels involved, must also be considered. However, the law is different for information transmitted on magnetic tape and for teleprocessing, where the publisher is not the owner of the 'raw material', and computer generation of data cannot be considered a 'form'.

Information transmission systems such as electronic downloading via telecommunications networks allow the end-user to retrieve data and modify its structure simultaneously. Legal problems arise from considerations such as the status of the end-user as an author or co-author, and from the difficulty of establishing the point at which a data compilation becomes subject to copyright.

In considering the application of copyright, the processes of research, collection, transmission and preservation, organisation and distribution of data have to be taken into account as well as the form and format of delivery. However, the immaterial nature of some of these factors poses problems for the legal process. Existing law protects software against unauthorized usage, and a similar status should be conferred on electronic databases. The form of protection determined should be exclusive, and not dependent on the concept of author as creator. Legislation in this area is in the process of being drawn up.

Références et notes

1. Directive dont la proposition a été présentée par la Commission de Bruxelles le 15 avril 1992, publiée au JOCE (C) 156/5, 23 juin 1992, V. Th. Desurmont, Chronique de la communauté européenne, Revue internationale du droit d'auteur, ci-après abrégée RIDA N°155, janvier 1993, p.89 et D.Delaval, Gaz.Pal.20 janvier 1993

2. Pourtant essentielles, les questions de la constitution des banques de données et de leur dépendance des droits sur les œuvres qu'elles incorporent d'une part, de la titularité des droits et de la qualité d'auteur de logiciels ou corpus d'informations d'autre part ne seront pas ici examinées. V. notamment Les banques de données face au droit d'auteur, in Banques de données et droit d'auteur, Colloque de l'IRPI nov.1986, Librairies techniques 1987; A.Dietz, le concept d'auteur selon le droit de la Convention de Berne, RIDA, janvier 1993, p.3-58.

3. Article L.112-1, code de la propriété intellectuelle; ancien article 2, loi du 11 mars 1957 codifié par la loi du 1er juillet 1992. Ce texte est visé par l'arrêt de cassation Société Williams Electronic rendu par l'Assemblée plénière le 7 mars 1986 à propos d'un jeu

électronique audiovisuel auquel les juges d'appel avaient refusé le bénéfice de la loi sur la propriété littéraire et artistique 'faute d'une quelconque préoccupation de recherche esthétique ou artistique de la part de son concepteur'.

4. Ayant de sa propre initiative écrit pour l'entreprise un logiciel de comptabilité pendant ses heures de loisirs, un chef comptable, Mr. Jean Pachot, l'avait repris après s'être opposé à ce qu'il en soit fait une copie de sauvegarde. L'employeur prétendait qu'il ne s'agissait que de simples méthodes et la Cour de cassation approuve la solution selon laquelle le caractère scientifique des programmes informatiques n'est pas un obstacle à leur protection par le droit d'auteur. Cette décision (Société Babolat et Maillot Witt contre Pachot) a donné lieu à de très nombreux commentaires: notamment JCP (N) 1986, II,14713; D.1986, Jur.405; Rev. dr.propr.ind. 1986, 3, 206.

5. ...et de découpage de lettres et autres éléments graphiques destinés à constituer des enseignes

6. Civ.1, 16 avril 1991, Bull. Civ.I, N°139, Revue de droit de l'informatique et des télécommunications (ci-après abrégée RDIT) 1991, N°4, 33, note Ph.Gaudrat. Cette décision pose par ailleurs la question de la distinction des programmes et des fichiers de données.

7. Le texte des principales décisions rendues dans cette affaire figure au Lamy Informatique, Télématique, Réseaux 1992 N° 1281 avec les références des commentaires et études suscités par cette jurisprudence dans une bibliographie sur l'accès aux informations couvertes par le droit d'auteur, N° 1237; V. aussi J.Huet et H.Maisl, Droit de l'informatique et des télécommunications, L'affaire Microfor et ses enseignements, Litec 1989, § 497 à 523

8. Prévues par l'article L.122-5-3° du code de la propriété intellectuelle, ancien article 41-3° de la loi du 11 mars 1957

9. Discutable, ce principe est d'ailleurs remis en question par l'arrêt rendu par la Cour de cassation le 2 mai 1989 dans l'affaire Coprosa, Bull. Civ.1, N°180 (V. infra)

10. Paris, 21 mars 1989, Société Harrap c/ Société Masson Editeur, Jurisdata N°20923; Lamy Informatique Télématique Réseaux Mise à jour sept.1989; RIDA octobre 1989, p.333

11. Trib.gr.inst. Grenoble 9 mai 1984, D.1985, IR, 309
12. Paris, 19 juin 1984, D.1985, IR, 309
13. Paris, 6 mai 1987, D.1987, Som.202
14. Paris, 29 juin 1992, Actualité de jurispudence et de droit des affaires 1993, 2, N°179
15. Paris, 23 septembre 1992, RIDA N°156, avril 1993, p.180
16. Civ.1, 2 mai 1989, LPEI/Coprosa, Bull.Civ.I, N°180; RDIT 1990/2 p.38; JCP 1990,II,21392
17. Trib.Com. Compiègne, 2 juin 1989, RDIT 1989/4 p.60
18. Jane C.Ginsburg, U.S.A.: banques de données et droit d'auteur aux Etats-Unis, RIT 1988/1 p.76
19. Ainsi en a-t'il été jugé à propos de mots (et contes) appartenant au folklore cadjin, répertoriés et retranscrits par un chercheur débouté dans ces termes de son action en contrefaçon contre le romancier qui les avaient réutilisés dans son œuvre, RIDA avril 1992, p.172
20. Paragraphe 101 du copyright Act de 1976; une telle définition invite à la perplexité dans la mesure où 'elle revient à dire qu'une compilation est une œuvre de l'esprit si elle est une œuvre de l'esprit', V. Jane G.Ginsburg, RDIT 1988/1 p.76
21. Cour Suprême, 27 mars 1991, Feist Publications Inc./Rural telephone service Inc., RIDA 1991,3 p.99, note P.E.Geller.
22. Qu'il s'agisse de personne physique ou morale
23. Les deux directives du 14 mars 1991 relative à la protection des programmes d'ordinateurs et celle proposée pour la protection des bases de données le 15 avril 1992 définissent en termes identiques la condition d'originalité au sens de 'crétion intellectuelle propre à l'auteur', celle-ci s'appliquant au choix ou au contenu de la base de données qu'il effectue.
24. Diversifiées, ces applications ont principalement pour objet la vérification et la correction orthographique, la traduction, la contraction ou l'analyse de textes.
25. Sur cette question, V. Ch.Poitevin, Contribution à une définition

du domaine des industries de la langue: l'élucidation des statuts juridiques, thèse dactylographiée en sciences de l'information, janvier 1993, Université de Paris VIII; également, Civ.1, 16 avril 1991, décision citée concernant les modules d'un logiciel de traçage.

26. A l'égard de ces produits, les solutions prévues pour des 'créations assistées par ordinateur' ou produits dérivés de systèmes informatiques qui désignent comme auteur l'utilisateur du système, c'est-à-dire celui qui en met les fonctionnalités au service de sa créativité, ne sont pas satisfaisantes. Ainsi, 'dans les cas d'œuvres (...) générées par un ordinateur, leur auteur est la personne qui aura fait les arrangements nécessaires pour que la création de l'œuvre ait lieu', (Copyright Act du 15 novembre 1988, Grande-Bretagne); et aussi, 'dans le cas d'œuvres produites au moyen de systèmes informatiques, les titulaires du droit d'auteur sont les personnes ayant fourni les éléments de création sans lesquels les œuvres finales n'auraient pu faire l'objet d'une protection par le droit d'auteur (Principe OMPI).

27. A propos de l'imagerie spatiale, V. A.Martin, Le statut international de l'imagerie spatiale, Thèse dactylographiée droit privé, décembre 1992, Université de Bourgogne.

28. Egalement à l'initiative de la loi du 5 janvier 1988 relative à la fraude informatique.

29. Entre autres règles de 'protection des connaissances scientifiques' prévues au Titre II du code de la propriété intellectuelle, le régime des topographies de semi-conducteurs organisé par la loi du 4 novembre 1987

30. V. Le Stanc, La propriété intellectuelle dans le lit de Procuste: observations sur la proposition..., D.1993, Chron. p.4

31. Ainsi, l'imitation de tout élément attractif de clientèle propre à susciter une confusion entre des entreprises ou des produits est sanctionnée comme un acte de concurrence déloyale. Et, en dehors de tout risque de confusion entre concurrents, la copie servile ou quasi-servile peut être qualifiée de parasitisme. 'Il y a (en effet) agissement parasitaire chaque fois que quelqu'un utilise de façon intéressée une valeur économique d'autrui, fruit d'un savoir-faire ou d'un travail intellectuel lorsque cette valeur n'est pas protégée par

un droit privatif', Ph. Le Tourneau, Emergence d'un droit de l'informatique, Ed. des Parques 1984, p.18

32. Articles 2 et 6

33. Respectivement défini à l'article 5 comme 'la personne physique ou morales ayant réalisé la création réservée sans être rémunérée à cet effet' et celle 'ayant assumé les coûts de recherche, d'étude ou de réalisation de la création réservée'.

34. Le Stanc, article cité V.note 2

35. JOCE (C) 156/4, 23 juin 1992, V. Th.Desurmont, Chronique de la communauté européenne, RIDA N°155, janvier 1993, p.89; D.Delaval, Gaz.Pal.20 janvier 1993.

36. Compte tenu des disparités dans la protection juridique des bases de données assurée par les législations des Etats membres et de la nature territoriale des droits de propriété intellectuelle. Elle leur applique notamment la règle de l'épuisement du droit de distribution dès la première vente d'un exemplaire.

37. (...alors qu'il est possible d'en copier le contenu à un coût très inférieur à celui qu'entraîne leur conception autonome), 6ème considérant

38. 19ème considérant

39. Article 2-1

40. Article 2-3

41. Article 2-4

42. L'article 4 relatif à l'incorporation d'œuvres ou de matières dans une base de données pose la règle énoncée par la Cour de cassation dans l'affaire Microfor de la non substituabilité d'extraits, citations ou résumés d'une œuvre à l'œuvre elle-même comme condition de leur libre insertion dans des bases bibliographiques. Et l'article 5 indique les différentes prérogatives de l'auteur tant à raison du choix ou de la disposition de son contenu qu'à raison de la matière électronique qui sert à sa constitution ou à son fonctionnement.

43. JOCE N° C19/02 du 25 janvier 1993

44. Article 2-3 c de l'avis du Comité économique et social

45. Droit d'interdire l'extraction de tout ou partie du contenu de bases de données à des fins commerciales

46. 'Actes soumis à des restrictions relatives au droit d'auteur': ces droits exclusifs portent sur la reproduction, la traduction, l'adaptation, l'arrangement et toute autre transformation d'une base de données, toute forme de distribution ainsi que toute communication au public.

47. Article 3-13 de l'avis: 'On ne voit pas bien pour quelle raison la durée précise de dix ans a été retenue' (et...) 'il ne semble pas que l'existence dans le cadre du droit d'auteur dans certains états membres de l'équivalent du droit d'interdire l'extraction déloyale y ait freiné la croissance de l'industrie'.

48. La Directive du 14 mai 1991 concernant la protection juridique des programmes d'ordinateur précise que 'seule l'expression du programme est protégée à l'exclusion des idées et des principes à la base de ses différents éléments y compris ceux qui sont à la base de ses interfaces'.

49. Jane C.Ginsburg, Banques de données et droit d'auteur aux Etats-Unis, article cité.

50. Disque compact à mémoire permanente

51. V. Sur la question, Banques de données et droit d'auteur, Colloque de l'IRPI, op.cit. p.115; A.Lucas, Le droit de d'informatique, PUF 1987, § 265; pour une opinion contraire et isolée, S. de Faultrier-Travers, Aspects juridiques de l'information, ESF éditeur 1991, p.95

52. V. Ph.Gaudrat, Typologie des plus-values de l'information, in Commercialisation des données publiques, La documentation française 1992, § 17

53. Sur ces questions, V. Nouvelles technologies et droit de la preuve, Fr. Gallouédec-Genuys, Notes et études documentaires, La documentation française 1990, Le droit et les NTI, Bibliographies, p.119

54. Ce que l'on désigne sous le vocable d'EDI, échanges de données informatisées

55. Echanges de données informatisées

56. Down loading

57. Article 8-4 de la proposition de directive

58. Affaire Harrap/Masson

59. Etant précisé qu'en droit positif, seules des personnes physiques concourent à la création d'œuvres de collaboration, Article L.113-2 al.1 code la la propriété intellectuelle; ancien article 9, loi du 11 mars 1957.

60. Article 3-14 de l'avis

61. A. Kerever, Colloque de l'IRPI, op.cit. p.71

62. Il convient de rappeler que l'insertion des logiciels dans la législation sur le droit d'auteru présente l'avantage de les faire accéder à une protection internationale dans le cadre de la Convention de Genève.

63. P. Nijhoff Asser, Le rôle et la place du droit d'auteur pour les éditeurs spécialisés, in Le droit d'auteur, enjeu économique et culturel, Union internationale des éditeurs, Litec 1990, p.55

64. Sociétés de service et d'ingénierie en informatique

65. Au demeurant, il y aurait là l'occasion de lever en partie et le moyen de prévenir les difficultés de qualification des corpus de textes annexés ou intégrés à des systèpes informatiques, dont on ne sait s'il faut les soumettre au régime particulier des logiciels ou au régime de droit commun des œuvres littéraires.

Irrational Innovation in the Transfer of Information

La Diffusion de l'Information: L'Irrationalité de l'Innovation

John Mackenzie Owen
De Bilt, The Netherlands

In the information chain, enormous investments in information technology have been made over the past twenty years. Publishers, libraries, information intermediaries, network providers and end-users are all users of technology and are linked through sophisticated electronic channels. Nevertheless, the distribution of published information still relies heavily on traditional printed media. Why is it that the large and continuing investment in information technology has not yet significantly changed the information chain? Is a fundamental change in information provision to be expected soon?

In this paper, I shall focus on aspects of the distribution of scientific information. I shall argue that there still are many barriers to the transition from paper to electronic distribution. These include technical, legal, political and financial barriers. I believe, however, that some of the main barriers are combinations of economic and psychological issues. These have to do with a lack of understanding of the value of information, the absence of a clear economic model of information provision due to this, and the subsequent irrational behaviour regarding IT-investments and innovation.

Fundamental issues

Technological innovation implies a significant change on a large scale. It will only happen when a large proportion of the people involved accept the new technology and adopt its use (Rogers, 1971; Mackenzie Owen and Van Halm, 1989). At the bottom line, innovation depends on what people are willing to do differently. Nevertheless, there are some preconditions that cannot be solved by willingness alone. These include a stable, working technology, the absence of legal barriers and the possibility to re-allocate funds towards the innovation. Let us look at these fundamental issues as related to the electronic distribution of information.

Technology

Although many people feel impatient at the slow speed at which paper is being replaced by electronic media, one has to admit that technology is not yet where it should be. Many technical issues remain to be resolved before the main body of scientific information can be distributed through electronic networks. These include electronic document formats, compression techniques, navigation and indexing methods and cost-recovery systems. Electronic document distribution is still in need of a major development and standardization effort.

Legal issues

Moving from paper to digital information creates all kinds of problems with copyright and reprography law. Libraries in particular have treated the copyright issue very carelessly. Publishers regard library photocopying as unfair practice. Libraries are reluctant to accept that electronic information cannot be copied and distributed freely, and that expensive copyright arrangements are inevitable. This situation makes publishers hesitant to distribute documents in electronic form. It also leads to a lobbying process towards over-restrictive copyright legislation. This makes copyright one of the major fundamental barriers to innovation of the information chain.

Financial aspects

Most innovative processes include a transition period where the new technology gradually supersedes the old technology. During this period, additional funds have to be available. Initially, these funds are used to 'subsidize' the new technology alongside the traditional approach. Then re-allocation becomes necessary, in order to transfer ordinary funding to the new technology. In the final stages, any additional funding is used for maintaining a 'fall-back' situation and for backlog reconversion.

In the information field, additional funding is extremely difficult to obtain. This means that innovation usually requires immediate re-allocation. Librarians find themselves in a dilemma. They have to cancel existing products and services in favour of a new technology which has yet to be accepted—and therefore does not yet really function. It is only natural that they are reluctant to do so. In practice, only very innovative librarians with access to major sources of additional funding can act as change agents. Carnegie Mellon, De Montfort and Tilburg Universities are good examples of this.

Problems in the information chain

Apart from these fundamental issues, the parties actively involved in innovating the information chain all have their specific problems. I shall not go into great detail here, but just summarize the main issues on the basis of a number of policy studies I have carried out over the past few years.

Authors

Creating and communicating information are essential for the advancement of science. But they also have the side-effect of creating status for the writer or speaker. The amount of status is determined by the impact of the communication on the one hand, and the status of the communication medium on the other. Uncertainty about the future impact, as well as the obvious relationship between status of the medium and potential impact both lead to predictable behaviour: the author will favour a high-status, high-impact medium. There is only one definition of that kind of medium: the refereed scientific journal from one of the prestigious international publishing houses.

The status-issue makes it extremely difficult to change from the traditional scientific journal to new formats such as 'electronic journals'. That is probably one of the reasons that most publishers have abandoned developing entirely new publication formats, and are concentrating on new—electronic—distribution models for the traditional product. Even so, one might expect authors to prefer the printed product as long as they have that alternative.

On the other hand, top scientists are using networks more and more for scientific communication. This is not confined to e-mail alone. Papers are distributed within closed networks of fellow researchers. Within these networks, one finds a kind of 'public network publishing'. As far as I can see, this is having two major consequences. One is that communicating through the electronic network is becoming more important to top researchers than publishing in scientific journals. Networks are faster and more interactive. Communicating through the network becomes more important in the minds of these people than writing an article. Actually publishing the article in a journal becomes something of an afterthought.

The other consequence is that the network is gradually obtaining more status for the very reason that it is being used, not by computer freaks, but by serious, internationally renowned scientists. One could argue that in some areas of science, electronic networks are slowly taking over from scientific journals as a communications medium, not because publishers are pushing that type of medium, but because of the behaviour of top scientists in using it.

This development is a mixed blessing. If it goes too far, publishers will go out of business. But we all know that uncontrolled networks eventually become chaos. It would be most unfortunate if we were to lose the added value currently provided by publishers in the way of selection, editing, abstracting and indexing, quality control, etc.

Publishers

I have already said a few things about publishers: that they have a legal problem with libraries, that they have given up developing new electronic publishing formats, and that they are now being threatened by new attitudes of scientists towards networked communication. Let me add a few more observations.

Most international scientific publishers agree that electronic distribution of scientific information is inevitable. Their major concern in changing from paper to electronics is the distribution model to be used. Publishers argue that electronic distribution has to provide added value by reducing cost and creating strategic benefits. What they would like to see is a model which provides much greater interactivity and market feedback from users. This would allow them both to create information products for which there is an expressed demand, and to tailor such products to specific, perhaps even individual user needs. What publishers therefore would like to see is a kind of 'vertical integration', a much tighter link between authors, publishers, intermediaries and end-users. It is not at all clear how this will have to be organized, what the roles of the various parties involved will have to be, and whether there is mutual agreement amongst these partners on the nature of such a new distribution model.

A second concern to publishers is that electronic information distribution models are based on assumptions derived from current network practice. The main issue here is that data transport incurs little or no cost to the end-user. If that were to change—for economic or political reasons—end-users would have to pay for acquiring scientific information in an unprecedented way. One cannot base the distribution model on the assumption that transport costs will be charged to end-users. Neither can one take the risk of not doing so. That is the publisher's dilemma.

Finally, the problem of copyright remains a barrier to innovation. If libraries, network services and end-users do with electronic information what they did with paper publications, viz. copying, publishers will soon be out of business. As long as this has not been settled through copyright law, licensing agreements, codes of fair practice and foolproof cost-recovery mechanisms, publishers will not dare to venture out into the network world.

Libraries

Libraries, too, are confronted with dilemmas in the transition from paper to electronic distribution of information. I have already mentioned the financial problem of re-allocating funds in favour of electronic information, and of obtaining additional funding when traditional budgets are decreasing at least in relative terms.

In general, librarians are keepers of books. It is their job to make sure that information remains available over a longer time. Libraries are not by nature dynamic, innovative institutions. One cannot expect librarians in general to be dynamic, innovative people. There exists a natural, and to a certain extent defensible resistance towards innovation. So in the library world, we see only a small number of change agents, champions of innovation. The reaction of other libraries towards these innovative colleagues is highly ambiguous. They are charmed by the fact that innovative libraries get media attention and increase the status of libraries in general. On the other hand they regard them as a threat to traditional library values.

It would be unfair, however, to accuse librarians of rejecting information technology. Libraries are heavy IT-users. But they use IT in a particular way, viz. to improve their internal business functions. They do not use IT as a means of adapting to a changing world which expects new and different functions from the library. By not doing so, they create new competitors and antagonize potential partners.

One of these potential partners is the academic computing centre. The development of information technology over the past decade has changed the role of computing centres. They no longer provide computing capacity, because the majority of users now have that on the desktop. They have had to change their role into that of service providers and infrastructure managers. Their strategic backbone has become the network: the main IT-component of the infrastructure that remains under control of the computer centre. Through the campus network, the computing centre also controls the vital access to the outside world through national and international networks. Most academic computer centres have been highly successful in making the transition from mainframe to network. Now they are wondering how to maximize benefits to end-users, in order to justify the cost of the network. Providing information services is the most likely way to do so. It is not surprising therefore that we are seeing both antagonism and cooperation between libraries and computer centres. But the driving force for either option is survival rather than the interest of information users.

Differing perceptions

One of the main barriers to innovation in the area of scientific information is the difference of perception between librarians and publishers. Librarians believe that the future model of distribution will be a digital copy of the current model. Instead of acquiring, storing and delivering documents in paper form, they will do so in digital form. Librarians regard this as an important step, but not as something fundamentally different from what they do already. According to this view, libraries will continue to perform their traditional functions. In other words: innovation yes, transformation no. I have already indicated that publishers envisage an entirely different distribution model for digital information. That is a model which calls for a different role for libraries, and therefore for very significant changes in their objectives, skills and organization.

As long as publishers and libraries do not agree on the future model for distribution of scientific information, not much, I fear, will happen. Publishers will keep publishing in paper mode, arguing that electronic publishing is not economically feasible. They will continue to accuse librarians of piracy, unfair behaviour and conservatism. Libraries will remain collection-based organizations in spite of some marginal innovative improvements, such as the provision of bibliographic information as part of integrated desktop services to end users. They will continue to accuse publishers of unfair pricing, monopolism and conservatism. Innovation of scientific communication will not be organized by those parties which regard themselves as responsible for the distribution of scientific information.

The economics of information

The value of *information* (as the resource provided through information services) is a concept not well understood. It is usually neglected in favour of issues such as the added value of information services, the cost of creating and distributing information, and—especially—economic aspects of information *technology*. Without sufficient understanding of the value of information to end-user organizations, any economic model of information provision has to be severely limited in scope. Unfortunately, our understanding of the value of information is very limited (Mackenzie Owen, 1992):

- The value of information can only be measured in a process involving a cooperation between information providers, end-users and their managers. Such cooperation is extremely rare.
- Investments in information technology are often based on mythical assumptions on the part of policy makers. Their expectation is that IT will solve all kinds of organizational and financial problems. Unfortunately, it usually does not.
- There is little understanding of cost-benefit relations in IT-investments. This is a well-identified problem which leads to many local efforts to clarify the issue.
- People with an interest in introducing new, IT-based modes of information distribution do not seem to have an interest in an economic analysis of the future situation they are creating. It is they who create 'technology push', not IT itself.
- Information technology changes the relationships between parties involved in information provision. Such changes are a challenge to some, and a threat to others, especially as they

involve changes in the allocation of funds. The outcome of this process is not rational and economic, but political.

In summary, one can argue: that we lack the basis for economic analysis, namely an understanding of the value of information; that investments in IT in this area are often based on false expectations and a lack of understanding of the economic issues involved; that a clear analysis of economic issues is even sometimes hardly welcome; and that people involved in IT create their own technology push, and innovation is primarily the result of a political process.

Information in the decision making process

The value of information is not a fixed quality. It depends on how people use it (their 'information behaviour') in relation to the purpose for which they do so (their 'information goals'). Using information to achieve specific goals would appear to be a highly rational process. But is this really true in practice? It is interesting to look at the way information is used in that prime example of rational behaviour: managerial decision making. I shall argue that decision making is not at all by definition a rational process, and that therefore the value derived from information is highly ambiguous. As one cannot assume that information behaviour in research and development is in principle any different from that in management, these findings point to interesting research issues in the area of scientific information.

Why do organizations use information? Daft and Lengel (1986) answered this question as follows. Organizations have to cope with uncertainty, and uncertainty can be defined as 'the lack of information', or 'not knowing what will happen and what one has to do'. Providing information therefore reduces uncertainty. But once information is available, a new problem arises: information creates equivocality. Here lies the origin of decision making: choosing between alternatives. Yet this is just another problem of uncertainty for which information provides a solution. Information can provide sufficient data on the various alternatives to allow a decision in favour of one of them.

The role of information is therefore ambiguous, even paradoxical. On the one hand, information helps to reduce uncertainty and to allow a choice between alternative options. On the other hand, it can offer too many alternatives, thereby frustrating the decision making process and creating even more uncertainty.

It is interesting to look at the way people behave in this paradoxical situation where they have to use information for decision making. Management is such a situation, and much research has been carried out in this area.

Cats-Baril (1990) of the INSEAD School of Management questions the traditional role of information in decision making. He makes the interesting distinction between the rational and the political approach.

The rational approach

This view is based on the belief that organizations have fairly constant goals and values which are public and constitute the organization's own culture. The behaviour of the organization is determined by a process of rational decision making. Within the organization, decisions are made by managers. Decision making is, in fact, one of their major tasks. Such decision making is based on a rational analysis of the current situation and on choosing alternatives, always related to the organization's goals.

This process needs information about the organization's own internal processes, as well as—at the level of strategic decision making—about the external environment. The amount of such information is increasing all the time. Because the information processing capacity of managers is more or less constant, ever greater investments are needed in information systems to prevent management from being overloaded.

In this approach, information is regarded as something which objectively reflects reality. It is accepted that it does not do so perfectly. But characteristics such as reliability, completeness and timeliness are regarded as desirable and quite well achievable. This is because of the belief that good information necessarily leads to good decisions. That is exactly why management information has value.

The political approach

One can also take a different view. According to Cats-Baril's political approach, an organization's behaviour is determined by ever-changing coalitions which influence the way the organization functions. That means that goals and values are also subject to change and varying interpretations. There exist different, conflicting ideas about goals, values and conduct. These views are not openly expressed, but they do guide individual behaviour.

In this view, managers are sense-makers. They try to create their own reality for the organization to live with. It is through the eyes of the manager that the organization looks to itself and to the outer world. People within the organization are supposed to share the management's views.

The tension between one's own views and those enforced by the organization lead to organizational dynamics or a political and non-rational nature. Decision making itself is a political process. Decision makers do not act rationally, they rationalize.

According to this view, people gather information in order to convince themselves and others, and to rationalize earlier decisions. In general, managers gather information to convince other people, and other people gather information in order to convince themselves.

Information is therefore not an objective representation of reality. On the contrary: information defines and creates reality. The value of information in this approach is determined by the way it helps to project a desired reality onto the organization.

Information versus ideology

The idea that people do not always behave as rational decision makers—nor show rational information behaviour—finds support from many other authors. Rice (1985), based on Cummings (1983), identifies two choices in the approach towards decision making:

- A choice regarding the *logic* to be applied, e.g. economic theory, law, social contribution, profit, religion or quantitative analysis.
- A choice regarding the *information* pertaining to that logic, its analysis and the conclusions to be drawn from it.

In other words, the 'logic' of decision making defines the information which can be relevant to that logic. But according to Rice, people often act in backward order. They take available information, and chose the logic from that, which often leads to a redefinition of the problem. The consequence of this is that only certain phenomena are recognized as a problem, and that very often a problem is not really solved at all by the information available.

Cummings distinguishes two kinds of management behaviour:

- *Management by information:* management activities are regarded as instrumental, involving linear causal relations.

People act logically and with clear goals in mind, based on generally accepted principles and assumptions.

- *Management by ideology:* management activity is an expression of the societal function of the organization. Causal relations are non-linear and often irrational. The coherence of the organization is not based on information, logic and argumentation, but on shared values, convictions and close personal relationships.

Rice draws the conclusion that managers can easily be drawn into irrational, non-productive modes of behaviour. The *value* of information in the decision making process seems therefore to depend on the *behaviour* of information users (in short: 'information behaviour'). Certain types of information behaviour can even lead to an extremely negative value of the information to the organization. Rice (1985), Cummings (1983), Daft and Lengel (1984, 1986) and O'Reilly (1983) provide interesting examples.

Irrational information behaviour

More than ten years ago, Feldman and March (1982) described the irrational behaviour of managers towards information. They demonstrated that information often serves a very different function than supporting decision making. A later study by Feldman (1989) provides additional support for this view. It is interesting to summarize their findings here.

Managers ask for large amounts of information, and they obtain even more. But a clear link between such information and their decisions is usually difficult to find. They spend much time on information that is not at all relevant to the decision they have to make. They gather relevant information without ever using it. They act first, and then gather information as an afterthought. This type of behaviour is so much in contrast with the 'rational' theory of decision making that it has to be classified as 'irrational information behaviour'.

Feldman and March put forward a number of reasons for irrational information behaviour. These include:

- Delegation of information gathering to information professionals who, understandably, make it their profession to gather information. More information makes their function more important. Users, however, believe that the more information is provided, the more important it must be. Information provision becomes an autonomous process, often unrelated to user needs.

- People tend to minimize personal risk. The punishment for being uninformed is much higher that the punishment for being over-informed. As long as people are not required to justify their information behaviour in terms of clear benefits to the organization, we shall have over-production and over-consumption of information.
- Information is often gathered 'just in case', in order to receive important information whenever it happens to pass by. Irrelevant information is the price one has to pay for being well-informed.
- Information serves a symbolic function, based on classical rational values of the organization. As people believe that more information leads to better decisions, they also believe that a well-informed person has better decision making qualities. One can 'symbolize' such qualities, i.e. make other people believe that one is a good decision maker, by creating an 'information intensive environment' for oneself, preferably highly visible for other people to see. An excellent way of doing this is to invest in information technology.

Many managers and staff members emphasize the importance of information. They invest highly in information systems. Sometimes, when it clearly leads to better business results, this is rational behaviour. But more often than not, the rationality of information behaviour can be questioned. Using and investing in information can also be a way to legitimize one's position. If there are few ways to measure the effectiveness of one's work—if you cannot demonstrate success—then the visible aspects of information behaviour become important. Such visible signs include library use, reading and attending conferences, but also purchasing new technology and developing information systems. Such irrational information behaviour can be expected in situations where people believe in the value of information rather than have to demonstrate it, where decision criteria are vague, performance appraisal procedures are weak, and the organizational culture is more political and ideological than rational and business-like. It is precisely such a situation which we usually find in research and development.

Apart from the studies mentioned, rather little is known about the behaviour of information users. Most of what we know has been studied in the management environment. What has been learned there indicates that in research and development information behaviour might well be more irrational than we commonly believe.

Conclusions

Supply-side and demand-side are two forces which can bring about innovation in the information chain, one by pushing new technology and changing the distribution model, the other by demanding new services and added value. We have seen that there are many reasons to believe that publishers and librarians will not easily adopt a new distribution model based on electronic documents and networks. Some of these reasons are 'ideological', i.e. they have to do with perceived roles and relationships within the information chain. Other ones have to do with uncertainty about the underlying economic model of the new modes of information distribution. It is uncertain that publishers can survive in an electronic world, and that electronic distribution can provide sufficient added value to justify the transition.

On the other hand, there is little evidence that a majority of authors and end-users are demanding a transition to electronic distribution either. I believe there are two reasons for this. One is that many irrational aspects of information behaviour are involved. Contrary to common belief, it is rather unlikely that end-users always demand relevant, reliable and timely information. Therefore, they might have little actual need for innovation which aims to improve precisely these qualities. Much more understanding of the irrational aspects of information behaviour is needed to develop successful information policies.

The other reason is the lack of economic models which clearly demonstrate the value of information in relation to the costs involved. Neither value nor cost seem to have any real meaning to end-users of information. This holds true both for information as such, and for the added value and related cost of information systems and services. There is, therefore, no economic incentive for end-users to improve their information behaviour and/or to demand better systems and services. In fact, it might well be that the lack of understanding of information economics is one of the main reasons for irrational information behaviour.

We may conclude therefore that innovation of the information chain towards a new, electronic distribution mode for scientific information cannot be expected in the short term, in spite of the important role IT appears to play in this area. We may also conclude that innovation in the information chain can benefit from research in the following three areas:

- Development of models which demonstrate both the cost aspects and the added value of a transition from paper based publishing to electronic distribution of scientific information. There is a special need for *transfer* or distribution models, as the information chain is primarily a distribution system.
- Development of models which demonstrate the value of information to end-users of scientific and technical information. These models would have to show the effect of information variables on performance variables of people, functions and the organization as a whole.
- Providing better insight into information behaviour, with special emphasis on its irrational aspects. For this, we have to look at the function of information when and where people use it. The question is not what people do in the library, but what they do at work. Cognitive psychology and task analysis seem therefore to be essentials ingredients of this area of research.

An understanding of information behaviour is essential to the understanding of information economics, and to economic as well as managerial solutions of information problems. I believe that the best approach will combine these three areas.

Résumé

La Diffusion de l'Information: L'Irrationalité de l'Innovation

L'investissement à grande échelle dans les technologies de l'information n'a pas eu un effet remarquable sur l'évolution de la chaîne documentaire. L'absence de tentatives pour la mise en valeur de l'information, et pour le développement d'un modèle économique de la provision de l'information est déplorée. Par conséquent, les activités d'investissement et d'innovation se caractérisent souvent par une certaine irrationalité. Des barrières légales, politiques et financières ont été créées à la diffusion électronique de l'information. De plus, la transition aux nouvelles technologies est empêchée par des problèmes de financement.

Des problèmes d'incompatibilité sont provoqués par les intérêts et les besoins des différentes parties de la chaîne documentaire. Les auteurs préfèrent la forme traditionnelle de la revue scientifique au 'produit électronique'; les éditeurs, craignant l'application peu rigoureuse des lois du droit de l'auteur, se bornent à créer un système de diffusion électronique pour le produit traditionnel; les bibliothèques éprouvent de la difficulté à autoriser un transfert de fonds entre les services traditionnels de bibliothèque et la diffusion électronique de l'information. L'absence de collaboration pour l'implémentation des nouvelles technologies de l'information a créé une certaine confusion dans les différents domaines de l'information.

La contribution de l'information à la définition de politique est mal comprise. L'approche rationnel se distingue de l'approche politique. L'approche rationnel vise la stabilité des objectifs de l'institution, donc une prise de décision rationnelle. Par contre, l'approche politique est déterminée par de différentes tendances organisationnelles, ce qui provoque une certaine tension entre les différents secteurs de l'organisation. L'irrationalité de l'innovation c'est la conséquence d'une liaison imprécise entre l'information requise ou fournie et les décisions qui en résultent.

L'imposition d'un mécanisme de l'offre et de la demande pourrait libéraliser le marché de l'innovation dans la chaîne documentaire. En ce qui concerne les développements dans l'innovation, l'irrationalité de l'innovation ainsi que l'absence d'un modèle économique sont mises en cause. Des propositions de recherche sont présentées: l'évolution d'un modéle économique des coûts et des bénéfices de la transition aux systèmes de diffusion électronique; d'un modèle pour représenter la valeur de l'information à l'utilisateur final; une étude de la méthodologie pour l'acquisition de l'information et en particulier, de ses aspects irrationnels.

References

Cats-Baril, W. (1990). **Executive information systems: developing an approach to open the possibles**. Fontainebleau: INSEAD.

Cummings, L.L. (1983). The logics of management, **Academy of management review**, 8, 532-546.

Daft, R.L. and Lengel, R.H. (1984). Information richness: a new approach to managerial behavior and organization design, **Research in organizational behavior**, 6, 191-233.

Daft, R.L. and Lengel, R.H. (1986). Organizational information requirements, information richness and structural design, **Management science**, 32(5), 554-571.

Feldman, M.S. (1989). **Order without design : information and policy making**. Stanford: Stanford University Press.

Feldman, M.S. and March, J.G. (1981) Information in organizations as signal and symbol, **Administrative science quarterly**, 26, 171-186.

Mackenzie Owen, J.S. (1992). **Waarde-aspecten van de informatieverzorging (Aspects of the value of information)**. The Hague: RABIN.

Mackenzie Owen, J.S. and Van Halm, J. (1989) **Innovation in the information chain: the effects of technological development on the provision of scientific and technical information**. London, New York: Routledge.

O'Reilly, Ch.A. (1983). The use of information in organizational decision making: a model and some propositions, **Research in organizational behavior**, 5, 103-139.

Rice, G.H. (1985). Available information and superstitious decision making, **Journal of general management**, 112, 35-44.

Rogers, E.M. (1971). **Communication of innovations: a cross-cultural approach**. 2nd ed. New York: Free Press.

What Price Research?

Le Prix de la Recherche

Barry Mahon
EUSIDIC, Luxembourg

Introduction

More than twenty years ago when I first came in contact with 'information' through being recruited from my life in the laboratory to the department, which was called TID, meaning technical information and documentation, at my then employer, I assumed I would be able to satisfy my considerable curiosity on subjects far removed from my specialization. I never imagined that information could have a research element. I was lucky enough to have been allowed, shortly afterwards, to attend City University where I discovered the research aspect, or at least that propounded by Jason Farradane.

I say 'that propounded by' because I had the impression that research in this field was rather personalized, depending on personal conviction and not necessarily related to a school of thought or a set of principles. In those far off days European researchers envied those who had been lucky enough to get to the USA where computers were plentiful and money also, and real research could be undertaken by people like Salton, Luhn, Jahoda, Borko and many others.

I also had the impression that things were simple, all the principles could be derived from a single document set. I sometimes had the profane impression that the document sets being used by Salton in the US and Cleverdon in the UK must have been rather worn, they had been subjected to so many counts and recounts and sorting into the retrieved/relevant or retrieved/non relevant, etc. categories.

I reminisce in this fashion not, I hasten to say, to occupy space or time in this paper but to put my thoughts into context. In asking the question as I have about the value (in monetary terms) of research I feel it is important to consider the beginnings so that the ensuing developments can be seen against that background.

I cannot confess to having scrutinized the literature of information research in detail for the intervening years in preparing this paper. I expect there will be some amongst the readership who will say that this would be an essential pre-requisite to a worthwhile analysis of the cost benefit of research but it is not the intention to extract a cost benefit equation. The intention is to examine the role and relationship of research to where information is today.

The need for justification

Throughout the relatively short history of information (as opposed to documentation or librarianship) there has been felt the need to justify the work, not only of researchers but even of those 'ordinary' people who were employed as information workers. This justification has centred around the need to distinguish the activity from that of librarians and others who were perceived to be concerned 'only' with the physical material and not with the content. This rather simplistic notion drove some of the early research, the examination of the efficiency of dealing with documents and their content through thorough indexing as compared to 'mere' cataloguing. The results were interesting if hardly surprising, showing that deeply indexed documents were on average easier to retrieve than lesser indexed materials. The same could have been said about different levels of cataloguing without too much fear of contradiction. The results—and here there is no implied criticism of those who either carried out the work or funded it—were hardly a justification of the difference with other types of documentation work.

The other strand of research undertaken was the use of computers to deal with some of the issues. Here, the mechanical capability of computing devices to do repetitive tasks was well harnessed in the creation of permuted indexes, the counting of word frequency, the analysis of stems and similar techniques. This area proved more beneficial in the sense that results could be applied to larger corpora of text with obviously greater effect, typically through the creation of multiple indices, the sorting by word count and the examination of Shannon theory based occurrences of terms in different subject literature. The justification here was the proof of certain theories using computing to treat large and relatively complex datasets.

The overall results did not and have not improved the credibility of computing devices to solve the problems. In fact, as will be touched upon later, the work done at that time was not even high profile enough to have been sufficiently recorded in the literature where it might have been found in time to avoid some of the less successful solutions offered, for example by the originators of word processing, at a later date.

The overall justification of information research in the early period was that the volume of information was expanding rapidly and needed new methods to deal with this flood. Of the flood there can be no doubt, of the need to deal with it there can also be no misunderstanding. Of how it was tackled there may now be questions raised on why there was so little effort placed on looking at a range of solutions within a framework, as opposed to separating work done in 'real' information environments from that done in academic surroundings. In many ways the amount of work done in 'real' environments was very small compared to the more theoretical work. This may be explained by the lack of arguments available to justify the research in commercial situations. The question to be asked today is why was it not felt necessary to develop the arguments?

The economic scrutiny

One of the reasons why there was little or no development of a framework may be because there was no overall economic scrutiny of what work was being done by whom and where. Money for research was relatively easy to obtain because there was perceived to be a serious problem of managing large volumes of information. Amongst the topics supported there was little or no work done on economics and not much effort was expended on cost analysis of the topics that were selected. The result would have been a corpus of work without much coherence were it not for the agencies who funded the projects. They did attempt, and of course they still do, to analyze the outcomes in an overall fashion. However, they were hampered by lack of a clear picture. Their own advisers were, and maybe still are, also confused by the seemingly limitless range of possibilities for research, many of which offered some hope in solving the still pressing problem.

Another reason may have been the emphasis on Scientific and Technical Information. One of the repeated arguments for better access to knowledge was to avoid repeating research. It was taken for granted that nobody wanted to do work that may have been done already and therefore there was need of better and more efficient information storage and retrieval, to avoid the risk. There has never been, to my knowledge, a study of what it might have cost to repeat the work against the cost of finding whether it had been done already. In the harsher economic climate of today it is very surprising to have been told by the Information Manager of the European arm of a major scientific multinational that they now apply strict cost analysis to that question and in many cases have found that it is cheaper to repeat the work.

So, the economic arguments were not, and are not, researched.

Technical credibility

Another of the issues which makes the credibility of information research difficult to support is the over-emphasis on technology. As was stated earlier, the beginnings of research in this field were driven by early work with computers and were promoted, even before the computer existed, by Vannevar Bush and the Memex. Whilst there can be no doubt about the contribution of computing and related technologies to dealing with some of the problems, there is also the nagging doubt that much was promised and little delivered. Typically this can be traced to an over-simplification of the questions to be dealt with. Early word processing engines were considered as big contributors to the information handling problem because they could be used to index material. In fact, all they could do was index every word in the texts, which did not contribute to solving the problem, but contributed to the problem itself. It appeared at one time that everybody who came from the computing world to the information world had a 'solution'—so much so that the information world became very cynical about the promises.

In addition, there was always the promise that more computing power would provide a better technique. There was much emphasis that online was the answer, until it was discovered that even the precision of scientific language was too loose for crude computer sifting.

There is no doubt that very high quality work has been done in areas such as substructure searching, concordance, citation analysis, frequency analysis and many other fields where the computer has made such work possible. Despite the undoubted success of these specialist outcomes from research, the basic problems remain, at least in the eyes of the 'average' user, typically: failure to distinguish sufficiently between terms; inability to 'record' questions in a meaningful way; and the more generic problems of Boolean incomprehension and 'false drops'.

It is not so long ago that Apple (or was it Microsoft?) promised that their next range of machines would be designed as information managers. We have also had Hypertext and Xanadu and various gurus who again promised much, so we need not feel too depressed, we were or are not alone in thinking that we can find the answer via technology.

Information and Information Technology

For almost a decade now we in Europe have been able to benefit from money made available from the EC for IT research. Much of this, in fact the vast majority, has gone to developing hardware of a basic nature: chips, ASICS, manufacturing custom built applications, etc. The 'I' piece has been a poor second. That may well be justified in terms of the long term development of Europe's manufacturing base, but the questions are now being asked as to when or whether the expenditure will pay off. The lack of applications, the continued need to subsidize European hardware companies and a lack of understanding of the objectives of the EC programmes have led politicians to raise some questions about their efficiency. Nonetheless the latest proposal—the Fourth Framework Programme—has recently been unveiled with a budget of 13 billion ECU for five years. The remarkable level of agreement on the budget is probably due to the fact that the officials who agree these things have realized that they can get more money under this umbrella than they can from their own Treasury or Ministry of Finance, so they agree to let the EC have the management, in principle.

In this programme 34 per cent is earmarked for 'information and communication'. What does this represent in terms of the requirement? How is this 34 per cent arrived at and what percentage of the figure is for information? I would guess, because the documents do not reveal that level of detail yet, that the vast majority is for (tele)communications. The remainder will be for 'information', but how much of what is included here is genuine research and not product or process development? The real question is, what input has information research had in the compilation of these programmes—very little from the evidence of what is published as the programme contents. I was recently asked to comment on the proposal from one part of the EC Commission to the detailed Fourth Framework programme. This proposal was a *mélange* of Information Engineering and Information Science and it was very disappointing to realize the low level of understanding of information research evidenced in the text. Just as an example: one of the objectives was stated as 'speeding up the transition from printed to electronic forms of publishing'—and this in a programme which spans 1994 to 1998! Where is the input from information research to this type of planning, where is the justification for expenditure of *x* per cent of the 13 billion ECU for information research? It is clear that the hardware needs information applications, it is obvious that information research needs hardware, neural nets, parallel computing etc., but where is the input and where is the cross-fertilization?

In another aspect of the I v IT issue there is now total confusion in the data area—at the level of misconception between data and information and in the loose usage of the word 'database' in discussing IT matters. This is not a plea to 'hijack' the words for the exclusive use of the information research community, but would it not be a good idea to try to create a taxonomy of these confusing terms?

Lastly in this territory littered with confusion, is there a price to be put on once and for all clearing up the anomalies that exist between the problems of dealing with simple, structured and unstructured data and the consequent problems of simple, structured and unstructured information? Again, an attempt at a taxonomy might make it possible to establish the territory where information research can flourish in this world seemingly populated by those who use the words without understanding the meanings, or—worse—use the words with a range of meanings to suit the circumstances.

The role of publishers in information research

The publishing community has been conspicuous by its absence in the field of information research. It may well be that they have funded work, it is almost certain that they have. However, a recent study by the EC (Consulting Trust GmbH, 1993) shows that the publishing community does not appear to have thought of the outputs of research in examining its future. The report looks at the options for publishers in the future, on the assumption that they will be moving more and more towards electronic products. It is interesting that the publishers themselves do not see 'electronics' as the major basis for products, a significant part definitely, but not dominant. They seem to be much more concerned about ownership of the material which might be published. They see multimedia as threatening their existing arrangements because the material is coming from different backgrounds and has different owners. The publisher has been accustomed to controlling the use of 'his' property and has apparently no plans for a world where this situation has changed. Is there an opening for research here? At what level? For individual publishers, or for publishing as a whole? If there is, it will have to be justified in terms of potential results to be expected against the support cost.

The legal environment

The discussion about publishers' 'problems' with ownership opens up the whole area of the legal environment in which information will find itself in the future. The arrangements which have worked in the past will simply not be sufficient in the future. Copyright is already becoming an outmoded concept in the face of electronic 'document' production and distribution. The Continental European concept of the *droit d'auteur* is becoming more the norm, where the only 'protectable' entity is the originality of the author, *where he or she wishes to protect that originality*. This latter aspect is very important. Up to now authors were more or less required to sign over their rights to a publisher in return for the publisher taking the risk in marketing their work. With the move towards network publishing this is no longer the case, and in the network world, at least today, the author does not seem to be overly concerned with claiming rights, since he or she is happy to have the recognition. This is acceptable when it concerns written text, but what about mixed media? If an author uses sound or video sequences to elaborate his or her work and publishes over a network, are we not facing some significant problems of recompense for other authors and rights holders, if the music or video was not the work of the original author? Are we doing any research on these problems? Will we have no alternative to systems that record usage in order to make sure that royalties are paid? Remember that the sound and vision industries are far more rigid in ensuring that 'broadcasting' is paid for.

There is a significant amount of work being done (by publishers) under the EC programmes mentioned earlier to ensure recording of use. This is to ensure the return to the publisher for the investment. The research is being part funded by them so they obviously expect to be able to use such systems in the future. The question that arises for the wider user community, and for the information researchers perhaps, is whether recording systems of the kind proposed will be acceptable to the information managers and the users. The managers will be faced with the issues which will arise concerning administration of the systems, authorizing use, being compensated for assisting in the scheme, their relationship with the publishers, etc. The users will certainly be worried about civil liberties aspects of the systems—it will be possible to know in detail what people are reading—as well as the general 'tax on knowledge' implications of any pay per view scheme. The information researchers do not (yet) appear to be involved in the research that is underway. It is a computing/technology problem being driven by a potential problem of revenue loss. Is it time to start looking at new legal and administrative environments to deal with these issues? If so, where does it fit into present information research? Again, what proportion of research revenues should be devoted to it?

Who should do the research, who should pay?

Having left a number of questions hanging in the air the time has now come to try to provide some answers.

The fundamental questions requiring answers are those surrounding who should do the research, who should decide what research should be done, and who should pay.

The simple answer to the first part is—the more the merrier: the more units, individuals, organizations, whatever, involved with research, the better. However, that desirable goal should be balanced by a modicum of coordination between the researchers to ensure that as many topics as possible are being covered. It is appreciated that researchers should not, to encourage original thinking, be overly managed in the selection of topics, but in the financial climate of today there must be some realism.

This raises the question about who should decide, and again the ideal answer is—the more the merrier. But the same problem arises: too many organizations involved will undoubtedly lead to a dispersal of topics. It is pleasing to recall that EUSIDIC has done its small part in encouraging research, which may have been less than optimum in the recent period of change in the administration of the organization, but is not forgotten. We would welcome a closer association with those who decide research topics in wider fields; we do have some of these bodies amongst our members, but we would also welcome a participation by other associations. There has been a tendency, again, to see the EC as a major source of funds for Europe and there has been a concentration on that source by some Associations. A workshop at the end of 1992 (*The role of Information in the Economy and Society*, 1993) suggested some more coordination of research at the European level and by implication suggested that the EC should provide the means for this. It might be better to consider a body which contained representation from the existing funding bodies, the Associations, non European interests and the researchers themselves, as a more efficient methodology.

Such a mechanism would also offer a means to discuss the funding and its sources. Earlier it was pointed out that the EC, again to take the European viewpoint, was being seen as a sort of 'neutral' place where research money could be diverted from national scrutiny while maintaining funding to national researchers. It is not advocated that this happen with information research. If it is too much to expect a worldwide coordination then at least in Europe would it be possible to link together the funding bodies and potential funding bodies, at least at the level of 'who does what' to ensure a minimum of coordination? Perhaps this happens already, but it not very obvious.

Finally, should there not be a concentrated effort to get a uniform tax treatment for research funding? This would have the effect of interesting and encouraging private funding, assuming the tax treatment was favourable.

What should be researched?

The final question is what should the research topics be? This opens up so many possibilities that it could be an excuse for some blue sky speculation. However, in keeping with the aim of this paper to look seriously at the role and contribution of research, the temptation will be resisted.

This seminar focuses on the issues of economics in the information sector. This area of research must be uppermost. There have been many attempts to define the economic bases for information activity and the cost/benefit formula continues to elude us. The concentration should perhaps be changed from the 'value' question to the 'role' question and the proportion of resources to be devoted to information. This was a fashionable area a few years ago, perhaps diverted by work which widened the concept of information workers to such an extent that it became almost meaningless in terms of the role of information and the proportions of resources to be devoted to information activities. There should perhaps be a revisiting of this area with a more focused objective of looking at different professional activities and attempting to allocate some relative proportions.

The next area should be a further push on the psychological basis for assimilation of information. This will become more critical as multimedia develops. The relative contributions of text, sound and video in information assimilation have been studied, but have those studies been associated with the present generation in education, for example—those who, compared to ourselves, were raised in an audio/visual world?

Associated with this is further work on the man-machine interface. It may have been well researched already and the computer people are working hard here. However, there are perhaps opportunities to cross-fertilize from 'classical' work in the information research field with work in computer supported cooperative work, hand held computers (personal digital assistants) and, for example, voice interaction.

Integration of computing and telecommunications is a holy grail which has been around as an objective of everybody in the IT field for what seems like forever. It is still held out as the ultimate goal, but it seems to be as far away as ever in some respects. There is probably an opportunity to re-examine just exactly what this might mean in terms of information use and value, if the integration were ever to be efficiently realized.

Finally, and this is perhaps blue sky, is there room for a re-examination of the medium/message equation? We are faced with so many media and their prospects are all considered equal in some way. It may be worthwhile to try to do some work on fitting medium and message together for greater information transfer efficiency.

Conclusion

This paper was not written to prove anything. That may seem like a way of avoiding coming to a conclusion but in reality the issues raised cannot be wrapped up in a set of results. They are ongoing, they are no less important today than they were when research started in this field. The main factor that has perhaps changed is the environment. Research generally is under scrutiny, information is one of those areas where it is difficult to define the territory with any precision, the number of potential topics is very large as also is the number of bodies with an interest in researching them. Without trying to make a specific case for receiving special treatment, information research needs to specify more effectively its fields of application and be able to justify it in the increasingly competitive environment of research funding today.

Résumé

Le Prix de la Recherche

Le rôle de la recherche dans l'industrie de l'information est examiné, ainsi que l'état de l'industrie, et le contexte économique et technologique de la recherche est défini.

La recherche dans la science de l'information a de la difficulté à l'origine à se distinguer des travaux effectués dans le domaine de la bibliothéconomie. L'évaluation économique des activités de recherche et de la sélection des sujets d'étude restent à faire. Etant donné l'importance de la gestion de l'information, le financement des projets ne présente pas un grand problème. La publication des travaux de recherche évitera la duplication inutile. La technologie semble représenter la solution idéale à tout problème de l'information, bien que ce n'est pas toujours le cas. La question fondamentale: comment intégrer les développements de l'automatisation à la recherche dans l'information?

Des fonds destinés à la recherche dans les nouvelles technologies ont éte affectés pour des initiatives de la Communauté Européenne. Pourtant, il arrive souvent que les objectifs des projets envisagés sont mal compris. Le résultat: c'est la technologie qui devient la priorité, et non pas l'information.

Les questions du financement de la recherche et de la sélection des chercheurs ne sont pas décidées. La coordination entre chercheurs dans les différents secteurs de l'information aurait l'effet d'introduire une plus grande variété de thèmes. Des institutions en dehors de la CE pourraient également participer dans le financement des projets. Les déductions fiscales imposées sur les fonds de recherche et les sources privées de financement devraient être prises en considération.

L'objectif de la recherche dans la science de l'information doit être clarifié. Des thèmes intéressants de recherche future sont proposés:

L'économie de l'information; la base psychologique de l'assimilation de l'information; le dialogue homme machine; les liens entre la recherche dans la science de l'information et l'automatisation; l'intégration des ordinateurs et des télécommunications.

L'environnement légal joue un rôle important. Le concept européen du droit d'auteur, qui protège l'originalité seule de l'ouvrage, va peut-être remplacer le 'copyright' du Royaume Uni.

Une étude récente de la Communauté Européenne a indiqué l'importance insuffisante accordée par les éditeurs aux résultats de la recherche dans la science de l'information. Le 'produit électronique' est mal compris, et les défis du multimédia font l'objet de crainte. La recherche sur la question de propriété intellectuelle serait accueillie par le secteur d'édition.

L'évaluation plus précise des objectifs de la recherche dans la science de l'information met en valeur l'importance d'une sélection plus rigoureuse des thèmes et des termes de la recherche. Il faudra spécifier les domaines de l'application, et les justifier pour des raisons économiques et intellectuelles.

References

Consulting Trust GmbH, for the Commission of the European Communities. (1993). **New Opportunities for Publishers in the Information Services Market**. Publication Number 14925 En. Luxembourg: Directorate General XIII E, CEC.

The Role of Information in the Economy and in Society. (1993). Proceedings of a workshop held in Luxembourg, 3-4 November 1992. Luxembourg: Directorate General XIII E, CEC.

An African Case Study: Higher Education Strategy and the Role of Information

Le Rôle de l'Information dans l'Enseignement Supérieur: Une Monographie Africaine

Peter Havard-Williams and Richard Neill
University of Botswana

Introduction

Recent reports of African universities make depressing reading. The African universities have undertaken some self-examination in a report published by the Association of African Universities (1991); the World Bank has underwritten a report by R.D.D. Blair (1991); a management consultant from Harare, Mr Trevor Coombs has produced a Consultation on Higher Education in Africa for the Ford Foundation (1991); and the Association of Commonwealth Universities has added its measure to the general map of gloom that has been charted. The International Institute of Educational Planning has more recently held a seminar which, it is understood, looked at more hopeful signs of coming to terms with the realities of life in African countries. The picture which has been painted is not very encouraging, and, as one who has written reports on situations in developing countries, one is cynical enough to ask, 'What difference will they really make?'. Yet things are stirring and the movement towards strategy management at Botswana is an interesting case study.

The University of Botswana is not altogether typical, one must admit: indeed it is a total exception, because the country is a relatively prosperous one and, for the past twenty years, it has been able to rely on its diamonds and its cattle exports to build up an astonishing monetary reserve. Thanks to the support of the first President, Sir Seretse Khama and his successor, Sir Ketumile Masire, and enlightened Ministers of Education and their Permanent Secretaries, in these prosperous times, the University has enjoyed exceptional support. On the whole, it would be true to say, the University has asked for what its administrators thought they could get—or get away with, and got it; and the mission of the present Bursar has been to see how much money he could return to the Government at the end of the financial year! On the other hand, the policy of the University and its predecessors has been cautious and its views have, in general, been in harmony with those of the Government.

A departmental analysis

In 1988, a few months after the arrival of a new head of the Department of Library Studies, it was realized that the Department, as it was then called, was grossly under-funded. What to do about it? I had been used to a department at Loughborough University of approximately 300 full-time equivalent students, with a budget of £500,000 ($750,000) a year, with about £250,000 ($375,000) coming in from research and development money and about £250,000 from foreign students' fees, of which the department actually saw 10 per cent and which in effect about doubled the departmental grant. The University budget was about £25m sterling ($37.5m). The department in Botswana was quite another case. There was the 'estimates' figure but that did not indicate the real amount, for instance, of salaries, and there was also the question of whether posts were filled. There was no computer facility, and the Department was treated as another humanities department. There were about 70 students. Neill and I were very conscious that the Department, albeit highly successful with a high profile in the University and in the region, and earning considerable income from research activity, consultancies and foreign student enrolments, was under-resourced compared with other departments. However, we hoped to get some financial support from a sponsor, whose representative was going to visit the University later in the year, and we got down to work immediately, producing our proposal document in time for the potential donor's visit.

We started from a description of the Department, and a fortunate quotation from *The Times Higher Educational Supplement*, 28 January 1988 (Supplement, p.iii):

> Although no longer formally linked with Swaziland and Lesotho, the University provide regional centres of excellence *in library studies* (our italics), nursing studies, primary teaching training and statistics.

We indicated that the Government of Botswana was making a substantial contribution to the programme, even though foreign students paid higher fees than Batswana. We stated that

> The Government, the University and the Department would therefore seem to deserve support for the further development of the Department of Library Studies, thus making a significant contribution to a major support service to education at all levels—literacy, research and development, to the general public, both in urban and rural areas.

Donors, we thought, would help those who help themselves. We pointed out too that we had always had more applicants than the Department could cope with, and we foresaw the need for a bachelor's degree programme, a master's degree programme, the regionalization of the school librarianship programme (which was just starting) an archives programme, converting some of our programmes into distance-learning modules, and training programmes for experienced librarians, documentalists, archivists and a programme for records managers. We also emphasized the importance of 'localizing', i.e. attracting Batswana to become lecturers in the Department. We also stated exactly what we were hoping to get from the sponsors, i.e., student awards, appropriate staffing, staff training and computer equipment. At that time, we had five established posts, together with a post funded by the World Bank. A further post had just been approved and we hoped that the World Bank post would be made permanent (as it was) by the University. (Today, incidentally, we now have ten posts, and have been fortunate to have had two years of supernumerary posts, through the generosity of the United States Information Agency—an ALA library fellow, Dr Wendy Simmons, and a Fulbright lecturer in mass communication, Ms Carol Pauli, both of whom were a huge success.) In our document, we provided a brief history of the Department, including our vacation programmes, and the sponsorship we had received from the various sponsors, especially the British Council, the ODA, the *Deutsche Stiftung für Internationale Entwicklung* (DSE) and UNESCO—from these and many others we still receive much appreciated support. In the document, details were given of our teaching duties, the amount of money that had been attracted into the Department from its beginning, including research grants, development grants, grants for short courses and the fees for foreign students. This indicated that the department had cost the University about P1.2m, but had brought in about P2.0m. This may sound a simple calculation, but in fact a great deal of hard work went into getting these figures together. The files of the relevant authorities of the university were not all in 'apple-pie' order, and some of the data was fortunately in the mind of Richard Neill who had been in the Department from the beginning (1979). He did a good deal of detective work on the figures relating to the beginning of the Department, and fortunately it had retained the annual reports. Sometimes we got contradictory figures, but we managed to reconcile them in the end so that the data we produced was reasonably accurate. The biodata for staff was easy enough to collect, but the list of project reports done from the beginning by students was much more difficult, because files tended to be incomplete, or spread around—a process all too easy when there have been changes of staff, and when the staff in any case has been only three or four members. In any case, young institutions are always careless about their records because they do not appreciate their importance, to, or interest for, later generations. We were also lucky to have the interest and support of the Bursar's department, which provided a lot of the data and with whom we had many interesting arguments on the status of various aspects of our financial affairs: they were taken by the fact that someone else, other than the Bursar's staff, was actually interested in the financial workings of the university. It was fortunate too that one of us had long and varied experience in building planning and design, so that we were able to include accommodation schedules for a new building, all within a very short time. The report was completed with some graphs, extracts from annual reports and the reports of external examiners, *curricula vitarum* of members of staff, a list of titles of projects undertaken by students, and proposals for a temporary and a permanent building. One hundred and thirty-two pages represented a lot of work done, among other commitments, within three months.

There were no standards to which to appeal. Budgeting, as I was to learn later as member of the Estimates Committee, was done on an historical basis, each department getting an added percentage for the next year, though exceptional cases were admitted from time to time. The major decision-making was that of the Bursar's Department. (The estimates were and in fact still are called for in June or July, the Estimates Committee, which is in effect the Senate Executive plus the financial officers, meets in August to October, and the Government's response comes in February or March. The Estimates Committee reports direct to Council's Finance Committee.) Foreign students were an important source of income. Were they a marginal cost or should they be counted only as the excess over domestic fees? What were all the costs of the Department? One could calculate the direct costs but what about the indirect costs—the Department's share of the Administration, Library, maintenance of the campus? How did one count residential costs? All this was very much a grey area. The importance of these figures was not to be found in the information they yielded, but in the questions they raised and the assumptions these revealed about university policy. One of the legendary figures was that of staff/student ratios—1:12. The Department had 1:11.5, better than the norm. But in fact the norm was 1.11.5 and we need not have been concerned. Indeed the University will not, in the present circumstances ever reach 1:12, because the faculty of science is calculated on 1:10.

The result

And what was the result? Immediately .... nothing, absolutely nothing. The sponsors for whom the report was prepared took the view (or that was what they said) that the Department was obviously very successful and did not really need help. In fact, the university administration did not then consider library studies as a priority area, and let us do all that work, and be interviewed by the donor, without telling us they would not support the proposal. However, with the help of my colleagues, we went on as if nothing had happened one way or the other, we applied for money under the regular procedures of the University, we applied for research grants and kept on going.

What was the real value of the exercise for which we received nothing in return? It was that, in preparing the case for the donors, we had the basis of a very quickly prepared strategic plan for the Department for the next three years, and perhaps for the next five to ten years, and we had it in a document to which we could refer from time to time when necessary and when opportunities might occur. For the staff, the exercise had provided a new way of thinking about the Department, and provided a strategic perspective. In fact, out of the various suggestions, the degree in library and information studies has been implemented, the master's degree is about to be established (with another ALA Library Fellow, we hope, to help us in developing the (second) 'information resource management option').

The professional Certificate in School Library Studies for teacher-librarians in secondary schools is about to be regionalized, the Certificate in Archive Studies would have started, but for another development which will be mentioned shortly, and the staff, particularly Kingo Mchombu, have also been working on a development which was not foreseen, viz., a Certificate in Rural Communication. In addition, all our syllabuses have been completely revised, and the direction of our research has been changed deliberately towards information rather than libraries. Though we did not know it at the time, the whole departmental process served as an introduction to the next stage, the major work in looking at the university-wide problems of considering the organization from an economic point of view.

So far, one might say that the Scout's motto is appropriate: Be prepared.

A university analysis

For the next stage, one must add: Be prepared for the unexpected. You could, I think, entertain for a few hours on good turns of fate, which have depended on the unexpected. In this case, a professor went on leave, leaving a vacancy on the Academic Planning Committee, on which Richard Neill and I were able to be members together for two years. In 1989, the Committee turned its attention to the subject of strategic planning. The Committee in April 1989, in considering an item dealing with the format for proposals on new programmes recognized that it did not really know a great deal about the University. It lived with mountains of paper, but this did not tell the Committee what it needed to know in the kind of accountable era in which it lived. Most of the information was either descriptive or administrative, and did not enable the Committee to consider planning in terms of the fundamental issues of university education nor, more important, enable the University to present a convincing case to a Government concerned with the possibilities of a diminishing economy in the next National Development Plan (1991-1996). Neill and I wrote a paper '*Information: a tool for planning*' (internal APC doc., 1989) in response to the Committee's concern. We already knew from our experience with the information sought for the Department that there were many grey areas in the University's administrative and managerial knowledge. *Information: a tool for planning* and succeeding papers sought to analyze the staff/student ratio department by department and to indicate the unit cost per student, and attempted to answer some basic questions as to the distribution of resources within the University, questions which at the time could not be answered. Although the costing was not absolutely accurate, the figures did provide a comparative guide to the difference in resource distribution between departments and the wide margin of costs between one category of student and another. In addition

> the exercise highlighted the fact that such information was not currently available in UB, nor (was there) a definite agreement as to how it should be calculated ... the figures also suggest some queries about the quality of some of the decisions previously made by (the Academic Planning Committee) and other committees of the University.
> APC 89/33, p.3(2)

The Havard-Williams/Neill paper also raised a number of topics for study. These were, for instance, a philosophy of higher education, institutional philosophy, goals and images of faculties and departments; staff, rank and activities; students, admission standards, background, social demand; curriculum; teaching and assessment; research and publication; resources and criteria, etc.; etc. The Committee responded by setting up a small Reference Sub-Committee to give attention to these matters and bring planning information to the attention of the Committee.

This Reference Committee eventually organized a university-wide Workshop on Strategic Planning in November 1991.

The work on the university's costing, etc. led to

a. a number of other papers,

b. involvement in the establishment of the University's automated system,

c. the installation of the Integrated Tertiary System,

d. a workshop on strategic planning, involvement in the planning for the next five-year planning period,

e. the compiling of the *University of Botswana Development Plan NDP VII 1990/91-1996/97* Gaborone, 1992,

f. major contributions to the Task Forces now recommending changes in the organization of the University.

In fact six members of the Department have been involved—and still are—in the Task Force operation. That in itself has helped to develop our research programme towards strategic management, assisted in giving the Department a high profile in the University, and allowed it to make many external contacts outside the University in the area of strategic management for higher education. We have been asked for *Information: a tool for planning* even from West Africa. How our colleague got hold of the title we cannot imagine. The paper focused on the kind of information needed 'in order to perform the function of strategic planning', and it was considered it would also improve the quality of the committee's decision-making.

> In addition, it is expected that much of the argument will be pertinent to the current exercise of developing the proposals for the next period plan (NDP7) as well as assisting in preparing for the forthcoming external review of the University (*doc.cit.* p.2).

The authors considered that, on the one hand, the quantity of paper generated by the committee provided a surfeit of information, on the other hand, the amount of real information relevant to decision-making was relatively small. Indeed it was a paradox that an institution entrusted with the task of generating knowledge for Botswana and the wider world community knew so little about itself (*doc.cit.* p.3). The University of Botswana is not peculiar in this: much the same could be stated of many other institutions.)

We turned our attention to staff/student ratios, a basic *datum* in planning. We found that this information was not available in the university, nor had it been systematically available. Nor was there any agreed policy on the methodology for calculating these figures. We found that much of the data was inconsistent, much of it was inaccurate, and had been insufficiently analyzed. Even tracing the data was sometimes difficult. The figures 'also suggest some queries about the quality of some of the decisions taken by committees within the University', we stated. The importance of that early exercise lay in the methodology, and the creation of a climate in which accurate and exact numbers were thought to be important, not in the accuracy of the figures. The aim was to allocate all University recurrent expenditure proportionately to each department, so that the University could know what it was actually spending on all the various individual departments. Finally, we gave a checklist of the kind of academic information which was needed for the planning exercise we had in mind. We included:

a. philosophy, goals, an image of the faculty/department;

b. academic staff and staffing (numbers, activities, etc.);

c. students (admission standards, numbers applying/admitted, progress; wastage, future employment;

d. curriculum, teaching, assessment, goals, structures, texts, quality of teaching, evaluation;

e. research and publication;

f. resources, facilities, costs per student; support services, organization, etc.

The whole analysis was to be part of the preparation for the establishment of an academic database for the university as a whole and for individual faculties and departments.

Looking back on this now, it seems so amateurish and sketchy and to those used to the elaborate statistics in industrialized countries, it seems quite elementary. However, the process could be repeated with profit in hundreds of institutions in developing countries, and there are even institutions in South Africa which could benefit from this kind of approach. Indeed in a recent visit to a South African University, involved in a five-year assessment of a department, it was noted that their statistics and figures were not as sophisticated as one had been given to believe. Over the next three years, then, we dug out information, facts and figures, until we got a rather more sophisticated model, and we were assisted by the installation of the automated Integrated Tertiary System, which has been, and still is, an enormous help. Moreover, a full-time Director of Planning and Information is being proposed for appointment in the near future: hence our work will be institutionalized. But it seems hard to convey just how much investigative work went into the various sixteen or so documents which we produced over the period: perhaps one example will give an idea of some of the difficulties. For one fourth-year class, we were given, from three different sources: 4, 25, 74 students. 'You takes your pick and makes your choice.'

The Reference Sub-Committee

The Reference Sub-Committee reported first in January 1990. Its purpose was to advise on a resource allocation model for the National Development Plan (1991-1996). It concentrated on two main areas:

- seeking to achieve an equitable way of distributing funds through the refinement of staff/student ratios;
- looking at the committee structure in order to make planning more objective and considered each year on a year-long basis instead of being done from August to September or October by the Estimates Committee.

It was also considered that the process of distributing resources should be related more closely to the work of the Academic Planning Committee. Further data had become available as Havard-Williams and Neill were able to give figures for 1988 and 1989 and actual staff ratios for 1979 and 1982 derived from an earlier study by M.H.Bond (internal paper, 1984). The apportioning of students to departments was analyzed 'in accordance with the governing regulations', and in detail with each student's registration forms. Since Neill had considerable experience in the Regulations Revision Committee (latterly as Chairman) the information could be guaranteed accurate—an important factor later when the figures were queried by the Dean of the Faculty of Science. This allowed the sub-committee to take into account loads in different teaching programmes. An attempt was also made to distinguish between the staff establishment and staff in post. The result was 'broad brush' evidence, but there were limitations. No attempt was made to account for the resources taken by

1. part-time courses;
2. teaching practice in the Faculty of Education (an extra six or eight weeks in the year);
3. contribution to teaching by demonstrators in the Faculty of Science;
4. teaching resources in the Botswana Polytechnic or the Botswana Agricultural College in respect of teaching for university degree and diploma programmes;
5. costs of service teaching among the three institutions.

These were mentioned as markers for future investigation. However, the comprehensive paper presented to the Academic Planning Committee and the NDP VII Committee showed staff/student ratios for all departments based on (1) actual posts filled and (2) the number of posts on the establishment. The distinction was important because in the Faculty of Science, for instance, it was said that a number of posts could not be filled. It has been interesting to note how many more posts have been filled since! The document also showed the relative size of departments in terms of full-time equivalent students—very different figures from those for students enrolled, because of complex degree structures. In addition, direct subventions to departments (departmental grants) were combined with indirect subventions (departments' share of general university expenditures). This was not calculated on the calculation of a proportion of the total budget (as had been done in the departmental exercise) but on the basis of the number of full-time equivalent students per department. Also, on advice from the Bursar's Office, monies from residences, refectory, text-book allowances, etc., were treated as revenue and also calculated on the basis of full-time students. (This seemed a dubious procedure since board and lodging for all 'home' students is provided by the Government of Botswana too). First year students represented input, graduates represented output, and the number of graduating students was provided year by year by year and subject by subject to 1989. Again, there were a number of *caveats*

> These figures are the best available but they are still to be treated with extreme caution: there are considerable limitations in the data itself and in the methodologies used in collecting it (Internal paper).

For instance, it would be possible to poke holes in the figures from the estimates. The *estimates*, for example, give only set figures for each type of post, not the actual figures of those in post. The method of calculating the indirect subventions is also rather uncertain in its accuracy. There is also the danger that the formulae will be mechanistically used, instead of being used as guidelines to support decision-making, which is what we intended. There was a significant variable to be factored into raw staff/students ratios: weighted student loads, e.g. large classes with heavy marking loads both during and at the end of the academic year. Along with that went department size, especially from the point of view of senior staff where the administrative load can be formidable. A high proportion of foreign students can also increase the administrative load, as they are all sponsored and each sponsor has different requirements, all of which have to be followed up. Different kinds of practical work and fieldwork need to be accounted for and indicators sought to calculate teaching load. For instance, the Departments of Environmental Science and Geology have field trips, at least three departments in the Faculty of Education have teaching practice commitments, the Department of French sends students, who have to be accompanied, each June to the University of Strasbourg, and other departments have vacation teaching commitments. Library and Information Studies has an extra semester fitted into the Long Vacation for the Certificate in School Library Studies and is proposing a Certificate in Rural Information and Communication with similar arrangements. Differences in departments can best be illustrated by comparing Library and Information Studies and English. LIS is a medium-size department, technologically-oriented, with commitments to teaching twelve months per year: English is the largest (or next to largest) department, vying with Accountancy and Management, with very large first year and second year classes, in which 96 hours or more per week are devoted to teaching groups in a first-year basic English course for the Faculties of Humanities and Social Science. Much more work needs to be done before we can begin to appreciate the differences in the workload of different departments. Unfortunately, since we did our basic analysis in 1991, it has not been possible to continue it, as the University is undergoing a wholesale re-organization, in which both of us are heavily involved. But the main lines of reform in allocating money and knowing how it is allocated have been laid down.

The University and manpower planning

There is a further complication. In a small developing country like Botswana (about the size of France but with a population of approximately 1.3 million), the University is very closed tied to manpower needs and can be affected very directly by changes in government policy. Numbers of students can vary very considerably depending on how many students can be released for study by different ministries. For instance, the Ministry of Health restricted entry to Nursing Education for several years, the Ministry of Education has restricted re-entry to the University of teachers, and has reduced entry to Primary Education, BA(Humanities), the M.Ed. and the Certificate in School Library Studies (programmes initiated at the request of the Ministry). This must also make programmes more expensive. The Ministry of Labour and Home Affairs for a while restricted a number of library studies students. The policy of sending students overseas for masters' degrees (over twenty a year in Education) has made masters' degree programmes barely viable, though in the last two years, the University has taken the initiative in establishing a series of masters' degrees, and this may change the picture in due course. These external variables can make long-term planning difficult, and there is no doubt there needs to be closer cooperation between the Government and the University in manpower planning at a micro as well as a macro level, through the Ministry of Finance and Development Planning's Manpower Planning Unit. Information on what is happening in the external environment (of which the University has taken too little notice) should form part of the planning effort. An effect of a different kind is the Government's policy of sending science-based students abroad after the first two years of the B.Sc. degree, when many of them could follow courses in Botswana. This is a major loss to the University, depriving the Faculty of Science of senior students who could be useful as demonstrators, and depriving staff of the interest of teaching the better students at a more advanced level.

Committee structures

The Sub-Committee, whilst concerned with measures designed to promote better and more accurate planning and target more finely the distribution of resources, inevitably became concerned with the process itself. The result was a document *Terms of Reference of the Academic Planning Committee*, which reviewed the terms not only of APC but also of other committees involved in planning (Estimates, referred to above, Estates, Development). The Academic Planning Committee, it was proposed, should be replaced by a Planning and Resources Committee. It would be concerned with current and future planning exercises which would be part of a continuous planning process, sufficiently dynamic and flexible to respond with some speed to changes in perceived needs and external initiatives.

> Within the bounds of the National Plan period, the evolution of the University's Academic Plan, both in the preparation and over the five year period, would be the consequence of regular interaction among the Depart-

> ments, Faculty Boards, Senate, the Planning and Resources Committee and the Administration (*doc.cit.*).

The Committee would consider overall planning problems, based on a 'rolling' five year plan, so that future years' planning would be modified in the light of actual annual planning with the modification of needs seen from this perspective. The Committee would need hard information such as had been already produced (but more and accurate) to get its work done satisfactorily. It would need figures for several years backwards and forwards to show trends for planning. It would need, for instance, the number of applicants per programme/faculty, the number accepted and the number registered—only the last is readily available still. Indeed the Government policy over the last ten years at least has been to encourage students to enter the Faculties of Education and Science in fact students have been more likely to enter the Faculties of Humanities and Social Sciences. Many decisions of students—and views of those in the community—are based on folk-lore rather than fact. Received wisdom is that the country does not want any more social scientists, but from a report by the body representing employers (BOCCIM *Survey of Botswana's manpower needs* 1991) it appears that more accountants, economists and managerial trainees are required for the development of the nation's economy. We need accurate information about trends in hard figures to make decisions as to how resources should be allocated, having not only the figures for the current years but those for past years and estimates for the future years based on past enrolments as well as the figures from the Ministry of Finance and Development. These figures would help to cut down the areas of uncertainty.

Most of the critical decisions will be in the area of academic activities. A planning committee will need to have a snapshot taken at various times of the current state of different university programmes. It will need to have information on staff and student numbers by programmes, years, faculty and department, the number of degrees and diplomas awarded for the last three years and the estimates for the next three years. It will require to know about accommodation, including residential accommodation, and relate the growth of numbers to the facilities available. What we need to build up is a climate of opinion which expects *a bank of information, a knowledge base* on which more precise planning can be formulated more expeditiously and more accurately. Judgements must also be based on quality. Information on teaching programmes should be available through regular reviews of departments, through information on job placements or placement in further study programmes, together with peer and student surveys of teaching.

From an internal university point of view, what the Academic Planning Committee has not considered sufficiently in the past, and the Planning and Resources will have to consider in the future (and generally what APCs in other universities have?), is the relationship of all these items to each other. Financial implications, physical resource, plant, accommodation, student facilities, external environment—all these need to be considered in relation to academic planning and development. They are often underplayed by academic committees, but their relationship in many of the decisions taken is nevertheless a real one, and a complex range of information, appropriately organized as a knowledge base is required if decisions are to be firmly based. Many departments need equipment, space and contiguity if they are to be effective. A drama department without an appropriately equipped practice theatre, a library and information studies department without bibliography, computer, conservation and indexing laboratories is like a chemistry department without test-tubes and laboratories. One needs to consider what the department will cost in the short term and what will be the cost long-term, what monies will it bring in? What will its programmes add to the University? How does it fit in with the overall programme? How does it fit in with the mission of the University? What *is* the mission of the University?

Our enquiry has been only a fraction of the whole process of self re-examination which the University is undergoing. We have had a University Commission, which recommended in the most general terms, we now have seven Task Forces (where the action currently is) which are examining the administration of the University, academic support services (including the library, computer centre, audio-visual resource centre and the bookstore) student services, the affiliated institutions, the academic structure, the establishment of a university press and a medical school. Whatever the outcome, our basic work on developing a sense of cost consciousness will be fundamental to the re-organization which is about to take place and will be fundamental to the future development of the University in the new economic climate with which the Government is concerned—one of recession. Our new Director of Planning and Information will at least have a precedent upon which to work.

Résumé

Le Rôle de l'Information dans l'Enseignement Supérieur: Une Monographie Africaine

Une série de rapports sur les universités africaines est analysée, parmi eux des rapports présentés par des organismes tels que l'association des universités africaines, la Banque Mondiale et l'association des universités du Commonwealth, mettant en valeur l'absence d'une stratégie d'enseignement dans ces institutions universitaires. La situation de l'Université de Botswana est meilleure, à cause de la prospérité rélative du pays. De plus, l'Université de Botswana peut compter sur le support du ministère de l'Education.

Une analyse du département des études de bibliothéconomie est présentée. En dépit du succès de ce département, avec son programme de recherche bien développé et ses activités de consultation, ainsi qu'un revenu supplémentaire provenant des étudiants étrangers, le département des études de bibliothéconomie à l'Université de Botswana éprouve une pénurie de fonds. Parmi les commanditaires précédents: le Conseil Britannique, l'Association pour le développement outre-mer, l'UNESCO.

Une offre de parrainage provoque en réponse la présentation des propositions pour le développement futur de ce département universitaire. Des programmes d'étude pour les cours de licence, pour la maîtrise, pour la bibliothéconomie scolaire, ainsi que des cours de recyclage pour les bibliothécaires et les documentalistes sont envisagés. Des fonds destinés à la provision du personnel et des ressources pour étudiants, et d'un nouveau logement universitaire sont exigés.

Dans le développement d'une stratégie générale, il a fallu prendre en compte l'absence des procédés standardisés pour la formulation des budgets, par exemple, ou pour l'estimation du rapport étudiants/enseignants. Les propositions du département de bibliothéconomie n'ont pas provoqué une réponse immédiate de la part de l'administration universitaire. Pourtant, il faut souligner l'importance de ces propositions pour la formulation d'un plan de développement départemental et pour la formation du personnel. Il faut noter aussi des conséquences pratiques telles que l'implémentation des cours de licence en études de bibliothéconomie, ainsi que la révision du programme d'études et la redirection des activités de recherche.

Une stratégie universitaire de développement pour l'Université de Botswana est également envisagée. Un article de Havard-Wiliams et Neill ('Information: a tool for planning') a servi d'identifier les 'zones grises' de l'administration universitaire en ce qui concerne la gestion et les connaissances de gestion, les thèmes de recherche, le programme d'études, l'enregistrement des étudiants, ainsi que la formulation d'une philosophie d'enseignement universitaire.

A la suite de l'établissement d'un comité responsable de surveiller le travail de réorganisation, plusieurs initiatives stratégiques s'évoluent: un atelier de planification universitaire, l'implémentation d'un système automatisé universitaire, la création des groupes de travail, et la présentation d'un plan de développement universitaire pour les années à venir.

L'article de Havard-Williams et de Neill a essayé de déterminer les information requises pour la définition de politique à l'Université de Botswana. L'absence des informations sur le personnel, le nombre des étudiants, l'évaluation du programme d'études et les services de soutien est notée. L'inconsistance et l'inexactitude de la plupart des données présentent un inconvénient sérieux. L'objectif de ce travail était la compilation d'une base de données universitaire.

Parmi les tâches envisagées pour le Comité responsable était l'évolution d'un modèle économique des ressources universitaires en vue de faciliter l'implémentation du plan national de développement universitaire. Des propositions équivalents sont susceptibles d'adaptation dans les autres pays en voie de développement.

Malgré l'absence de l'action directe à la suite de l'initiative entreprise par le département d'études de bibliothéconomie à l'Université de Botswana, la formulation d'une stratégie de développement a facilité l'amélioration de la situation économique de ce département et sa reorganisation future.

References

Association of African Universities. (1991). **Study on cost effectiveness in African Universities: synthesis report**. Accra-North.

Blair, R.D.D. (1991). **An assessment of progress and the potential for financial diversification and income generation of selected African universities: a report to the World Bank**. Harare.

Coombs, T. (1991). **A consultation on higher education in Africa**. London.

PAPERS SUBMITTED BUT NOT DELIVERED AT THE CONFERENCE

Communications reçues; non prononcées à la Conférence

Information and Organization: Questions and Clues

L'Information et l'Organisation: Défis pour la Recherche

Donald Lamberton
Research School of Social Sciences,
Australian National University,
Canberra

Much effort in developing an information economics has been based upon and has used the language of neo-classical economics. This has been dictated by several circumstances: first, this has been thought necessary in order to keep open a dialogue with both the economics profession and the decision-makers, both national and international, in industry and government; and, second, the intellectual capital in which information economists, the radical and the less radical, have made substantial investments. On this second point, the economics profession as an 'organization' is subject to the same Arrovian tendency toward obsolescence as are other organizations.

The more radical now press for a reframing of economics, a revolution, a new paradigm. What may seem less radical voices (e.g. Lamberton, 1992a and 1993) note that, despite the rather severe limitations at times imposed—some focus entirely on information asymmetry (Phlips, 1988)—much research has been concerned with matters that lie outside the well-defined, rigid boundaries of neo-classical economics and would have been an anathema to its practitioners, e.g., the concept of the secondary information sector, organizational design, human/organizational capabilities, learning processes, and the probing of the use of information. These are all matters increasingly to the fore in information economics research and they do not belong in the neo-classical world of given technology and tastes, given institutions and given organizational units.

If we turn the clock back two decades, we find a major assessment of information economics placing heavy emphasis on the role of information in improving the efficiency of markets (Spence, 1974). Ten years later a similar exercise for the ARIST series (Lamberton, 1984), noted that much more of the literature was addressing the role of information within organizations.

I readily concede that the change of focus was in part a product of the perspective I brought to that task. I had earlier sought to explore the role of organization and information in the context of the economics of disequilibrium (Lamberton, 1965; Ribet-Petersen, 1972) in order to better understand the role of profit. The dominant uncertainty bearing view seemed a little naive in light of the significant resource allocation to the creation of information and information-using organizational capital. This was 'investment', even if it was not recognized as such in the accounting practices of either the business world or national income statisticians.

Economics was changing in a general way: its concerns were extending more to non-market aspects of the economy.[1] This trend has continued and is inextricably interwoven with the information theme. Simon, for example, has continued his attack, from an information perspective, on the conventional optimization approach, blending together lack of information, bounded rationality and the design of organization, to reach his conclusion that what goes on in organizations is more important than what goes on in markets (Simon, 1991).

Simon relates his own efforts to the new institutional economics: transaction costs, opportunism, agency theory, etc., which he sees as wholly compatible with and conservative of neo-classical theory. He does, however, rightly point out that these approaches have failed to draw in a significant way upon the empirical work on organizations and decision-making for auxiliary assumptions. This is, of course, no cause for surprise: economics has shown a marked unwillingness to draw from other disciplines like psychology.

---

1. Here as always there were those who anticipated the change. When I paid tribute to E.R. Walker (1942) in a paper at the American Economic Association meeting in 1992 a participant, Beth Allen, inferred incorrectly from his mention of 'behaviour' that he was a behaviouralist. After all, the classic work of von Neumann and Morgenstern was entitled *Theory of Games and Economic Behavior*!

I draw attention also to the growing recognition that information problems and interrelated problems of strategic behaviour together constitute the major attack on the relevance of neo-classical modelling for a modern economy (Vines and Stevenson, 1991).

Should we join the forces seeking the new information paradigm? There is a good deal of empirical backing for the continuity of economic thought. Both monopolistic competition theory and Keynesian economics are now seen as less revolutionary and more evolutionary—the former was more about information assumptions than the number of firms and the latter was about uncertainty and the other side of that coin, information. It is possible that both might take their places in the process of developing an economics that recognizes the pivotal role of information, as the neo-classical model eventually becomes an incident in the longer evolution of thought.

A time when governments around the world are relying more on 'the market', deregulating and selling-off state-owned assets, is not opportune for scrapping, retooling or reframing. Perhaps with the pendulum swing, the opportunity for lasting change will come. Meantime, we must recognize that markets will not disappear, so the model of the market system will be retained. I suspect that the evolution of economic thought may well see the combining of the market model with an organizational model: the market model has to take account of organizational constraints and changes and the organizational model cannot be impervious to price and cost influences.

Some of the questions and clues can be seen if we look at contrasting analytical problems. Analysis of short-term movements in stock prices, for example, demands attention to the role of information but modelling can legitimately assume a great deal about the stock of information, technology, land and buildings, and human and organizational capital. If we turn to the search for the missing pieces in the productivity puzzle there must again be attention to the role of information: e.g., to R&D and the many other forms of exploratory behaviour, learning, changing human and organizational capabilities are all relevant. The role of information enters in vastly different ways needing very different models.

I wish to suggest that we have erred in thinking of information like lubricating oil: a small quantity in the right places can, so we are told, bring low-cost benefit to everyone. There are many different kinds of information. To develop appropriate taxonomies, we have to specify the characteristics of information—applying the Lancaster approach that has proved useful for goods.

Studies of the information economy, either aggregative or micro studies, have at last created wide recognition that information is costly and this is a good starting point for a treatment of organization and managing. Organizations need a great variety of information, and efforts to meet that need generate many forms of exploratory behaviour that are reflected in expenditures. Business firms, for example, spend on organizational change, marketing, industrial intelligence, computing, employee training, risk assessment, competition and cooperation with other firms, and attempts to reduce the margin of error in regularly used flows of information. Much of this can be brought together under the heading of business intelligence, which has been defined as the ability to acquire new information and knowledge, make judgements, adapt to the environment, develop new concepts and new strategies and act in a rational and effective way (Dedijer and Jequier, 1987).

One aspect of this exploratory behaviour merits particular attention in view of the excessive emphasis it has received in recent times, and that is networking (e.g., Antonelli, 1992). Several comments are called for. First, networking is an extension of the Simon thesis, in that it is non-market and we can define the firm, as Kenneth Arrow has done, as an incompletely connected network of information flows. Such a definition captures both the internal and external patterns of communication. Second, networks are not a new phenomenon and we should be careful about describing them as *the* new form of organization. After all, the recent experience of firms like IBM and Saatchi & Saatchi gives cause for doubt. Technological linkages should not lead us to infer that there are information flows; and, even if there are information flows, to infer that the information is used effectively.

The successful use of intelligence by a business firm or any organization calls for the protecting and enhancing of organization-specific information. Four major determinants of the rate at which, for example, a business firm acquires technical knowledge have been distinguished (Rosegger, 1991):

- The rate at which the firm produces new knowledge internally;
- The rate at which the firm acquires public-goods type knowledge from its environment;
- The rate at which the firm acquires other firms' proprietary knowledge;

- The rate at which the firm generates new technical knowledge jointly with other firms.

But production and acquisition of information do not ensure effective utilization. They need to be complemented by learning processes. This calls for a wider view, wider than that provided by the 'learning by doing' ideas that have slowly penetrated economics. A recent typology (Malerba, 1992, p.848) holds promise, distinguishing as it does between:

a. Learning by doing, internal to the firm and related to production activity;

b. Learning by using, internal to the firm and related to the use of products, machinery and inputs;

c. Learning from advances in science and technology, external to the firm and related to the absorption of new developments in science and technology;

d. Learning from inter-industry spill-overs, external to the firm and related to what competitors and other firms in the industry are doing;

e. Learning by interacting, external to the firm and related either to the interaction with upstream or downstream sources of knowledge such as suppliers or users or to the cooperation with other firms in the industry; and

f. Learning by searching, internal to the firm and related (mainly) to formalized activities (such as R&D) aimed at generating new knowledge.

Can these categories of learning be fitted together with the property rights/control aspects? And what of the missing pieces—the considerations internal to the organization. The essence of management lies in coordination and control and it seems useful to think, not of the learning organization, as so much management and organization studies literature asks us to do, but rather of the learning manager. It might help to treat the learning manager as the embodiment of a form of organizational capital, i.e., a capability of minimizing the seeming uniqueness of the events about which major decisions have to be made.

Earlier I criticized a too sharp focus on information asymmetry. I suggest it can be helpful to split this into two: asymmetry of information and asymmetry in the ability to gather and use information. Once we have introduced the capability asymmetry—or differences in organizational capital—we have to break that down to component parts: inquiring, gathering, processing, computing, communicating, deciding. Such unbundling makes the analysis both more realistic and more complicated; and opens the way for trade-offs between these components.

Some recent information science writing seems to raise similar issues. Devlin (1991) builds on Dretske's ideas (1981) about analogue-digital conversion, distinguishing two stages in the extraction of information from the environment: perception and cognition. His concern lies with the conceptual information of the cognitive stage, the agent being assumed to have the capacity of cognition, So here again we meet the need to develop some concept of capability, 'that condition in virtue of which one is *able* to do something' (Nussbaum, 1992, p.47).

Information and the capability of transmitting or using that information are complementary forms of capital. Absent such capability and transmission costs will be high, so there will be inappropriability on the part of imitators in the innovation process. This serves to strengthen the monopoly power of the original inventor or innovator. As this capability of using information is partly internal, e.g., the state of readiness of the person or organization, and partly external, e.g., institutional (public and private) support, it can be augmented or weakened through state policy interventions and business strategies.

This reinterpretation of appropriability (Lamberton, forthcoming) has both analytical and policy implications. So too does reinterpretation of the notion of indivisibility of information which has supported the existence of pervasive economies of scale. The legal approach to intellectual property has emphasized the discrete nature of the information embodied in a grant of property rights, e.g., a patent or copyright, and that discrete nature is compatible with the notion of indivisibility.

The basic complementarity between information and capability requires reinterpretation of the role we have been assigning to indivisibility. Xeroxing is a simple process and much has been inferred from the low cost of that process. However, even in that case there are equipment and operating costs. Someone must be assumed to have capability of perceiving the value of the information and of using the information. As the information becomes more complex, the likelihood of having to replicate a substantial part of the informational and organizational costs grows.

If we assume that capability is more likely to exist where there has been prior related experience, then it becomes possible to analyze these implications of capability or lack thereof, and to ask whether they strengthen or undermine traditional market structure forces.

The argument in favour of an organization-oriented approach to information economics research can be posed in another way. A plausible case can be made against efforts to assess the contribution of information (or technology) to economic growth because it has permeated all forms of production and consumption (Rosegger, 1993) and its value lies in its quality. 'Neither changes in the costs of inputs nor in the prices of outputs provide anything but the crudest approximations to the qualitative role of knowledge and information flows in economic performance. On the other hand, organizational change can be observed...' (Rosegger, 1993, p.124).

In conclusion, therefore, I should like to say I believe that the national accounting-type studies should proceed but with efforts to disaggregate the data. Comparisons between industries, between regions and between countries, approximate though they be, may tell us something useful about the contexts of organizational studies; and they are essential to the study of international economic relationships.

The organizational studies, I believe, deserve priority. As to our efforts to persuade our economist colleagues to pay sufficient attention to information problems, we should now design measures of informational efficiency and advocate their application. Just as it is often conceded that cost:benefit analysis fails to obtain a precise measure but enforces more careful investigation, so a combination of economic efficiency and informational efficiency measures might give better value. Whether there will be genuine interaction between the market and organizational models, and whether it proves to be only cooperative or generates a new discipline will be known in due course, as paradigms and disciplines do not seem to be created by exhortation.

My writing has been interpreted by some as too neo-classical but I share the wish for and hope of a new 'new institutional economics' that grows from our current efforts in information economics. If I am not as optimistic as some would like, it is because the economics profession, with its wide-reaching networks, exhibits sclerosis—a conclusion firmly based in Arrovian information economics.

Résumé

L'Information et l'Organisation: Défis pour la Recherche

L'histoire de la pensée économique est liée aux développements dans l'économie de l'information. Pourtant, les concepts de l'économie ne sont pas toujours assimilés à ceux de l'information. Dans la recherche, l'étude des organisations devrait remplacer l'étude du marché. L'évolution de la théorie de l'information pourrait associer le modèle économique au modéle organisationnel.

Il y a un besoin de spécifier les caractéristiques de l'information et ses coûts, de développer un modèle des activités de l'information telles que la recherche et le développement, et d'évaluer les facteurs humains et organisationnels. Les investissements dans les nouvelles technologies de l'information mettent en valeur les avantages des réseaux d'information. C'est en utilisant l'information spécialisée que le succès de l'entreprise est assuré. Pourtant, l'existence d'un réseau d'information technologique ne garantit pas la communication de l'information. L'implémentation d'un programme d'apprentissage continu atteindra cet objectif.

L'acquisition de l'information et sa transmission sont des procédés complémentaires. Il faut réévaluer le concept de l''indivisibilité': les parties d'un procédé, telles que le coût, ne doivent pas être considérées séparément. Trop d'imporance a été accordée au concept de l''asymmétrie de l'information', que ce soit dans la compilation de l'information ou dans son utilisation.

Dans la recherche de l'économie de l'information, l'approche orientée vers les organisations est préférée à l'approche axée sur le marché. Le développement et l'implémentation d'une méthodologie de mesure pour l'efficacité informationnelle gagnerait le respect des économistes. L'oeuvre de Lamberton est critiquée pour être trop néo-classique; pourtant, la pensée de Lamberton se penche en même temps vers une nouvelle économie institutionnelle.

References

Antonelli, C. (ed.) (1992). **The Economics of Information Networks.** North-Holland.

Arrow, K.J. (1984). **Collected Papers of Kenneth J.Arrow, Vol.4 The Economics of Information**. Oxford: Blackwell.

Dedijer, S.and Jequier, N. (1987). **Intelligence for Economic Development: An Inquiry into the Role of the Knowledge Industry.** Oxford: Berg.

Devlin, K. (1991). **Logic and Information.** Cambridge, Mass.: Cambridge University Press.

Dretske, F. (1981). **Knowledge and the Flow of Information**, Cambridge, Mass.: MIT Press.

Lamberton, D.M. (1965). **The Theory of Profit.** Oxford: Blackwell.

Lamberton, D.M. (1984). The Economics of Information and Organization. In **Annual Review of Information Science and Technology (ARIST)**, 19, edited by M.E.Williams. American Society for Information Science.

Lamberton, D.M. (1992a). Information Economics: 'Threatened Wreckage' or New Paradigm? In **Interfaces in Economic and Social Analysis**, edited by U.Himmelstrand. London: Routledge.

Lamberton, D.M. (1992b). **Information and the Internal Organization of Firms**, paper presented at the American Economic Association meeting, January.

Lamberton, D.M. (1993). The Information Economy Revisited. In **Information and Communication in Economics**, edited by Robert Babe. Dordrecht: Kluwer.

Lamberton, D.M. (forthcoming) Innovation and Intellectual Property. In **Handbook of Industrial Innovation** edited by M.Dogdson and R.Rothwell. Cheltenham: Edward Elgar.

Malerba, F. (1992). Learning by Firms and Incremental Technical Change, **Economic Journal**, 102, July, 845-59.

Nussbaum, M. (1992). Justice for Women, **The New York Review of Books**, 39(16), October, 43-8.

Phlips, L. (1988). **The Economics of Imperfect Information**. New York: Cambridge University Press.

Ribet-Petersen, C. de (1972). Les derniers developpements de la theorie anglo-saxonne du profit: la 'Theory of Profit' de D.M.Lamberton, **Economie Appliquée**, 25(4), 645-80.

Rosegger, G. (1991). Advances in Information Technology and the Innovative Strategies of Firms, **Prometheus**, 9(1), June, 5-20.

Rosegger, G. (1993). Review of G.Eliasson et al., *The Knowledge Based Information Economy*, **Prometheus**, 11(1), June, 122-4.

Simon, H.A. (1991). Organizations and Markets, **Journal of Economic Perspectives**, 5(2), Spring, 25-44.

Spence, M.A. (1974). An Economist's View of Information. In **Annual Review of Information Science and Technology (ARIST),** 9, edited by C.A.Cuadra *et al.* American Society for Information Science.

Vines D. and Stevenson A.A. (1991) (eds). **Information, Strategy and Public Policy**. Oxford: Blackwell.

Walker, E.R. (1942). **From Economic Theory to Policy**, Chicago: University of Chicago Press.

Investments in Education for Information in Africa: Tradeoffs, Benefits, and Sustainability

Les Investissements dans l'Education pour l'Information en Afrique: Bénéfices et Entretien

M. Adisa Tiamiyu and W. Olabode Aiyepeku
Africa Regional Centre for Information Science,
University of Ibadan, Nigeria

Introduction

One of the endemic characteristics of Sub-Saharan Africa has been lack of sustainable growth and development. This phenomenon, alongside the spectre of life-threatening malnutrition, endemic and epidemic diseases, and debilitating ignorance, puts Sub-Saharan Africa in a two-level resource allocation dilemma which often begets controversy (Olden, 1987; Aiyepeku, 1988a; Tiamiyu, 1989). At the first level is the challenge of striking an appropriate balance in the resources devoted to meeting immediate critical human needs, such as food, basic health and hygiene, shelter and basic literacy, compared to resources devoted to the longer-term need for expansion in the capacity for producing and providing more of these basic necessities in the future. This is the problem of choice between present and future consumption.

At the second level there is the challenge of balancing investments in 'tangible' activity sectors, such as agriculture, manufacturing and physical infrastructure (roads, dams, buildings, vehicles, etc.) compared to such 'intangible' and difficult-to-quantify activities as, basic literacy, primary-secondary-tertiary education, formal information systems and services, and research and development. This is the problem of choice between the 'visible' *growth* needs and the 'transparent' *developmental* needs.

All of us here are very much aware that knowledge is a non-depletable, self-reinforcing resource for increasing efficiency in specific activities in the short term, and a catalyst for long-term growth and development. We are also aware that most of Sub-Saharan Africa is characterized by:

- a dismal and almost exasperating developmental record, despite substantial and increasing investments in development projects;
- a declining natural resource base, combined with huge external debts;
- life-threatening malnutrition, epidemic diseases, and basic ignorance;
- a low information, knowledge and technological base in a global world increasingly being dominated by knowledge super-powers.

The outlook, clearly, is dismal, but certainly not hopeless. We believe that an effective programme of education for information in Africa is a strategic option for meeting the challenges of the evolving information age, and that well articulated and coordinated action by both Sub-Saharan African countries themselves and the international community is required to mobilize investment resources for resolving Africa's resource allocation dilemmas. We are confident that this approach stands a good chance of attracting increased investments of local and external resources in sustainable African programmes in information and knowledge activities generally, and in education for information in particular.

The purpose of this paper is to articulate a framework that might be used by African governments and institutions, as well as donor countries/agencies, to evaluate the benefits and tradeoffs of various options in the programming of requisite investments in education for information in Sub-Saharan Africa. In other words, this paper hopes to initiate an important effort to identify and evaluate possible investment options and strategies, with a view to mobilizing and sustaining resources for investment in education for information in Africa.

But what do we mean by 'investments in education for information in Africa'?

The phrase is defined here to include, foremost, investments in programmes for building high-level human and infrastructural capacities required to create the executive capacity for further investments in education for information in Africa. Among such investments are those on programmes to train trainers, to develop local institutional capacity for training trainers, and to fund technical aid and exchange programmes.

Additionally, the phrase is also used to encompass selective investments in programmes for producing appropriate information workers at all levels for the design, implementation and evaluation of information systems, products and services tailored to Africa's growth and developmental needs. Such programmes include formal training courses, workshops, seminars, symposia, conferences, and on-site training.

Our definition of 'information' in the phrase 'investments in education for information' is oriented more towards specialized 'hard' information which is often required for decision-making in specific productive activities or sectors, than the generalized 'soft' information needed by all persons in modern societies. However, we are aware of the empirical findings of various macro-economic and social studies of information activities (e.g., Borko and Menou, 1983; Okada, 1978) that higher levels of both the specific, 'hard' information (data, scientific and technical information (STI), etc.) activities, as well as the more diffuse 'soft' information activities (postal, telephone, radio/TV, newspaper, etc.) are often required to stimulate and sustain growth and development in every society.

What, then, is the operational framework envisaged for the realization of sustainable investments in education for information in Africa?

Articulating an operational framework

The framework articulated in this paper is illustrated in Figure 1. The framework highlights six areas that require attention in efforts to stimulate, rationalize and sustain investments in education for information in Africa. These are:

- Objectives of investments in education for information in African countries and regions;
- Programme components of investments in education for information;
- Potential sources of investible resources;
- Institutional machinery for investment initiatives;
- Institutional machinery for investment administration; and
- Potential beneficiaries of the investments.

***Figure 1**: A framework for evaluating the tradeoffs, benefits and sustainability of investments in education for information*

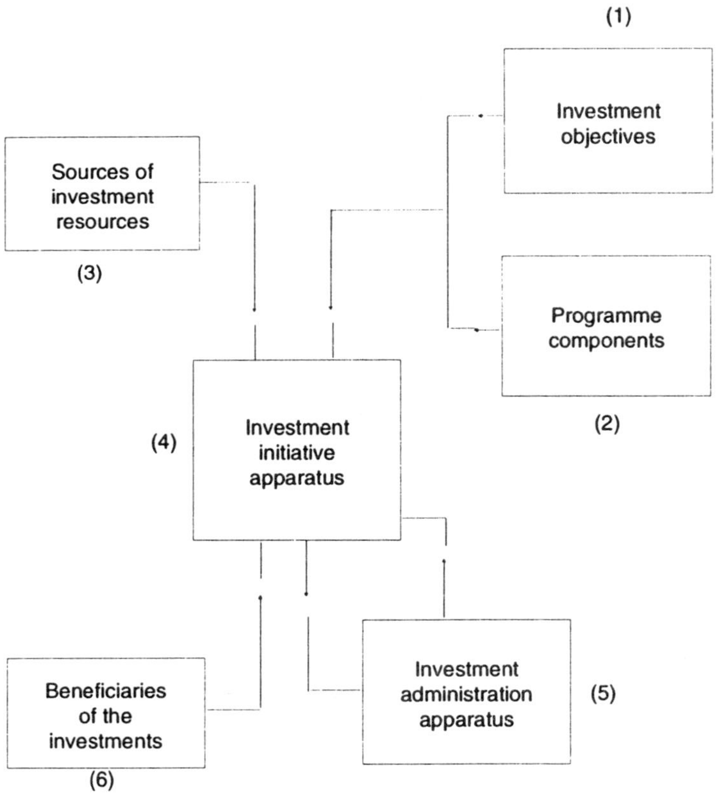

The figure should be understood as follows: starting with a well-articulated set of objectives for investments in education for information in Africa (1), it would be equally important to identify the candidate programme components (2) that might be implemented separately or in combination towards achieving the objectives. Another important input task would be to identify the potential sources of investible funds (3). Indeed, initial investments might be required for identifying and articulating input tasks (1) through (3). And it is probably inevitable that an investment initiative apparatus (4) would be required to spearhead and implement such catalytic types of investments. However, in order to sustain, expand the scope and reap the fruits of such initial investments, a longer-standing investment administration apparatus (5), is also required. Such apparatus would also serve to relieve the investment initiative apparatus (4) of the fears of the self-sustainability of their investment initiatives. Finally, at each stage, actual and potential beneficiaries of investments in education for information in Africa must be identified and encouraged to actively participate in input tasks (1) through (5).

We believe that this is a dynamic framework for highlighting the various options, tradeoffs, advantages and limitations that might be explored in each of the six areas listed above in order to enhance cost-benefit analyses and, thus, the effectiveness of efforts to mobilize and use resources for investments in education for information in Africa.

We shall now discuss the six areas in some detail under four broader sub-headings.

Objectives of investments in education for information

What are, or should be, the objectives of investments in education for information in Africa for individual African countries, for regional groupings of African countries, and for international donor countries and agencies which would be expected to continue to invest in Africa's developmental efforts? Among the possible objectives, at least six may be considered, as follows:

- **Awareness of information in society**. A desirable improvement in the general level of awareness in African societies of the importance of information and knowledge for making decisions at the personal, community and national levels is urgently required. Strategies for achieving this necessarily broad objective of education for information in Africa would include literacy campaigns, formal and informal public information/propaganda programmes, as well as programmes for stimulating information awareness and use by specific groups.
- **Decision-maker awareness and use of information**. Improving the level of information awareness by specific groups (e.g. farmers, or policy-makers) of specific types of information

needed in decision-making in specific situations constitutes a major objective of all development efforts in Africa. Unfortunately, commitments to expenditures in this sector are not easily discernible in the budgets of African nations.

- **Data collection and accessibility**. A recurring theme in African development plans is how to improve the capacity of African countries to design and operationalize systems for collecting and processing data to support growth and developmental efforts in individual countries. However, despite substantial resource allocations to such efforts, tangible results have been, at best, spotty.
- **STI and local technological development**. All African countries acknowledge the potential value of science and technology in their development strategies. Most of them also recognize the need for appropriate technological transfer to address local problems. Not so well recognized or acknowledged, however, is how significant investments in scientific and technological information might boost their absorptive capacities for imported technologies and enhance the development of local technologies.
- **Information exchange for regional integration**. Improvements in the capacity of each African country for regional integration in terms of the capability to gather, document and share data and information with other members of regional or global networks, in a manner explored by one of the authors at a recent Conference on West African Integration (Aiyepeku, 1993), are urgently required.
- **Reduction of negative global externalities**. The capacity of African countries to design information systems and conduct research studies as the basis of improved policy-making aimed at combating national problems with global negative externalities (e.g. the AIDS menace, degradation of the global environment, etc.) is severely limited. An important objective of education for information in Africa would be to demonstrate the organic link between access to, and use of, appropriate information and the success of efforts to ameliorate the effects of these global phenomena in Africa.

One can think of other possible objectives as well. We have carefully selected only six to highlight some of the salient undercurrents and implications of the often unstated or inadequately articulated objectives of investments in education for information in Africa in particular. For instance, although the six objectives are complementary, programmes and strategies for fostering their attainment could vary from massive public enlightenment programming in the case of the first, to implementing a project to collect and evaluate data on the incidence of AIDS in a particular country, region or area, in the case of the last.

However, there are other dimensions of these objectives which are vital in the African context. In particular, one may attempt to discern the relative importance accorded education for information in Africa by looking at investments in sectors that are recognizable as actual or potential sources of information of different types. For example, what is the relative emphasis by African countries on investments in institutions which generate and use general, 'soft' or propaganda information vis-à-vis investments in institutions which specialize in the production and use of data/information/knowledge for development? How are investments in basic scientific and technical research and documentation activities vis-à-vis investments in applied research and development activities prioritized? It is our view that questions such as these (and others) are best put and systematically addressed in the context of formal education for information in Africa. Not only must answers to these questions be found, but a clear demonstration of their implications for African development at all levels and stages would constitute a continuing focus of education for information in Africa, especially at the tertiary level.

Another important dimension of the objectives earlier enumerated concerns current investments in library and documentation services on the one hand, and investments in computer and communications systems and services on the other. Much has been written about the lowly status of librarians in Africa compared to other professionals such as lawyers, doctors and engineers, and lately, computer scientists. Since modern information services are heavily technology-driven, how should investments in computer and telecommunications infrastructures and services be re-packaged and sold to ensure that requisite investments in information activities are not unduly compromised in favour of the high-status sectors and professions? What are the inherent tradeoffs in this scenario between education for librarianship on the one hand, and education for information science on the other?

Finally, there are also tradeoffs to be considered at national, regional and sub-regional levels in regard to the perceived benefits derivable from the implementation of specific programmes of education for information in Africa. Pertinent questions here include: What would be the relative benefits for particular African nations, regions and sub-regions of specific types of investments? Arising from the perceived differential benefits to be derived, what should be the equitable contribution of each country, region or sub-region to such investments? And how about the international community?

Our discussion of possible alternative objectives of investments programmes in education for information in Africa is intended to stimulate efforts to identify and articulate all relevant objectives and dimensions against which alternative components of programmes on education for information in Africa (discussed in the next section) could be measured. Such consideration also implies continuing research on appropriate yardsticks that could be used to gauge the extent of achievement of each objective at any particular point in time.

But what are the possible programme components?

Programme components

As was highlighted in a policy discussion paper by Aiyepeku (1988b), investments in programmes of education for information in Africa must be prioritized, implemented and evaluated from the perspective of producing an initial critical mass of high-level African executive capacity for implementing and sustaining subsequent investments in the sector.

We suggest that decisions on the optimal mix of programme components must recognize the following imperatives:

- Remedies must be found for the currently low motivation of African policy-makers for incremental investments in education for information, over and above their already heavy and continuing investments in primary and tertiary education in particular. It would be unrealistic, for example, to contemplate sustaining investments in regional education for information programmes without substantially increasing the collaborative inputs of governments of Sub-Saharan Africa.
- The currently low executive capacity in Sub-Saharan Africa for designing and operationalizing computer-based information systems and networks, especially in the area of

documentation, records management, and library services, and the completely absent capacity for the local manufacture of computer and telecommunications equipment needed for instructional purposes at all levels of education for information in Africa, need to be urgently addressed, primarily at the level of education for information.

- The wide differentials in the remuneration of information workers across economic sectors and across national and regional boundaries which often trigger undesirable mobility of trainers, researchers and other highly skilled personnel, threatening the sustainability of programmes, is a real and serious issue. Consequently, programmes of education for information must include components for overcoming this potentially destabilizing problem.
- The relatively low commitment of resources to information science education at the tertiary level compared to library and archival science education is, perhaps, partially a function of the relative youth of information science as a discipline. The perpetuation of the situation will, however, do most havoc in Africa where the need for the application of modern information technologies to development is most acute.
- The dismal record of Sub-Saharan Africa on the issue of the sustainability of investment programmes must be addressed. Specific strategies for improving the situation need to be carefully articulated and systematically implemented to cope with Africa's changing socio-economic realities.

Table 1 (overleaf) lists the probable components of an investment portfolio in an education for information programme for Africa. Four major categories and their corresponding components of investment initiatives are identified in the Table as follows:

- **Establishing a core of indigenous academic personnel**. Such initiatives would be oriented towards developing individuals as trainers and researchers, and to attracting brilliant young individuals from established academic disciplines, economic sectors and organizations to a career in teaching and research in information science. The long-term objective of these initiatives would be to constitute a self-renewing bank of indigenous trainers and researchers in education for information.

Table 1: Probable components of investments in African education for information programmes

A. Establishing a Core of Indigenous Academic Personnel

1. Teaching-fostering initiatives
   (a) Formal training in teaching
   (b) Supplementation of teacher's local remuneration
   (c) Curriculum development
   (d) Development of teaching materials
   (e) Local and foreign travel
   (f) Exchanges and visits
   (g) Awards/prizes for excellence in teaching

2. Research-fostering initiatives
   (a) Research assistantships
   (b) Part-time higher degree programme for teachers
   (c) Research grants
   (d) Exchanges and visits
   (e) Local and foreign travel

B. Building and Consolidating Vital Infrastructure.

1. Fixed and long-term capital assets, including buildings

2. IT hardware (computers and peripherals, telecommunications equipment and accessories)

3. General-purpose computer software

4. Specialized information and information-related software for instructional use

5. Instructional software development tools

6. Development of information science literature resources

7. Development of IT media resources

8. Resources for facilitating instructional information access and delivery:
   (a) Access to online databases

(b) Demonstration CD-ROM databases
(c) Telecom and E-mail networking

10. Resource sharing networking among education for information institutions

11. Cooperating networking with industrial training institutions

C. Building the Institutional Machinery for Sustaining Regional Investment Initiatives and Cooperation

1. Institutional organs for on-going investment initiatives

2. Regional communication and networking on investment administration

3. Sourcing resources for regional investment initiatives

4. Sponsorship and placement of regional trainees

5. Networking and tracking of teachers, researchers, and former trainees in information

6. Measurement and evaluation of executive capacities in different aspects of education for information

D. Building Managerial and Operational Capacity

1. Formal post-graduate degree programmes
   (a) Trainee tuition, board and lodging
   (b) Trainee practical projects
   (c) Awards, Prizes, etc.
   (d) Industrial training/visits

2. Continuing education programmes
   (a) Participation in workshops, seminars and conferences
   (b) Exchanges and visits
   (c) On-site training of information end-users

3. Sensitization initiatives for raising the level of policy-maker and societal awareness of the value of education for information

- **Building and consolidating vital infrastructure.** Infrastructure would comprise the institutions, networks of institutions, data and communications networks (for instructional use), training resources (e.g. books and journals), etc., needed for the education of trainers, researchers and all categories of students of information.
- **Building the institutional machinery for investment initiatives and administration.** Such institutional machinery is needed for identifying, on a continuous basis, areas of need for investments in education for information, for articulating investment initiatives and programmes in the sector, for sourcing investment funds, for evaluating and selecting programmes, and for making investments with a particular emphasis on sustainability, in all critical aspects of education for information in Africa. Also included under this category are initiatives to establish viable networks of African countries and institutions which would be required to contribute resources and trainees to regional education for information institutions, as well as those for networking among the beneficiaries of education for information programmes.
- **Building managerial and operational capacities.** The objective here is to build capacities at the managerial and operational levels of information services. Some of the beneficiaries of the investments in this area would also augment the capacity for the trainer and researcher-oriented initiatives itemized under category A in Table 1. However, most beneficiaries would end up as operators and managers of information services, rather than as trainers of information service personnel. Investments in these areas only indirectly benefit education for information by sensitizing policy-makers, information managers and end-users of the importance of long-term investments in education for information. Consequently, only occasional, carefully evaluated programmes are envisaged.

Each of the four categories of investment initiatives, along with their associated components, would be evaluated from the perspective of advancing the attainment of specific educational objectives, using such criteria as impact, penetration, knowledge transfer and empowerment, and using different data collection and evaluation techniques, including, for example, the Delphi and case study methods.

We can now consider the probable sources of funds and potential beneficiaries of the programmes envisaged.

Potential sources of funds and potential beneficiaries

Who are the likely beneficiaries of investments in education for information in Sub-Saharan Africa? What are the potential sources of resources for the investments?

Each of the alternative investment initiatives discussed in the previous section could be assessed from the perspectives of potential short- and long-term benefits to: individuals (as trainers, researchers, or trained end-users); organizations (in the private or public sectors); particular African countries or sub-regions where specific investments are located; donor countries or agencies; and the global community. In order to ensure a comprehensive coverage of the entire terrain of potential beneficiaries of, and contributors to, investment initiatives on education for information in Africa, the following categorization of persons and corporate entities may be considered:

- **Private sector organizations in individual African countries**, which often benefit from the normal flow of information personnel from educational programmes funded by public-sector and not-for-profit organizations. Various sub-sectors of the private sector of African countries are able to attract highly qualified personnel essentially because they offer better remuneration packages. However, such organizations have not been known to be significant contributors of resources to public education for information programmes. Vigorous and systematic efforts should be initiated to motivate them to contribute to such programmes.
- **Non-African and Middle-East countries** which, because of their comparatively higher remuneration packages than can be obtained in Sub-Saharan African countries, often benefit from the brain drain of personnel from publicly-funded or subsidized African training programmes in information. Until recently, Africa had been losing highly trained human resources through migration to Western European and North

American countries. More recently, the oil-rich Middle-Eastern countries have been the primary beneficiaries of the net outflow of qualified human talent from Africa. This situation poses a barrier to the consolidation of executive capacity for investments in education for information. We should be thinking of how Africa can source investible resources from these net beneficiaries of African talent, and motivate them to contribute to education for information programmes in Africa.

- **Governments and agencies of governments in African countries**. The key issue here is that African governments often control the bulk of investible resources available to their countries, from both domestic and foreign sources. Quite often, however, political considerations favour 'visible' voter-captivating projects, rather than investments in 'transparent' sectors, such as information and education for information activities, as was highlighted by Tiamiyu (1993). Vigorous and sustained efforts are required to change this inclination of African governments and decision-makers in order to guarantee a sustainable commitment to funding information services and education for information programmes at national and sub-regional levels.
- **Regional organizations in Africa**, for example, the Economic Community of West African States (ECOWAS), the United Nations Economic Commission for Africa (UNECA), the Council for the Development of Social Science Research in Africa (CODESRIA), etc., should be veritable sources of funds. Such organizations should be persuaded not only to fund programmes for operational information systems and networks, such as PADIS, but also to actively participate in funding training programmes in order to build human executive capacities for such systems and networks in various countries and sub-regions of the continent.
- **Donor countries and agencies outside Sub-Saharan Africa**. In this category are Canada's IDRC, UNESCO, and the Ford Foundation, among numerous others. It is on record that these organizations have made substantial investments in development-oriented projects in Africa. However, the present precarious resource position of all countries in Sub-Saharan Africa makes it inevitable that they would be called upon not

only to invest more resources for development programming in Africa generally, and in education for information in Africa in particular, but also in investments to ensure the sustainability of their investments.

- **Individuals within and outside African countries and subregions as potential sources of funds**. These are, as yet, a largely untapped potential source of resources for investments in education for information. Although per capita incomes in Sub-Saharan African countries are among the lowest in the world, there are African billionaires (in whatever currency) in Africa and in diaspora who should be appropriately targeted and motivated to endow specific aspects of education for information, such as buildings, professorial chairs and scholarships. For instance, the black caucus of philanthropists in the United States appears to be a promising source of investible funds for education for information in Africa. One must mention here that, already, development assistance efforts that might eventually have a positive impact on education for information in Africa are already being provided by, for example, the Global Coalition for Africa, the Africa Capacity Building Foundation, and the Donors to African Education (DAE) programmes. However, there is the need to make concerted efforts continuously to alert such organizations to Africa's critical need for investments in education for information as a strategic foundation for ensuring the effectiveness of investments in other sectors.
- **Individuals as beneficiaries of education for information programmes**. These are the individuals who, as trainers, researchers and trainees, benefit directly from participation in education for information programmes. To avoid losing such trained talent to other sectors, such individuals, and especially new trainees, must be motivated on a continuous basis. Effective tracking and networking programmes which link researchers, trainers and former trainees, to a long-term commitment of a career in education and service for information in Africa should prove particularly helpful in ensuring long-term sustainability and expansion of executive capacities in African education for information.

It is generally recognized, however, that the measures we have outlined will not have the desired impact without putting in place appropriate institutional organs for investment initiatives, appraisal and administration. Such issues are now considered in the final section of the paper.

Institutional organs for investment initiatives, appraisal and administration

Discussed under this heading are such factors as the organization, motivation and driving force for sourcing investment resources, for executing investment programmes, for evaluating the impact of investments, and for ensuring the sustainability of initial investments.

Among the well-documented reasons often adduced to explain the dismal developmental showing of Sub-Saharan African countries, despite substantial aggregate investments, has been lack of managerial commitment and local financial support of projects after seed resources are spent (Agha and Akhtar, 1992). International donor countries and agencies, in order to avoid being accused of paying the piper and dictating the tune, had previously often adopted the policy of acting as motivators and funders of initial investments only, in the belief that the investments would be self-sustaining thereafter. However, the hostile environmental factors (political interference, lack of a long-term outlook, loss of executive capacity, etc.) often combine to make it difficult to sustain the investments. The key issue here is: can an investment administration *process* for ensuring the sustainability of initial investments be designed and implemented without running the risk of being accused of undue interference in the development processes of individual countries of Sub-Saharan Africa?

The possibility of Africa's inability to maintain and sustain investments in education for information, as had been the case with many other developmental programmes, should be carefully addressed. Our thinking is that the sustainability of education for information programmes might be threatened by both the scarcity of local resources (in the face of diverse basic societal needs), and the currently inadequate social awareness of the potentials for increased productivity through investments in information resources. Adopting a longer term perspective of initial investments, based on a carefully evaluated and selected mix of complementary investment initiatives on education for information is, therefore, strongly advocated.

It is further contended that the effectiveness and overall success of investments in the depressed African environment depend on a careful selection and mix of programmes, *as well as* on the implementation of appropriate strategies for administering the investments. This involves paying a closer attention to the ways in which funds are sourced, the sustainability of the sources of funds, and the nature and continuity of administrative and political participation and controls by local institutions, national governments, regional bodies and donor countries/agencies. The basic questions here are: Who would provide the seed funds and for how long? Who should provide on-going, maintenance funds? To what extent should the responsibility for contributing funds be divorced from, or balanced with, the responsibility for programme decision-making? What should be the correct mix of donor, executing and participating institutions in the decision-making machinery for programmes of education for information in Africa?

The following are some of the alternatives in investment funding and administrative arrangements whose relative effectiveness should be constantly evaluated for specific programmes in the African context:

- **Completely anonymous funds by philanthropic institutions and individuals.** This presupposes maximum trust by donors that the funds would be judiciously expended towards the attainment of the objective(s) for which funds were sought and obtained.
- **Publicly acknowledged funds by philanthropic and donor countries, agencies and individuals** (e.g. naming donated buildings or endowments after donors) but with no involvement by donors in the decision-making processes of programme selection, implementation and evaluation, other than periodic accounting for expenditures to the donors and/or third parties.
- **Funds tied to specific programmes with active participation** in the decision-making processes of programme articulation, design, implementation and evaluation by donor countries, agencies or individuals, and/or third parties.
- **Funds tied to technical aid from specific donor countries, regions or institutions to specific recipient countries, regions or institutions** for the initial design and implementation

of the programme, and for institutionalizing the local capacity to sustain initial investments.

- **Funds sourced from commercial activities within and outside the information sectors of African economies.** For obvious reasons, the bulk of such funds must be derived initially from profitable investment activities in developed countries, or in the non-information sectors of African and other less developed countries. Usually, a fund or foundation established for the purpose assumes full administrative responsibility.

Additionally, the following options in institutional arrangements for investment administration should be comparatively evaluated alongside the funding options already proposed in this paper:

- **Investments undertaken through individual African university/research institutions**, each of which could then be eventually transformed into centres of excellence in specific areas of education for information in Africa. This option could be used to consolidate existing infrastructure, but there might be constraints to adequately fostering regional capacity building objectives within the existing organizational structures of such independent institutions.
- **Regional bodies (e.g. regional research and training institutions)** grouped, funded and administered by a number of African countries with assistance from donor individuals, agencies and countries. Although such institutions would be located in specific countries, they would be truly regional institutions providing their own education for information programmes tailored to regional needs, and in collaboration with other similar institutions within and outside Africa.
- **Regional consortia of Africa institutions with funds obtained independently from African and other sources**, but dedicated to the sourcing and using of funds for programmes in education for information in Africa.

The options that have been enumerated here are obviously not exhaustive; other potentially viable and effective administrative arrangements could have been considered. It is important, however, to bear in mind that whatever options are preferred, the ultimate goal is to initiate, consolidate and sustain investments in African education for information in the face of fiercely competing demands for the region's meagre resources.

Concluding remarks

Very little has been written or published on the economics of education for information in Africa. Specifically, we are not aware of any previous attempts to address the critical issues of investments and sustainability as they relate to tertiary-level education for information in the world's most economically depressed region. And yet, it is clear that the global investible resources for education are getting short and that Africa's share is getting shorter.

This paper has merely presented, with minimal discussion, issues that we believe deserve greater attention and commitment by the international community. The enormous challenges that lie ahead are essentially for Africans who need all the help they can get from the Americans, Canadians, Europeans and Japanese in particular, as well as the international development assistance agencies, in order to succeed. Canada's International Development Research Centre (IDRC) and, to a lesser extent, UNESCO, have pioneered short-term investments in two regional post-graduate training programmes for information science in Africa. Evidently, Africans, like the authors of this paper, who are closely involved in the implementation of such programmes, will have to continue to do their utmost to convince African governments, IDRC and similar international development assistance agencies that their confidence is not misplaced. This paper has, therefore, initiated a dialogue on an important subject that should command the attention and positive response of all levels of investment policy and decision-making authorities in Africa, as well as outside the region. Only time will tell whether or not the crusade being launched, through the medium of this paper, will produce the desired results.

Résumé

Les Investissements dans l'Education pour l'Information en Afrique: Bénéfices et Entretien

Un mécanisme pour l'évaluation des coûts et des bénéfices des objectifs proposés, du contenu des programmes d'implémentation et des stratégies d'investissement dans l'éducation pour l'information en Afrique est présenté. Un tel mécanisme pourrait être adapté par les gouvernments et les institutions africains aussi bien que par les associations internationales pour le développement. La recherche des sources de financement ainsi que l'établissement d'un système d'administration de l'investissement sont proposés. Dans ce contexte, la responsabilité des associations internationales pour le développement de venir à l'aide des pays africains dans le lutte de survie politique et économique est signalée.

Une crise de ressources dans l'Afrique subsaharienne pose des problèmes d'allocation des fonds. Il faut contrebalancer les exigences humaines de l'alimentation et de la santé avec le besoin d'expansion économique, les activités 'concrètes' telles que l'agriculture et la fabrication avec les activités 'conceptuelles' telles que l'éducation et la recherche. Dans le contexte d'une maîtrise globale des connaissances technologiques, l'Afrique subsaharienne est caracterisée par une infrastructure insuffisante de l'information, des connaissances et de la technologie. Le rôle de l'éducation pour l'information est mise en valeur en option stratégique pour les pays africains voulant s'adapter à l'ère de l'information.

Dans l'implémentation des programmes d'enseignement, l'importance des initiatives d'investissement est soulignée. La discussion de l'investissement comprend les initiatives suivantes: la perception sociale de l'importance de l'information; la perception de l'information par les décideurs; l'acquisition de données et l'accès aux données; les investissements dans les informations scientifiques et techniques; l'établissement des réseaux régionaux d'échange de l'information; les implications nationales des initiatives de l'information telles que les programmes pour le contrôle du SIDA et les connaissances de l'environnement.

Les initiatives d'investissement doivent comporter les éléments suivants: l'établissement d'un personnel universitaire national; le développement d'une infrastructure essentielle; l'implémentation d'un mécanisme de surveillance des initiatives de l'investissement; la provision des ressources de gestion et d'opération.

Une catégorisation des bénéficiaires et des sources de financement comprend: les organisations du secteur privé dans les pays africains, qui profitent du 'drainage des cerveaux' du personnel de l'information sans contribuer aux programmes de l'éducation pour l'information; les autres pays, qui profitent également du drainage des cerveaux et qui sont capables de financer les initiatives de l'éducation; les gouvernments et les agences de gouvernement des pays africains qui préfèrent les investissements 'visibles' aux investissements dans les activités de l'information; les organisations régionales africaines, comme la Communauté économique des Etats de l'Afrique de l'Ouest, la Commission économique des Nations Unies pour l'Afrique; les pays et les agences donateurs, tels que le Centre de Recherches pour le Développement International (CRDI) au Canada et l'UNESCO; les individus dans les pays africains et en dehors de ces pays, en particulier, les résidents de la diaspora africaine; les bénéficiaires des programmes de l'éducation pour l'information, dont l'identité a été établie par les réseaux de liaision entre les chercheurs, les instructeurs et les apprentis.

L'établissement et l'implémentation d'un mécanisme pour la surveillance des initiatives de l'investissement sont essentiels pour l'entretien des investissements initiaux sans provoquer l'interférence dans les procédés de développement des pays individuels de l'Afrique subsaharienne. Parmi les mécanismes alternatifs pour le financement et la surveillance de l'investissement sont: les donations anonymes provenant des agences et des individus; les fonds publics provenant des agences et des individus; les fonds liés à des programmes spécifiques; les fonds liés à l'aide technique fourni par le pays donateur; les fonds dérivés des activités commerciales en Afrique et en dehors de l'Afrique; l'investissement par les institutions universitaires et par les centres de recherche africains; les organismes régionaux de formation et de recherche qui ont établi des programmes internes de l'éducation pour l'information; des groupements africains et étrangers de financement.

La littérature sur l'économie de l'éducation pour l'information en Afrique est peu évoluée. Les organisations internationales sont obligées de confronter les problèmes de l'investissement et de l'entretien par rapport à l'enseignement tertiaire. En même temps, la communauté africaine doit convaincre les gouvernements africains ainsi que les associations internationales pour le développement de leur faire confiance.

References

Agha, S.S. and Akhtar, S. (1992). The responsibility and the response: sustaining information systems in developing countries. **Journal of Information Science**, 18, 283-292.

Aiyepeku, W.O. (1988a). Comments on the paper entitled: Sub-Saharan Africa and the Paperless Society. (Letter to the Editor). **Journal of the American Society for Information Science**, 39(1), 219-220.

Aiyepeku, W.O. (1988b). Producing the critical mass of information professionals. In **Papers Resulting from the Meetings to Develop an Information Strategy for IDRC in Africa**, (Manuscript Report 206 e,f). Ottawa, Canada: IDRC, November, pp.58-67.

Aiyepeku, W.O. (1993). **Integrative and value-added properties of information in space and time**. Paper presented at the International Conference on West Africa Integration, Dakar, January 11-15.

Borko, H. and Menou, M.J. (1983). **Index of Information utilization potential (IUP): The Final report of Phase II of the I.U.P. Pilot Project**. Paris: UNESCO, General Information Programme and UNISIST (October).

Okada, N. (1978). Some aspects of Japan as an information society. In **Information societies: comparing the Japanese and the American experiences**, edited by A.S. Edelstein, et al. Seattle: International Communication Center, University of Washington. pp. 15360.

Olden, A. (1987). Sub-Saharan Africa and the Paperless Society. **Journal of the American Society of Information Science**, 38, 298-304.

Olden, A. (1988). Rejoinder to W.O. Aiyepeku's Comments. (Letter to the Editor). **Journal of the American Society for Information Science**, 39(1), 220.

Tiamiyu, M.A. (1989). Sub-Saharan Africa and the Paperless Society: A Comment and a Counterpoint. **Journal of the American Society of Information Science**, 40(5), 325-328.

Tiamiyu, M.A. (1993). The realities of developing modern information resources management systems in government organizations in developing countries with particular reference to Nigeria. **Journal of Information Science**, 19(3), June, 189-198.

SUMMING UP

Vue d'ensemble

Summing up

The conference brought together researchers and practitioners from many different fields, and the papers and discussions had enabled them to exchange experiences and broaden their outlook. The final session was intended to bring out the major topics that had emerged, to identify any important topics that had been missed during the earlier deliberations of the conference, and to indicate any areas for further research. A brief indication of the principal points arising from this final discussion is given below.

One theme common to nearly every paper was the need to focus on *information*, rather than *technology*; the bias had been too much towards technology over the past few years. This emphasis was confirmed by the final discussion.

While several papers, such as the keynote paper given by José-Marie Griffiths, did attempt to define information, the fact that we still do not have a widely accepted definition of what information is, nor strategies for how we should focus on it to improve effectiveness, remains a major problem for researchers in the area of the economics of information.

Three categories of information were suggested as possible ways of approaching this problem:

1. Information which transfers knowledge from generation to generation, for example through learned papers or their substitutes

2. Information which measures processes or status, where information, for example about processes, can become hard information and progress to (1)

3. Information which is normative or provides a framework, such as patents, legal cases, or standards such as ISO 9000, where again some information can become hard and progress to (1).

Although the emphasis should be on information, technology and information are interdependent. The changes in individual and group characteristics—for example, people's readiness to use information, and a better understanding of information flow—are now critical. We cannot understand, or change, anything unless we have a good picture of the people involved and their readiness and capacity to use information. Those who do use information tend to do better in various fields. Why is this, and what can we do about it?

One important point was the need to differentiate between the various kinds of information, their uses, and the benefits they bring. It is not simply a case of private good and public good: use, value and benefit depend very much on environment, function, patterns of use, etc. For example, the users/providers of humanities information are very different from those of financial information.

We need better models of the information economy and information use. Are we bringing together the various sectors now becoming involved in the new discipline of the economics of information, or are they diverging? There are shared values and a shared language even where there are different paradigms, and we must all be hospitable to new ideas in the development of modelling techniques.

It is possible to see the importance of modelling from two different positions, and these coincide with the lines for different research options which are now being drawn up:

- modelling information as an object, i.e. a conceptual clarification of information as an object
- modelling the information system, e.g. the type of empirical work done by King Research to build indicators and models

One problem is the underlying assumption of considering information as a social, behavioural, neo-classical model, traditionally associated with marketing and libraries. We need to go beyond these models to look at industrial evaluation techniques, such as competitive advantage. For example, how do firms learn to define their position through information flows?

In conclusion, it was agreed that the main issue arising from the conference was how we can look at information through the different modelling techniques available. We need empirical, case-study research in the economics of information field; the time for purely theoretical modelling is past and it is essential that we now use real people and real information in order to test the models.

Vue d'ensemble

La conférence a réuni des chercheurs et des professionnels venant de domaines différents. Les communications et les discussions leur ont permis d'échanger leurs expériences et d'élargir leurs perspectives. La séance finale avait alors pour objectifs de mettre en avant les principaux sujets qui étaient apparus lors de la conférence, d'identifier les sujets importants qui n'avaient pas été abordés et d'indiquer des pistes de recherche ultérieures. Une brève présentation des principaux points ainsi apparus est présentée ci-dessous.

Lors des différentes interventions, il est apparu qu'une orientation était récurrente: celle de se concentrer sur l'information plutôt que sur la technologie, l'accent ayant été trop mis, ces dernières années, sur la technologie. Cette réorientation s'est trouvé confirmée lors de la séance finale.

Alors que dans plusieurs communications, dont la comunication introductive de José-Marie Griffiths, on essayait de définir l'information, il est notoire que le fait de ne pas avoir une définition largement accepté de ce qu'est l'information, ni de stratégies pour savoir comment il est possible de l'utiliser afin d'améliorer l'efficacité, est et reste un problème majeur pour l'ensemble des chercheurs en économie de l'information.

Trois catégories d'information ont été proposées qui pourraient permettre de développer des approches économiques:

1. L'information qui communique, de génération en génération, les connaissances à travers, par exemple, les textes érudites ou leurs équivalents.

2. L'information qui n'est encore que mesure des processus ou des statuts. Cette information étant une information 'dure', elle acquière progressivement le statut de la catégorie 1.

3. L'information normative, qui fournit un cadre, comme les brevets, les décisions légales, ISO 9000, où, à nouveau, une partie de cette information peut devenir 'dure' et acquèrir le statut de la catégorie 1.

Bien qu'il faille mettre l'emphase sur l'information, technologie et information sont interdépendantes. Les modifications des caractéristiques des individus et de groupes—par exemple une plus grande propension des gens à utiliser de l'information, une meilleure compréhension du flux de l'information—sont actuellement trèscritiques. Nous ne pouvons pas comprendre ou changer quelque chose sans une bonne connaissance des gens qui sont impliqués et de leur propension et capacité à utiliser l'information. Ceux qui font usage de l'information font beaucoup mieux, et dans des domaines variés. Pourquoi en est-il ainsi et que pouvons nous faire pour l'améliorer? Un besoin est apparu important: celui de différencier les différents sortes d'information, leurs usages et les bénéfices qu'elles apportent. Ce n'est pas simplement une question de bien privé ou de bien public: usage, valeur, bénéfice dépendent beaucoup du contexte, de la fonction et des modes d'usage, etc. Par exemple, les usagers/fournisseurs d'information en sciences humaines différent de façon importante des usagers/fournisseurs d'information financière.

Nous avons besoin de meilleurs modèles de l'économie de l'information et de l'usage de l'information que nous avons actuellement. Allons-nous regrouper les secteurs variés qui se sont engagés dans la nouvelle discipline que représente l'économie de l'information ou allons-nous les laisser diverger? Même lorsque les paradigmes sont différents, il ya toujours des valeurs et un langage partagés. Aussi devon-nous être accueillant aux nouvelles idées qui nous aideront par exemple à développer les techniques de modèlisation. Il ya deux approches importants de modèlisation qui correspondent aux orientations des recherches entreprises:

- modèliser l'information objet, c'est-à-dire conceptualiser l'information comme un objet
- modèliser le système d'information, comme le fait par exemple, de façon empirique King Research, pour arriver à construire des indicateurs et modèles.

Le problème, c'est que l'on continue à considérer une information situé dans un cadre social, comportemental, néoclassique, associé traditionnellement avec le marketing et les bibliothèques. Nous devons dépasser cette vision pour regarder plus du côté des techniques d'évaluation industrielles comme par exemple l'avantage compétitif. Ainsi, coment les entreprises apprennent-elles à définir leur position dans les flux d'information? En conclusion, il ressort de cette conférence que la question principale reste de savoir comment aborder l'étude économique de l'information à travers les différents techniques de modèlisation disponibles. Nous avons besoin, en économie de l'information, de recherches empiriques, d'études de cas: le temps de la modèlisation purement théorique est dépasseé. Il est essentiel maintenant que nous utilisions des gens et des informations réels pour tester ces modèles.

Conference Programme

Changing Information Technologies: Research Challenges in the Economics of Information

The Third International Information Research Conference
11-13 July 1993

Sunday 11 July

Registration

Opening Remarks: Yves F. Le Coadic, CNAM, France.

General Overview of the Economics of Information: Michael Hill, Retired Director of the Science Reference Information Service, The British Library, UK.

Monday morning 12 July
Economic implications of information technology
Chair: W.A. Turner, Ceresi/CNRS, France.

Keynote address: Nigel Gardner, University of Ulster, UK. [Paper delivered but not submitted for publication]

The information industry in the Republic of Ireland: a critical examination of a possible model for information sector development: William J. Martin, Belfast University, UK.

Nouvelles technologies de l'information et structures matricielles: Alain Bompard, Université de Lyon, France.

The new role of information technology in the international division of labor: Vijai P. Singh, University of Pittsburgh, USA.

Electronic publishing: new opportunities for public sector libraries: Ian Hunter, Gateshead Libraries and Arts Service, UK.

Monday afternoon 12 July
Measures of economics of information and information economics
Chair: Toni Carbo Bearman, University of Pittsburgh, USA.

Keynote address: José-Marie Griffiths, University of Tennessee, USA.

L'Impact de l'information sur le développement: les résultats d'une première investigation: Michel Menou, CIDEGI, France.

A commodity, but what kind of commodity?: Michael Heine, University of Northumbria, UK.

Approche analytique du coût de l'appui documentaire dans un établissement de recherche: J-F. Giovannetti, CIRAD, France.

Information spécialisée et formation de l'avantage compétitif: J-L. Coujard, Cerise/INPL, France.

Tuesday morning 13 July
Changes in the political and legal context
Chair: Brian Perry, The British Library Research & Development Department, UK.

How can digital information be protected?: Michael Lesk, Bell Communication Research, USA.

Automatisation et dématérialisation de l'information: les défis juridiques: Martine Barré, CREDIMI, France.

Irrational innovation in the transfer of information: John Mackenzie Owen, De Bilt, The Netherlands.

What price research?: Barry Mahon, EUSIDIC, Luxembourg.

An African case study: higher education strategy and the role of information: Peter Havard Williams, University of Botswana.

Tuesday afternoon 13 July
Concluding session—discussion
Chair: Michel Menou, CIDEGI, France.

Index to English text

Page numbers in **bold** denote main chapter-length treatments; page numbers in *italics* denote end-of-chapter résumés; *n* denotes a footnote.

Index du texte français

Les numéros de page en caractères **gras** indiquent les références principales; les numéros en *italiques* indiquent les résumés à la fin des chapitres; *n* indique une note en bas de page.